G.I. Messiahs

G.I. Messiahs

Soldiering, War, and
American Civil Religion

Jonathan H. Ebel

Yale UNIVERSITY PRESS

NEW HAVEN AND LONDON

Columbia FLI Partnership
BL 2525. E245 2015

Published with assistance from the Mary Cady Tew Memorial Fund.

Yale University Press books may be purchased in quantity for educational, business, or promotional use. For information, please e-mail sales.press@yale.edu (U.S. office) or sales@yaleup.co.uk (U.K. office).

Set in Ehrhardt type.
Printed in the United States of America.

ISBN: 978-0-300-17670-4 (hardback; permanent paper)

Library of Congress Control Number: 2015936435

A catalogue record for this book is available from the British Library.

This paper meets the requirements of ANSI/NISO Z39.48-1992 (Permanence of Paper).

10 9 8 7 6 5 4 3 2 1

To Mom and Dad
Thank you

Contents

Acknowledgments   ix

INTRODUCTION   1
CHAPTER 1. Incarnating American Civil Religion   25
CHAPTER 2. Symbols Known, Soldiers Unknown   46
CHAPTER 3. In Honored Glory, Known but to God   69
CHAPTER 4. Saint Francis the Fallen   100
CHAPTER 5. The Vietnam War as a Christological Crisis   134
CHAPTER 6. Safety, Soldier, Scapegoat, Savior   164
CONCLUSION. Of Flesh, Words, and Wars   189

Notes   201
Credits   231
Index   233

Acknowledgments

I began work on this book in the fall of 2009 and have, over the past five years, benefited from the generosity of numerous friends, colleagues, and institutions, and from the love and support of my family. One of the great pleasures of this work is the frequent reminders of human goodness it provides. Another great pleasure is the opportunity to say thank you. David Price, head of the Department of Religion at the University of Illinois, Urbana–Champaign, has given me more encouraging words than I can count. I owe him and my colleagues in the department a tremendous debt of gratitude. I appreciate very much the encouragement and support I have received from Dianne Harris and the Illinois Program for Research in the Humanities, Masumi Iriye and the Center for Advanced Study, Nancy Abelman and the Office for the Vice Chancellor of Research, and Rajeev Malik and the Office of International Programs and Studies. I am thankful as well to Nancy Castro, James Hansen, Valerie Hotchkiss, Lilya Kaganovsky, Rick Layton, Rebecca Linder Blachly, Justine Murison, Kathy Oberdeck, David O'Brien, Ned O'Gorman, Michael Rothberg, Rob Rushing, Renée Trilling, Anna Stenport, Ruth Watkins, Olof Westerstahl, Gillen Wood, and Yasemin Yildiz, wonderful colleagues, past and present, who have made the University of Illinois such a vibrant intellectual community.

Major sections of this book would have been impossible to write without the generous support of the American Academy of Religion, the William and Flora Hewlett Foundation, and the Louisville Institute, whose grants helped me to both travel to research sites and have the time to think through what it was that I found there. I am especially indebted to the Young Scholars in American Religion program. This program, led by Phillip Goff, has done a service to the field of American religious history that can hardly be measured. As a program fellow, under the mentorship of Clark Gilpin and Tracy Fessenden, I received professional and personal support for which I will always be grateful. I owe particular thanks to Clark and Tracy, and also to Heather Curtis, Jennifer Graber, and Kip Kosek, who read and commented on substantial pieces of this book, and who have kept the experience of the Young Scholars program alive, even though the "young" part may not fit quite as well as it once did. I would also like to thank my friends and colleagues Edward Blum, John Carlson, John Corrigan, Kathryn Gin Lum , Alison Greene, Kathryn Lofton, William Munro, Erik Owens, Brent Plate, and Skip Stout for reading and advising and encouraging me over the course of this project, and for making this corner of academia such a pleasant one. I had the incredible good fortune to study under Catherine Brekus as a graduate student at the University of Chicago. I am forever grateful for the many things that I learned from her and for her continued friendship and support.

I am also thankful to Jennifer Banks at Yale University Press, who helped me think through this project from its very earliest stages and has shown great patience along the way. She is everything one could hope for in an editor. Heather Gold at Yale answered many questions down the stretch and helped me get this project over the finish line. Heartfelt thanks also to Eliza Childs for her stellar copy editing and good humor, and to Margaret Otzel for coordinating every aspect of production. During the research process I also had valuable assistance from archivists, librarians, and staff at the American Battle Monuments Commission, the American Cathedral in Paris, the Lafayette Escadrille Memorial, the George Marshall Foundation, American Legion Headquarters, Princeton University's Mudd Manuscript Library, the Southern California Social Studies Research Library, and the magnificent libraries of the University of Illinois. Had it not been for the help of two capable and generous research assistants, Sarah Jackman and Joshua Young, I could never have found or kept track of much of the material in this book. I owe special thanks to Joshua, whose assistance in the last year of work on this project was crucial.

I have neither enough words nor the right ones to express the love that I feel for my wife, Meredith, who sustains me, and my three amazing daughters, Sophia, Charlotte, and Beatrice, who inspire me. Not only do you all give me energy as I work, you give me great joy in the many other things we do together. Thank you for that. Who knew ballet was so fun? I love you all very much.

I dedicate this book to my mom and dad, Holly and David Ebel, who for forty-four years have loved, understood, supported, and even traveled alongside. For the many ways in which you have provided nourishment, refreshment, challenge, relaxation, and safe harbor for me and my merry band, I offer my love, my gratitude, and this for the cabin bookshelf.

Introduction

In the beginning was the Word, and the Word was with God and the Word was God. He was with God in the beginning. Through him all things were made.
—JOHN 1:1–3

This book is about the religious dynamics of soldiering for America from the Great War, which I mark as the emergence of the United States as a global power, to the conflicts in Afghanistan and Iraq, which future historians will certainly describe as national crises, perhaps even as engines of American decline. Hundreds of histories have been written of the wars waged in the so-called American century and of exercises of American might—both violent and not—that have, in one way or another, fallen short of war. A significantly smaller historiography of religion in the modern United States has emerged over the last half century, sometimes attending to moments of national crisis and war, sometimes treating governmental institutions and American actions on the global stage as disconnected from or irrelevant to the faiths of Americans.[1]

The focus of this book is the men and women without whose bodies no wars could be fought, no diplomatic challenges backed up, no histories of either written. But in keeping this focus, I have found it necessary to tell two stories. The first involves the presentation of the American soldier to America's publics, moments of public connection with the soldier as a living symbol. The second considers the ways that soldiers have interacted with America's publics and with their symbolized selves, the ways that real servicemen and -women shape and are shaped by expectations, beliefs, and memories of the soldier. My aim is to weave together these two stories and to relate them to what scholars often call American civil religion: the narratives, symbols, practices, and institutions that create and sustain a sense of America's special purpose and place in the world.

This is also, then, a book about religion, which may seem odd at first blush. Judging by appearances, there is nothing necessarily religious about either the warrior or the warrior image. In the first decades of the twenty-first century we are accustomed to thinking of religious themes and identities as clearly marked and as matters of choice, whether presented by an artist in a sculpture or by a believer in a word or an act. My interest here is in matters that frequently go beyond clear markings and conscious choices. In fact, a central presupposition of this book is that both the imagined soldier and his more fragile, more complicated, human counterpart participate inevitably in American civil religion. Presentations of American soldiers and soldiers' own engagements with the myths, rituals, and symbols that inform those presentations are expressions of American civil religion; in them we can often see both the theological substructures of American civil religion and its complexities as a lived religion.[2]

From its earliest stages *G.I. Messiahs* has been both a work of religious history and a work of interpretation. The sources and stories, situated as they are in places where religion, nation, and war converge, are saturated with the intentionally and the accidentally hybrid, with loyalties described, embodied, and enacted in ways that, though familiar, are far from simple. As a historian of religion in America, I choose to attend most closely to the religious aspects of these convergences and to think about the ways that the life of a nation and the lives and deaths of its soldiers can be understood as religious. The resulting narrative describes a nation that has looked upon its soldiers not simply as protectors and preservers of the nation and its ideals, but as incarnations of those ideals—the Word of the nation made flesh—whose willingness to suffer and die brings salvation to an often wayward but nevertheless chosen people. It also tells the story of soldiers across the twentieth and into the twenty-first century who have, in a range of ways and with varying motivations, welcomed, reshaped, and resisted this role and the accompanying veneration. In doing so, they have shown that American civil religion, like all religious traditions, is characterized by the tug and pull of official versus lay understandings, institutional versus popular expressions. The lives and deaths of soldiers, in whom American civil religion invests so much, show the creative force and the destructive power of these tensions.

Myths, Symbols, and Realities

A recent observer of American civil-military relations noted that people often "fill gaps in understanding of others with stereotypes and assumptions," and that because "few Americans have direct experience with military service," the army, and presumably the other branches of the military, are "especially susceptible to this dynamic." It is a common observation: Americans see soldiers in particular ways and expect of them particular attitudes and behaviors. But the images and ideals that fill the physical and psychological spaces between civilians and the military are not randomly generated. As Edward Linenthal has argued, these images generally emerge from a narrow, if not perfectly stable, range of images sanctified by their connection to America's canonical wars. The American Revolution gave the nation the Minuteman, a ready volunteer, patriotic to the core, able to move easily between the farm and the fight. The Civil War produced the sacrificial warrior, who fought fiercely and died honorably even if the cause for which he fought and died was something other than honorable. From World War II emerged another version of the citizen-soldier: "the homely hero," to use Linenthal's phrase. However hesitant this young man was to traverse the Atlantic or the Pacific, he recognized his duty; did his job; and was, "thanks to his moral superiority, a fierce warrior."[3]

These images have resonated down through American martial history— "fantasy echoes," in the words of Joan Scott—touching soldiers and civilians in the midst of wars that were quite different and quite distantly removed from one another, not only chronologically and geographically but strategically and tactically as well. Americans involved in the Great War, for instance, made regular use of imagery from the American Revolution and the Civil War, connecting their spirit and their work to that of Patriots, Yankees, and, sotto voce, Rebels as well. American pilots flying in support of France took the name of the French general who supported the revolutionary cause and called themselves the Lafayette Escadrille. A Jewish author encouraged readers of the *Jewish Advocate* to do their martial duty by invoking the spirit of George Washington. The editors of the soldier-authored *Stars and Stripes* described battles fought in the summer of 1918 as recapitulations of pivotal Civil War battles. The fighting around

Chateau-Thierry was, they proclaimed, "as fraught as Gettysburg in its consequences to the world" and "the Gettysburg of the A.E.F."; the battle of Ourcq was nothing less than "another Antietam." War in the trenches and forests of France was, of course, dissimilar in degree and in kind from war under Washington or Sherman or Custer. Later in the twentieth century, soldiers of the Korean War were drawn to service by images of World War II: dutiful older brothers and friends rallying to the cause of freedom and fighting doggedly against fascism. Despite a chronological gap of a mere five years, this army of volunteers and draftees soon discovered that such images were inadequate to their experiences of war in a land of questionable relevance to the United States and of marginal interest to its citizens.[4] Fifty years after Korea, Vice President Dick Cheney also drew on images of World War II when he predicted that American soldiers would be welcomed in Baghdad as liberators. Seoul in 1951 and Baghdad in 2003 were not Paris circa 1944.

Indeed, it is an open question whether "Paris circa 1944" was Paris circa 1944. Wars are, after all, unstable cultural objects. How we see, read, and interpret them changes over time, sometimes subtly and slowly, but nevertheless surely. The memory of the Great War and the experiences of those who fought it changed with the collapse of Wilson's effort to win support for the League of Nations. It changed again with the rise of Nazi Germany and the descent of Europe and Asia into war. It changed once more with late twentieth-century struggles over and around borders drawn following the armistice of 1918. The memory of World War II—the Good War—has the appearance of stability in the United States, but the mythic status it has attained over the last seven decades was no fait accompli. With the Cold War dictating the possibilities and the limits of global engagement and hot wars in Korea and Vietnam raising questions about America's martial efficacy, questions lingered about what exactly the defeat of Germany, Italy, and Japan had achieved. Ongoing discussions about U.S. conduct in World War II—toward its own citizens of Japanese descent and toward Japanese civilians subjected to relentless napalm bombings and, finally, to nuclear attack—keep the memory evolving.[5] This is all to say that, appearances to the contrary, wars are fought and recalled in history, not above it.

But symbols and images of war, not to mention the myths that inform them, work powerfully to obscure this fact. Indeed, it is a common characteristic of American civil religion to emphasize and extol America's martial tradition with little consideration of the different ways in which military service has been understood and embodied. The soldier, I argue, is a particularly important pillar in the construction of a timeless, sanctified "American military tradition." Weapons, battlefields, and justifications change in obvious ways, but the soldier—always young, strong, brave, and until very recently always male—appears to resist history's corrosive effects. The soldierly body stabilizes that which is constantly shifting in war memory; it miniaturizes, simplifies, and personalizes that which is grand and complex in American foreign policy; it makes tangible, visible, and apparently timeless the virtues of honor, courage, and sacrifice. But the soldiers at the center of so many civil religious moments, the soldiers in whom Americans often see so much that is good and true or, at least, meaningful, are as shaped by time as the wars they sometimes wage. Not only are they subject to the same forces that change, age, and eventually erase us all, but their soldier-ness and our perceptions of it are products of roughly a century and a half of developments in the military and in American society. The American military and American soldiers have not always been as they are now. Americans have not always thought as highly of either as they do today.

In the decades following the Civil War, the military moved far from the notion that soldiering was one civic duty among many—a vision most famously embodied by George Washington and articulated by the likes of Thomas Jefferson and Andrew Jackson—toward the belief that soldiering ought to be a line of work to be chosen, practiced, and theorized. During this same period West Point and Annapolis departed from their founding purposes as technical schools and became academies where would-be officers received an education that balanced the liberal arts, the sciences, and the study of war. As a result, officers and soldiers moved away from the approaches to war and service that were on display through the mid-1860s, becoming far more astute observers, analysts, and students of war-craft. They developed a sense that war was not an occasional eruption to be confronted with the tools at hand but was rather so woven into human existence, so much a part of the world of nations and empires, that to ignore it was as foolish as it was dangerous. These attitudinal and institutional developments were, in the main, very good for the military. For it was in the decades following the Civil War that the army and the navy became professionalized and that through focus on military leadership, soldiering, and the art of war, the seeds were planted for future success on the battlefields of the world and for greater respect in American society.[6]

It was also during this post–Civil War period that the military stood at its furthest remove from the wider American public. The army was geographically quite distant—garrisoned on the frontier, sequestered in military academies—and was, many argued, just as distant ideologically and culturally from progressive, liberal, individualistic America. The hierarchical military was a square peg in the round hole of egalitarian America. When involvement in the Great War brought the military into closer contact with society and made its existence a matter of relief to those who thought militaries either hopelessly reactionary or merely obsolete, it was the institutions, practices, and professionalism of the regular army that made the training of four million citizen-soldiers and subsequent battlefield successes in Europe possible. In other words, it was not continuity with traditions of American warfare dating to the Revolution but departure from them that made the army and the navy viable global fighting forces in 1918 and beyond.[7]

Military successes, of course, come at a cost. Throughout the century and a half following independence, many Americans voiced concerns that a well-trained, professional standing military was out of synch with the spirit of the young republic.[8] It would be far better and more American, critics proclaimed, to rely on the raw martial prowess of American men and on state militias than to transplant to American soil the antidemocratic spirit and tyrannical ways of Europe's professional armies. In theory and in practice the individualism and love of liberty so often equated with the American spirit hardly had a place within the realms of the military, where order, obedience, and communalism mattered above all else. This long-standing antipathy between the perceived soul of America and European militarism was at the root of numerous prophecies of doom, predictions that a professional army would transform a great and progressive people into a nation of cogs.[9] Such sentiments, especially common in the Progressive Era and in the interwar period, were quieted significantly by America's involvement in World War II and the Cold War and, in spite of a twenty-first-century resurgence, remain rare today. The nature and frequency of global threats in the last century have something to do with the general acceptance of a large, professional, standing military force. The many heroic images and mythic narratives that Americans associate with military service are, without question, important as well.[10]

The topic of civil-military relations in America's past and present has drawn ample attention from historians, cultural critics, novelists, and filmmakers. But few observers of America have attended to the place of religion, Christianity for the most part, in forging and solidifying connections between the military and society.[11] Throughout much of the past century, even in the midst of eras characterized by societal ambivalence toward the military, individual writers, sculptors, ministers, and missionaries have drawn on the images, narratives, and rituals of Christianity when describing soldiers, their sacrifices, and the wars they have waged. When this sanctification has not been overt, it has often been at work quietly but powerfully, translating the untranslatable, making pure that which is gruesome, massaging chaos into coherence. American civil religion has performed this sanctifying work and has also benefited from it. The evidence is all around us. It is in the monuments we build, the films we see, the rituals we observe, even the words we choose. But the existence of such evidence does not answer the question of how best to interpret it. What are we to make of the Christian narratives, symbols, and theologies that are so frequently connected to soldiering? Are they relics of a bygone era? Do they still do theological work in service of the nation?

G.I. Messiahs is at least the study of an American cultural and civil religious metaphor or trope—that of the soldier as savior. In its most delimited form this trope encourages Americans to acknowledge the service, the suffering, and the sacrifices of the men and women who wage America's wars. It presents as fact that soldiers have, literally and figuratively, saved America and encourages reflection on their saving actions. Soldiers, the trope points out, have saved the nation as a geopolitical entity by beating back global enemies before those enemies could reach our shores ("Freedom Is Not Free"). They have saved American influence and American values by staring down international bullies ("Don't Tread On Me"). In doing these things they have also saved Americans from a jaded conception of the nation, from the sins of wandering, forgetting, declining ("We Support Our Troops"). Soldiers do and have done this saving with their bodies, enduring suffering and sometimes sacrificing their lives.

The soldier-savior trope has emotional power and staying power because it makes sense. Soldiers *have* served, suffered, and sacrificed. Soldiers *do* demonstrate altruism in the extreme. The Congressional Medal of Honor citation for Nelson Holderman, an army captain in the Great War, reads in part: "He was wounded on 4, 5, and 7 October, but throughout the entire period, suffering great pain and subjected to fire of every character, he continued personally to lead and encourage the officers and men under his command with unflinching courage and with distinguished success. On 6 October, in a wounded condition, he rushed through enemy machinegun and shell fire and carried [two] wounded men to a place of safety."[12] Captain

Holderman was hurt in ways that few can imagine. He suffered immensely. Yet he led those around him to fight on and risked his life to save two of his men. Nelson Holderman actually sacrificed, suffered, and saved. Private First Class Daniel R. Edwards's Medal of Honor citation for action in the same war is similarly compelling. "Reporting for duty from [the] hospital where he had been for several weeks under treatment for numerous and serious wounds and although suffering intense pain from a shattered arm, he crawled alone into an enemy trench for the purpose of capturing or killing enemy soldiers known to be concealed therein. He killed [four] of the men and took the remaining [four] men prisoners; while conducting them to the rear one of the enemy was killed by a high explosive enemy shell which also completely shattered [one] of Pfc. Edwards' legs."[13] Private Edwards repeatedly gave his body, parts of it at least, in service of America. He bore the suffering of war in his body and remained both determined and lethal. American civil religion names and honors men like Holderman and Edwards, publicly drawing tight connections among suffering, sacrifice, and heroism. The soldier-savior trope provides a nation deeply influenced by the narratives and symbols of Christianity with a generally intelligible conceptual language—expressed in word and in symbol—with which to recognize the suffering, celebrate the heroism, and mourn the deaths of its soldiers.

A more expansive interpretation of the material in this book points to the possibility that to study the soldier-savior, the G.I. Messiah, is to study the emotional and theological core of American civil religion. On this interpretation, the trope described above and its myriad textual, monumental, rhetorical, and filmic manifestations interact with and express a genuine civil religious theology in which "the soldier" operates as the second person of an American godhead, the first person of which is the nation itself.[14] The connection of the American soldier to Christianity thus extends beyond semiotic patterns and linguistic tics. The trope explains soldiering, yes, but it also reveals soldiers, both living and fallen, to be the Word of the nation made flesh; America among us. And American civil religion seems to require this incarnation. American civil religion is deeply concerned with the veneration of those who have served and suffered and sacrificed for their country, or who have, at least, surrendered themselves to this possibility. Whatever other forces have divided America—and those forces have been myriad—the nation has often gathered around and celebrated, in different ways and often to vastly different ends, the saving power of the G.I.

Messiah. A barely submerged incarnational theology, frequent invocations of theories of atonement, regular equations of the fallen soldier to Christ crucified are appropriations from Christian tradition that give both coherence and binding power to a religious tradition focused on worship of the nation.[15] This reading of the evidence requires more interpretive work than the first. There are a few more gaps and it is sometimes harder to see. One can walk among the graves of fallen soldiers of the two world wars and readily note the trope. One must climb a ladder (or request an aerial photograph) and look down on those graves to note the theology. These interpretive moves, minor for the most part, make credible, if not inevitable, a more robust reading of the G.I. Messiah through twentieth-century America and down to our current moment.

The biographical material woven into this book is both methodologically and historically crucial to a full accounting of the trope and the theology. The sufferings and sacrifices asked of soldiers are and have been real and individual. The Word of the nation made flesh is no mere abstraction.

Intro:1: Suresnes American Cemetery in the Parisian suburb of Suresnes, France, holds 1,541 dead from the Great War and 24 dead from World War II.

Intro:2: The graves of twenty-four unknown American soldiers, arranged in the shape of a cross. Suresnes American Cemetery, Suresnes, France.

Whether viewing the soldier with pride or with concern, public commentary often obscures his particularity with a thick veil of rhetoric, symbol, and tradition. By examining some of the men and women behind or underneath that veil, we can at least note their individuality and recover something of soldiers' own struggles with the burdens of civil religious incarnation. Whether or not one finds explanatory power in naming the military a sacrificial system or drawing attention to the blood-soaked altar of the nation, it is an irreducible fact that individual soldiers have struggled and suffered in public and in private, in wartime and in peace, both because of what the nation has asked them to do and because of the ideal that they and others imagine themselves to embody.[16]

Interpreting the G.I. Messiah

This book is a work of American religious history. It is based on archival materials, newspapers, periodicals, published memoirs, films, and

Intro:3: Intersecting walkways at Normandy American Cemetery form a cross, visible from the air. In the lower right-hand corner of the picture is a path that winds down the bluff to Omaha Beach. (Photo courtesy of the American Battle Monuments Commission)

memorial environments, which I have approached with an eye for religion and religious messages traditionally understood. As noted above, my understanding of religion and the religious extends beyond these traditional sources, locations, and labels, which has led me to consider other sites and archives—parades, state funerals, award citations, even the ordeal of basic training. In these, too, I have looked for religious meaning: discourses, practices, communities, and institutions that orient a person or people toward a higher power.[17] This book is also, like many in the field of religious studies, a work of interpretation, a study of subjects, actions, and attitudes beset with the ambiguous and the hybrid. I have done my utmost to interpret subjects in context, to read them reasonably, and to fill historical gaps in ways that make sense. I am, however, aware of and interested in other interpretive possibilities. To help readers better understand the interpretive choices presented and developed here, I would like briefly to describe and analyze three presentations of the soldier from three moments of American military consciousness. For each case I present two brief readings, one that engages the soldier-savior connection primarily as a civil religious trope, another that examines its connection to a civil religious theology. In addition to demonstrating something of my approach to the sources for this study, these three examples allow a preliminary engagement with the larger historical questions that I address throughout the book. In what ways has the G.I. Messiah and popular engagements with it changed over the past century? What do these continuities and changes reveal about the nation, its soldiers, and its faiths?

The first sources, literally the most solid in the book, are the brilliantly white, cruciform headstones—hewn from Italian-quarried marble—that populate America's overseas military cemeteries. Walking through these sacred spaces and interacting with thousands of white crosses and a far smaller number of Stars of David, one is easily impressed by the scale of suffering and sacrifice soldiers have incurred on behalf of the nation. There are just so many. Each stone marks a life ended, a family's tragedy, the world-changing realization that the uniformed man on the porch has come with the worst news imaginable. Many stones are evidence of a once-and-for-ever decision that, as one woman put it, "he should be buried in the ground he fought for." The scale and the aesthetic of the cemeteries work together to create something "monumental" and impressive. White crosses over the Christian dead, a civil religious memorial trope, are one aspect among many that help visitors comprehend the meaning of service and appreciate these remarkable cemeteries.[18]

The white marble crosses can also tell a more theological story to those who visit Suresnes, Meuse-Argonne, Normandy, or any of America's twenty other overseas military cemeteries.[19] This story uses the words service, suffering, and sacrifice and takes in the brilliant whiteness of the crosses. It also notes that these crosses are doing civil religious work. For beneath them lie men, women, even a few children, whose lives and deaths and faiths varied. Some volunteered to serve, some were compelled. Some fought, some did not. Some lived lives of virtue and heroism, some lived lives of sin and cowardice. Most lived somewhere in between. The white crosses make these bodies uniformly noble, uniformly sinless, uniformly saved. The crosses and the cemeteries of which they are a part argue the incarnation of the nation's will, death on behalf of the nation, and salvation as the reward. At the same time, the crosses and the cemeteries encourage devotion to a nation that has so loved the world that it has given its sons.

The G.I. Messiah as trope and as theology is not hard to spot in official contexts—cemeteries, tombs, monuments, funeral orations—from the 1920s through the 1950s. What makes this figure so fascinating, though, is the extent to which it has permeated other eras and other realms of American culture, from film to sports journalism to television commercials. These sources as much as the official sources help to pinpoint both change and stability over time. The 1954 film *The Bridges at Toko-Ri*, adapted from James Michener's novel of the same name, is not set about with white marble crosses and excerpts from Christian scripture, but it is intensely focused on suffering and sacrifice and, like the overseas military cemetery, allows at least two levels of analysis.

The Bridges at Toko-Ri stands out among mid-century war movies for the fact that its hero dies. After crash-landing his jet, Lieutenant Harry Brubaker (William Holden) and a rescue pilot (Mickey Rooney), hopelessly outnumbered, are overrun and killed by North Korean soldiers. Yet the film is also quite orthodox. It is long on admiration for those who serve; it acknowledges that service brings suffering to those who wear the uniform and to their families; it depicts American sacrifice in the struggle against the forces of Communism. The soldier-savior trope is woven into the film in obvious ways.

This message of sacrifices made and remembered also features narrative devices and bits of dialogue that weave civil religious theology into and around the trope, encouraging audiences to see the soldier (or, in this case, the navy pilot) as the G.I. Messiah. Most compelling in this regard is the film's presentation of Lieutenant Brubaker's growing intuition that he is going to die in combat. Brubaker, who has a wife (Grace Kelly) and two daughters, struggles mightily with his premonition of death as the day of the aerial attack on the bridges at Toko-Ri nears. In fact, he is so affected during a preflight briefing that he leaves his squadron's ready room to be alone. Brubaker's twentieth-century Gethsemane moment deepens when his commanding officer finds him writing a last letter to his wife and offers to let the cup pass from him. "Look Harry," he says, "This is an important mission, very important. We've got to do a first rate professional job. I can't afford to take chances." The CO continues, "A guy comes clean and grounds himself, I'm grateful. But if he tries to bluff it out and endangers an entire mission, that's unforgivable. Think it over Harry." Faced with the weight and the consequences of an unforgivable sin, Brubaker takes the advice of a salty rescue pilot (Rooney) and makes his way to the bow of the ship to be calmed by the ocean spray. His head wet as if by baptism, Brubaker is finally prepared to let the nation's will, not his, be done. American soldiers fear and doubt, the narrative confirms, but doubts and fears do not prevail against them. As surely as the nation lives within them, they will fight for the right and die if they must.

In the film's final scene, with Brubaker's death confirmed, the admiral (Fredric March) who commands the aircraft carrier from which he flew mourns Brubaker and praises his type, demonstrating soldier veneration and calling audiences to its practice. "Where do we get such men?" he asks. "They leave this ship and they do their job, and they must find this speck lost somewhere in the sea. When they find it, they have to land on its pitching deck." Once again for good measure, he asks, "Where do we get such men?" The answer, implied but crystal clear, is that "we" get such men from the heart of the nation, from true, pure America, perhaps even from the audience seated in the theater. What the audience knows but the admiral does not is that Brubaker's heroism exceeded his exploits as an aviator. On the ground, against overwhelming odds, he fought. He died fighting. Surrender to "communist forces" was never an option. Brubaker the soldier revealed the nation to the nation. He did his part to save the nation from the forces of evil. He was the nation made flesh.

One final source, this from a network television broadcast, requires that we sharpen our attention to the G.I. Messiah. This source is far more compact than the film, far more ephemeral than the cemeteries. It involved oblique references to Christianity—an image and a mention of a church, a child shown kneeling in prayer—but no references to scripture. Instead, soldiers and the civil religious trope were woven into a tapestry dominated by American commercialism and communalism. The advertisement appeared during halftime of the Super Bowl in February 2013. For two minutes, the most recognizable female voice in America spoke to America of America. Oprah Winfrey, on behalf of the automaker Jeep, communicated first through text, white letters on a black background: "We wait. We hope. We pray. Until you're home again." Thus began one of the most earnest advertisements of Super Bowl XLVII. Voiced by Winfrey, the spot, "Whole Again," focused on the soldier-shaped empty spaces that have characterized American families and communities for more than a decade. As the images began to flow, viewers saw those spaces and the men and women traveling homeward to fill them. Winfrey spoke, "There will be a seat left open, a light left on, a favorite dinner waiting, a warm bed made. There will be walks to take, swings to push, and baths to give. On your block, at the school, in your church, because in your home, in our hearts, you've been missed."[20]

The poetry leaves much to be desired, but the civil religious lesson is powerful nevertheless. American families live in American homes near American schools and American churches, all part of an American nation that waits and hopes and prays for its soldiers. Oprah continued: "You've been needed. You've been cried for, prayed for. You've been the reason we push on." The "you" in this narrative is at once elastic and needle-sharp— all soldiers / our soldiers / my soldier. The "we"—the advertisement's imagined community—is defined by needing, crying, and praying for a uniformed "you." In Oprah's final line, bodies real and metaphorical come together in a statement of civil religious doctrine worthy of Lincoln, Kennedy, Reagan, and Obama, "Because when you're home, we're more than a family; we're a nation that is whole again."

At the level of the image and the text "Whole Again" is uncomplicated. Living soldiers of many racial and ethnic groups make smooth returns to attentive communities and eager, loving families. Christianity is one strand among many binding soldiers and their families. Madison Avenue and Oprah take us back to a future in which men and women, black, white, and Hispanic, return from war smiling, striding, ready to embrace, clear-eyed, strong, eager to live. This beloved mythology draws additional strength from the "we" that the advertisement asks us to imagine. Narrator, narrative, and image tell us that America is not only post-racial and post-secular, but post-civilian as well. With the soldier as integral to our national body and therefore as close to our hearts as Oprah tells us he is, his tragedies and triumphs become our tragedies and triumphs, her uniform our uniform, his homecoming our homecoming.

In order to read the theology of "Whole Again," it is important first to ask a few questions: What is the point of this civil religious psalm? Why are bodies deployed as they are, praised as they are, embraced as they are? In short, what is really going on here? Here I borrow from Jonathan Z. Smith, who has argued of ritual that it often provides communities with an "ought" that is precise and unambiguous not because this is how the world works, but rather because the ambiguities that ritual environments eschew are felt so powerfully in the non-ritual world, the world of "is."[21] Applying Smith to Winfrey as she applied herself to Jeep, and keeping in mind the civil religious moment of 2013, we must note the powerfully ambiguous reality on which "Whole Again" depends for its emotional force, that darkness at the edge of the screen. This reality involves and inhabits soldierly bodies that, whether destroyed or merely broken, can't walk up the front stairs or give a child a bath; bodies that look out on the world with darkened eyes, that resist communal embrace, that too often turn violence back on themselves or on those they once loved. This reality inhabits a nation that, some believe, has remained too distant, even disinterested, as bodies have marched forth to fight in Iraq and Afghanistan while the wars have come and gone from the news cycle.

Oprah and the Chrysler Corporation offer unambiguous salvation to that fallen, ambivalent nation. They show the way, the truth, the light to a community troubled by war and its multiple cultural and individual aftermaths. Mediated through those who have offered their bodies to the nation, this salvation involves a highly public embrace of the soldier, a commercial confession not only that "we" (America) need "you" (the American soldier) but, more important, that whether or not we *actually* need you, "we" must *acknowledge* our need of "you" if we are to be saved. The Gospel of Oprah gives us the G.I. Messiah.[22]

The range of discursive and ritual moments that I examine in this book extends beyond a two-minute Jeep commercial, a mid-century war film, and the cemeteries described above, but includes quite a few sources that have more in common with them than with more traditional sources for the study of civil religion. These choices are not meant to imply the irrelevance of more canonical materials. Abraham Lincoln's Second Inaugural and Gettysburg Address remain crucial texts in the history of American civil religion. But taking guidance from not only Smith but Sacvan Berkovitch and Perry Miller, I suggest that we attend to realities and dynamics beyond and beneath these texts, and behind and within their authors and orators. Lincoln's rhetorical positioning and community imagining are truly masterful. But what was the sine qua non of Lincoln's political and his moral power, especially late in his presidency? Whose deaths did he present to the American people as sacrifices of which they had to prove worthy? What happens when the prominence of soldierly bodies in scholarship on civil religion rises to match their prominence in the American civil religious imaginary?

Civil Religion and Soldiering

"Civil religion" has been a controversial and contested term since Robert Bellah brought it into American scholarly discourse in the 1960s.[23] I am applying the concept throughout this book because it has descriptive and analytic utility that reaches beyond the related terms "nationalism" and "patriotism," and because I am interested in continuing the work of those who have engaged with civil religion before me. For most of its life as an analytical category, civil religion has referred, in Bellah words, to "formal speech" and "original texts," as well as to public observances of moments of national import.[24] These sources and moments highlight the role of political leaders in expressing and shaping America's sense of itself and its place in the world.

When Bellah first described civil religion in America, he called fellow scholars to study it with "the same care in understanding" they would apply to any other religious tradition.[25] Many answered this call and carefully applied the methods that they believed would lead to the deepest understanding of a complex, compelling, and infamously elastic tradition. There is much to be learned from their work. The field of religious studies has, however, changed dramatically in the decades since Bellah first wrote, and scholars have increasingly engaged religious traditions not only through words spoken and written but also through embodied practices and lived patterns.[26] Such efforts have enriched the field with accounts of discord and tension between elite articulators of a faith and the lives and thoughts of laymen and -women (be it Puritanism in colonial New England, Judaism and Catholicism in mid-twentieth century Chicago, evangelicalism today). My aim is to bring similar concerns and similar questions to the study of civil religion. To wit: How and where is this religion practiced? By whom? How do these practitioners shape and engage this religion with their bodies?[27] This is, to my mind, akin to asking whether civil religion is just a heuristic mirage, or if there really is a there there? Are we really talking about religion, or are we happy simply to say the word?

It is a central contention of this book that the American military and American soldiers provide an excellent setting for inquiries into the complexity of American civil religion as practiced, lived, and died. Soldiers are indeed agents in the shaping of their civil religion. Like the faithful of America's myriad religious traditions, they accept, resist, and otherwise negotiate their relationships to orthodoxy and hierarchy.[28] It is perhaps more difficult to see soldierly agency because the mechanisms of the military and of American civil religion work so actively, so powerfully to obscure it, but its existence is a matter of historical record.

This book considers soldiering as civil religious practice. It is about the things soldiers do, are asked to do, expected to do, and are portrayed doing to embody devotion to the nation. By examining individual and communal attempts to articulate these demands and to reconcile them with experiences, I hope to provide a fuller accounting of civil religion as a lived religion full of contradictions and aspirations, half-made connections, meanings forged and forgotten and forged again, at the same time that I provide an accounting of its Christian theological frameworks. My intent is to think through the ways in which soldiers' bodies and experiences of war are woven into the community of faith, the ritual life, and the symbols of this religious tradition. The ubiquity of soldier veneration is staggering, its gravitational pull tremendous: political events, parades, civic gatherings of all types; car bumpers, novels and films. Never far from these moments are the practitioners themselves, often forced to work against civil religious orthodoxies to make sense of their war experiences and to live in the aftermath of having given flesh to the Word of the nation.

Very few works of American religious history have worked on this particular braid: religion, soldiering, and war. The reasons for this deficit range from the habits, attitudes, and methods of the relevant disciplines to broader cultural and political inclinations toward imagining American war-craft as disconnected from religion and vice versa. Scholars are working toward a more integrated picture of religion and warfare in American history, making their way, war by war, from the colonial era to our current moment, but few attend to soldiers and soldiering as closely as they study sermons, periodicals, and political rhetoric. By far the most comprehensive treatment of the soldier as a civil religious symbol is Edward Linenthal's 1982 study *Changing Images of the Warrior Hero in America,* which examines the interaction between images of the soldier and the changing nature of warfare from the Revolutionary period to the aftermath of Vietnam. Works by Catherine Albanese, Kelly Denton-Borhaug, Stanley Hauerwas, and Andrew Huebner have also drawn connections between images of the soldier and American self-understanding, describing and analyzing patterns that are as fascinating as they are troubling.[29] I have chosen to focus on lives (and on locations for remembering lives) in addition to patterns because they serve as windows onto the lived experiences and the complex relationship between the nation—understood as the nation-state and as the *Volk*—and American soldiers. The tension between individualism and the peculiar communalism of war service, between personal aspirations and national need, provides ample opportunity for describing and theorizing the appeal, the effects, and the costs of service both for soldiers and for the nation.

In addition to the generally humanistic task of noticing and rehumanizing individuals who so often stand as symbols, increased attention to the place of the soldier in American civil religion generates an interesting body of evidence regarding secularization and ecumenism in American civic life. Much recent scholarship has noted that insofar as twentieth-century scholars conceptualized secularization as the removal of religion from public life and the diminution of its influence across society, they failed not just as prognosticators but also as describers of the thing—secularization and the secular—they thought they saw.[30] Some observers would take the bits of evidence presented above (the cemeteries, the film, the advertisement) as proof positive that our current moment is indeed more secular, more ecumenical, than the moment that gave us the cruciform grave markers and the intensely Christian chapels of America's overseas military cemeteries. "Whole Again," they might say, is far less Christian than the American cemetery at Normandy.

It is significant that one needs to work harder, in general, to see Christian assumptions today than one did in 1923. Americans are more alert today than in 1918 to the problems with referring to the U.S. Army as "Pershing's Crusaders" or, as happened regularly in the Great War, with overt equations between the dying soldier and the suffering Christ. This change might lead one to argue that not only the G.I. Messiah but also more general

Christian influences have vanished from American civil religion. Just as plausible, though, is the argument that from Normandy to Hollywood to Super Bowl XLVII the civil theological assumptions connected with and to the G.I. Messiah have remained strong and influential and are at least as widely embraced today as they were a century ago. Modern media has certainly played a part in disseminating and arguing for particular conceptions of the American soldier. These conceptions have, I believe, simultaneously become more acceptable as the theological discourses have become more substructural, the messianic discourse phrased not in New Testament language but in terms of embodied virtue, supreme sacrifice, and atonement. A brief return to a mid-century war film in which the G.I. Messiah is subtly but undeniably present helps illustrate this point.

Only eight years after the release of *The Bridges at Toko-Ri*, another film about soldiering in the Cold War arrived in American theaters. *The Manchurian Candidate* (1962) told the story of Major Bennett Marco (Frank Sinatra) and Sergeant Raymond Shaw (Laurence Harvey), leaders of a platoon captured during the Korean War, brainwashed by a Communist International, and returned to the United States as part of a plot to control the United States government. It is easy to see in *The Manchurian Candidate* only critiques about soldiering as civil religious practice and none of the veneration that dominates *The Bridges at Toko-Ri*. The story is indeed more complicated. It is in the midst of war that Communists lay claim to the minds of the American soldiers and turn Sergeant Shaw into both a war hero and an assassin. Upon returning home, Major Marco struggles mightily with what we now call PTSD. Sergeant Shaw's mother (Angela Lansbury) is relentless in her attempts to exploit his ill-gotten Congressional Medal of Honor to bolster her own political power. Yet *The Manchurian Candidate* develops these negative portrayals of soldiering for America only to overturn them. Major Marco recovers from the psychological wounds of war and helps Sergeant Shaw to understand and counter his own more sinister postwar affliction. Marco and Shaw, two veterans, are the only men in the entire nation who are both fully aware of the Communist plot and able to thwart it through properly directed violence. In the end Shaw takes his own life but only after saving the nation from possible Communist takeover.

In the film's final scene, Major Marco is at home with his wife Eugenie (Janet Leigh) trying to make sense of an evening of violence, most particularly Shaw's suicide. "Poor Raymond. Poor friendless, friendless Raymond," he says. "He was wearing his medal when he died." Marco is holding a book, a history of American war heroes, consisting of Congressional Medal of Honor citations. With a rain-spattered window behind him, Marco continues: "You should read some of these citations sometime, just read them. 'Taken eight prisoner, killing four enemy in the process while one leg and one arm were shattered, and he could only crawl because the other leg had been blown off.' *Edwards.* 'Wounded five times, dragged himself across the direct line of fire of three enemy machine guns to pull two of his wounded men to safety amid sixty-nine dead and 203 casualties.' *Holderman.*" Marco then extemporizes a Medal of Honor citation for Shaw, revising the tainted, Communist-authored original. The new, spoken version acknowledges that though Shaw was physically whole "the enemy" had "captured his mind and his soul" leading him to commit "acts [a string of political murders] too unspeakable to be mentioned here." Marco concludes in a highly orthodox register: "He freed himself at last, and in the end heroically and unhesitatingly gave his life to save his country." Marco's grafting of Shaw onto the heroic tradition of soldiering for America argues for continuity in the face of rupture. What happened to Shaw and what Shaw did are made meaningful by their perpetuation of a sacred history of service, suffering, and sacrifice.

Marco is not, however, simply adding one more soldier to a long line of heroes. He is reinterpreting and elaborating upon that tradition and, like the narrative of which he is a part, hinting at its theological substructure. The stories Marco relates of Daniel R. Edwards and Nelson Holderman are based on their Medal of Honor citations (quoted earlier in this introduction), but they are not those citations. Edwards's citation mentions previous injuries but describes his leg injuries differently and counts four not eight prisoners taken; Holderman's citation focuses as much on his leadership of a group in extremis as on the rescue of his comrades. Marco is not lying to the audience, but he is amplifying a mythology and taking liberties with his sources. These liberties extend beyond the content he cites to the structure of his citation. The standard citation for a Congressional Medal of Honor includes the soldier's name in the first sentence if not in the first words. Marco presents the acts of heroism first and adds names only at the end. The tradition of service, suffering, and sacrifice endures. Edwards, Holderman, and Shaw are incarnations of it. Through them we know the nation. Through them we can be saved. In the beginning is the Word. Then the Word is made flesh.

Finally, my focus on the soldier may well fuel conversations about the boundaries around a dominant type of American civil religion and prompt reflection on the relationship among competing varieties of American civil religion.[31] There are, after all, many Americans who would not place the soldier near the center, much less *at the center* of the nation, and who do not share the theology, whether explicit or implied, discussed throughout this book. This does not negate the historical phenomenon to which I am attending, nor does it mean that the trope and the theology are tangential to American civil religion. What it does mean is that, as with any religion, there have been multiple ways of confessing and embodying American civil religion. Interestingly, though, the soldier has often figured meaningfully if not centrally in other varieties of civil religion, countertraditions if you will. He has regularly embodied damning truths about the nation, about war, and about particular policies or administrations. Both praise and critique of the nation have been mediated through the G.I. Messiah.

Chapters and Approach

G.I. Messiahs is built around six case studies. The first three examine moments from the first half of the twentieth century; the second three focus on the Cold War, Vietnam, and the War on Terror. I have chosen these cases because they illustrate well the enduring dynamics of soldiering as civil religious practice, the recognizably religious valences of that practice, and active soldierly engagement with religious and civil religious authority. These cases also suggest two recognizable phases of American civil religion as a lived tradition. The first phase, 1917–60, during which the United States fought three major overseas conflicts, made military and cultural sense of the outcomes, and mourned its soldier dead, saw the working out at official and lay levels of a civil religious orthodoxy vis-à-vis the American soldier. During these decades of American ascendancy the G.I. Messiah was draped in the symbols and narratives of Christianity. His military service grew out of a sense of duty to the nation and devotion to its causes. Death in combat was rendered meaningful in powerfully Christian terms and was imagined as redemptive for the nation and salvific for the soldier. The second phase, covering the remaining years of the twentieth century and the first decade of the twenty-first, has been marked by the persistence and, in many ways, the strengthening of civil religious orthodoxy. But as the cases I examine highlight, these five decades have seen public contestation of orthodox renderings of the G.I. Messiah—some arising from soldiers themselves—and attempts by public and private voices to make civil religious sense of the space between the orthodox soldierly ideal and discordant soldierly realities. American civil religion and the place of the soldier in it are not immune to change, but neither are soldier practitioners or the civil religious devout fickle in their devotion. In short, this is not a story of orthodoxy crumbling under the pressure of ritual failures, of a Christological crisis, and of democratized engagement with soldierly sacrifice. It is not the story of civil religious paralysis in the face of complex moral and devastating martial realities. It is, rather, a story of contestation, adaptation, and reassertion.

I have chosen these cases also because they are challenging as subjects of interpretation and because I am aware of the hazard of tautology posed by the study of a symbol. In this work on the religious dynamics of soldiering and the Christian valences of the imagined American soldier it would be convenient but ultimately self-serving either to attend to evidence with little connection to broader national communities or to find a crucifix wherever straight lines intersect. There is no sure way to avoid the overly narrow or the biased hermeneutic other than to read and analyze carefully, to step away from a project regularly, and to rely on friends, colleagues, and reviewers to ask difficult questions. The cases described in this book were all simultaneously public and private, social and individual, about "the American soldier" and about an American soldier. My hope is that they connect both among themselves and to cases not discussed here. Where that connections fails, further discussions of theology, history, and methodology in the study of soldiering and civil religion may well bear fruit that renders this endeavor worthwhile beyond my original framework.

Analogies such as the one woven throughout this book (soldier to Christ, nation to God) are by definition imperfect. They bring together two objects or qualities of objects, two ideas, two things that are not the same for the purpose of encouraging sustained reflections on their similarities and, through reflection on similarity, to better understand the two distinct entities. Imperfect as they may be, analogies have exerted considerable force on American imaginings of the nation's place in the world and those who fight on its behalf. This book demonstrates that American civil religion—as practiced in the twentieth and twenty-first centuries—has drawn deeply and consistently on Christianity, subtly encouraging (through analogy, symbol, myth, and ritual) a Christian identity in its practitioners. Christian norms structure many public moments of civil religious devotion and have been especially visible in the public veneration of the simultaneously Americanized and Christianized bodies of American soldiers. Nevertheless, as with all norms, there are those who contest these from within—within the nation, within the military.

I am interested in describing and analyzing the religious dynamics of soldiering for America and the place of the soldier in American civil religion not to belittle or reduce. My own experiences in the military—four years of active duty in the navy, over six years in the reserves—are one indication of the seriousness with which I take this subject. Rather, I hope that this study and its constituent chapters will contribute to a more sophisticated understanding of how American civil religion works as a religion, will heighten sensitivities to the human dilemmas posed by soldier veneration as it has been configured and practiced in twentieth- and twenty-first-century America, and will encourage greater attention to the complex and sometimes tragic modes of thought, feeling, and action with which soldiers have engaged a religious tradition that makes more space for myths and symbols than for voices and people.

While I find some of the cases described in this book troubling and occasionally present these troubles as part of my analysis, I will leave to others representing the kaleidoscope of religious traditions in the United States the task of raising questions in a sustained way about the theological propriety of American civil religion in general and soldier veneration in particular. Were the answers to questions about service to earthly power (and the imagination of that service) and service to the divine (and imagination thereof) obvious and uncomplicated, they would have been presented and embraced long ago by observers far more astute than I. We need only look to any American war of the past two centuries to see people of good will and good faith balancing earthly and heavenly loyalties in radically different ways. Disagreement on this constellation of issues is here to stay. If my interpretation of the religious dynamics of soldiering and the difficulties to which they contribute tilts the debate one way, awareness of the profound sense of duty that soldiers embody and of the battles they have helped wage against corrupt, despotic, murderous regimes may well tilt the debate back in the other direction. What I hope to impress upon readers—whatever their ideological or theological inclination—is the value of thinking carefully about soldiers and wars as we imagine, celebrate, and memorialize them and the importance of noticing and studying the men and women whose bodies and lives we ritually revere and defame, celebrate and ignore, remember and forget.

CHAPTER 1

Incarnating American Civil Religion

The dead body on the jail cell floor confirmed what the ten men suspected. Their comrade had been lynched. Led from the jail by an angry mob under cover of darkness, he was beaten, hung, and then shot repeatedly. He was then dragged back to the jail in Centralia, Washington, where the living prisoners had to share an already cramped space with his broken, lifeless body. Though we cannot know what the jailed men thought, it is reasonable to assume that their minds were numb with fear, shock, anger, exhaustion, revulsion. November 11, 1919, had been a long and bloody day.[1]

The body count stood at five. Four of the dead were veterans of the Great War and members of the American Legion, shot to death when their Armistice Day parade somehow devolved into a raid on the Centralia offices of the Industrial Workers of the World (IWW). Bullets fired by IWW members killed Warren Grimm, Arthur McElfresh, Dale Hubbard, and Ben Casagranda. The fifth body was that of the lynching victim, Wesley Everest, also a former soldier. Everest began the day as an IWW organizer struggling against the timber industry in the Pacific Northwest. When violence erupted out of the Legion parade, he was the triggerman allegedly responsible for killing Casagranda and Hubbard and wounding another Legionnaire. His day and his life ended in a tempest of violence, pain, and darkness as local men, many of whom were likely Legionnaires, ripped him from the jail and took the law into their own hands.

The mob lynched only the former soldier that night, but the town and the Legion wanted the body count to climb. Reports from the scene described Centralia residents promising, "There won't be any I.W.W.s left in the jail by morning." For its part the Legion hoped, after a trial, to throw "a first class hanging party" for those IWW members who had not tasted the full measure of vigilante justice.[2] The United States, they believed, was not big enough for people with un-American ideas: Communists, socialists, anarchists. The mutilated corpse of Wesley Everest was a ghoulish memo from the Legion and its supporters: the rights of radicals in America were being foreclosed.

Theirs was not an isolated position. Newspapers from San Francisco to Chicago to New York screamed for vengeance—arrest, expulsion, violence—against radicals of all types. Guests at the annual dinner for the Indiana chapter of the Sons of the American Revolution heard the organization's president, Chancellor L. Jenks, proclaim, "We have jails and scaffolds . . . and vessels sailing away daily. Let us use them all. The blood of those men killed at Centralia calls for vengeance and the men who avenged the sinking of the *Lusitania* and the rape of Belgium [America's Great War veterans] will not let that call go unheeded." An editorialist at the *Indianapolis Star* warned faithful patriots to be on guard against "Parlor Bolshevism" which was taking hold among "Americans from whom better things are expected."[3] Federal and state authorities drove home lessons in the limits of liberty nationally by launching raids on the headquarters of suspected radicals. These same lessons were driven home locally as the IWW men jailed in Centralia were forced to build a coffin for their dead friend and to dig what would become his unmarked grave. Wesley Everest's horrific demise and his unresurrected return to his imprisoned comrades culminated in his erasure from the American memorial environment.

News of the bloodshed in Centralia radiated quickly across the country and surely reached the small town of Astoria, Oregon, within hours. Separated by roughly one hundred miles of mountain, forest, field, and river, Centralia and Astoria were linked at least by commerce. In 1919 Centralia's economy depended on agriculture and timber—cultivation, harvest, and milling. Astoria was and is a site for shipping product to market. The town sits on the south bank of the Columbia River just inland from the point where the Columbia tears its way into the North Pacific. Residents of Astoria have a front-row seat at the infamous Columbia River Bar, a uniquely treacherous and yet crucial passage for commercial vessels carrying cargo out of the Pacific Northwest and bringing goods to inland markets via the Columbia, the region's freshwater artery. The battle between the forces of river and ocean, often exacerbated by violent North Pacific storms, creates currents, surf, and variations in depth that are, for those who must navigate the bar, at best nerve-wracking and dangerous, at worst bewildering and deadly.[4]

Reverend Aaron Allen Heist moved to Astoria in 1918 to become the pastor of the First Methodist Church. He and Elsie, his wife of two years, had married during his previous pastorate at Rose City Park Methodist Church in Portland. Reverend Heist had also served churches in Warrenton and St. Helens, Oregon, with a three-year break for studies in divinity at Garrett Theological Seminary in Evanston, Illinois, all before his thirty-fourth birthday. News of the Armistice Day violence and the looming murder trial may well have been pushed from the headlines in Astoria by a winter storm that struck Washington and Oregon on December 9, 1919, and raged across the region for three days bringing historic snows and arctic temperatures.[5] Nevertheless, as he sat down to prepare his sermon for Christmas Day 1919, Reverend Heist had the American soldier on his mind. Like many ministers before and since, Heist sought to explain to his congregation the nature of the miracle of Christmas and the words of John 1:14: "And the Word became flesh." The American soldier, he thought, was an especially apt analogy.

Reverend Heist delivered his Christmas sermon, "Present Day Incarnation," from a collage of typed and handwritten notes. The print varies, but the message is constant. The Word has been in the world for ages, filling "hearts and consciences of poets, prophets and lawgivers," but the Word reached "full flower" only when it appeared in the "flesh." As was common among liberal and modernist Protestant clergy, Heist took events described in scripture as important less for their historical uniqueness than for what they said about the ongoing relationship between God and humanity. He continued, "This is what we celebrate at Christmas. Not the coming of a new word . . . but the setting of the well known word in terms of flesh and blood. . . . In actual life real things are done only when a spirit takes on flesh." Christmas, Heist declared, celebrates more than a past miracle, "What God did in Christ that first Christmas, God is always waiting and longing to do." As proof of the ongoing reality of incarnation, Heist asked the Methodists of Astoria to think about the recently concluded world war. "America spoke great words as she entered the war, words that have shone far and will be long remembered. But that which has given power to the words is that they became flesh; sacred flesh that lies buried in a soil once alien; clean flesh that marched and fought and suffered for the honor of the country and the safety of humanity. The flesh without the word would have been brute force; the word without the flesh would have been a bit of paper. It was when the word became flesh that the word became mighty." As Jesus Christ was to the Christian God, so was the American soldier to the United States of America. Flesh alone—mere bodies—whether moving through villages and teaching in parables or running through fields and brandishing weapons—would spread error or violence. The word alone— from Roman-occupied Palestine to the trenches of Europe—was without influence in the shaping of the world. American soldiers made the "great words" of the nation real and efficacious. The great words of the nation made American soldiers righteous.

Reverend Heist continued, "This is the present and undying meaning of Christmas—that God brings about his mighty ends by incarnation, by setting forth truth not in words of wisdom but in deeds of love. . . . Christmas comes to remind us that infinitely more effective than the most glowing vision or the wisest plan is a single human life that puts into flesh and blood something of the vision of the ideal." Worshippers at Astoria's First Methodist Church made their way home with Heist's soldier-savior analogy on their minds and with his concluding words in their ears, "Not the word, but the word made flesh, is ever the power of God unto salvation."[6]

On the surface, there is little to connect Centralia's Armistice Day killings and Astoria's Christmas Day sermon. A regional map that accompanied the *Chicago Tribune*'s initial reports of the events in Centralia depicted both towns, but readers certainly focused on the "Scene of Outrage" and the public drama unfolding in Washington State knowing little about the hamlet on the Oregon coast. Regardless of where one lived, there was little reason to think of the civil religion and bloodshed on display in Centralia through the theological framework deployed in Astoria. A patriotic parade marking the first anniversary of the end of the Great War explodes into violence. An articulate young Methodist minister delivers a Christmas sermon. What hath Sparta to do with Jerusalem? What connects these events, in addition to their Pacific Northwest setting, is their engagement with civil religion even if the "civil" or civic in one case and the "religion" in the other, are less than obvious, and their use of soldiers' bodies as sites in and over which to work out civil religious doctrine.[7]

Reading a Parade, Mapping a Sermon

No assumption was more central to the American Legion in its first two decades than the sacred nature of soldiering for America. The Legion was founded in March 1919, just eight months before the Centralia Massacre, by veterans of the Great War. It was established for the purpose of keeping alive "the spirit of the Great War" in the lives of the four million men and women who had served the nation, both in France and on other foreign and domestic fronts.[8] The veterans' organization grew dramatically in membership and influence in its first year, enlisting 800,000 members and establishing local posts across the nation—from Washington, D.C., and Charleston, South Carolina, to Los Angeles and, of course, Centralia, Washington. Out of a desire to distance this body of former soldiers from national politics, Legion leadership chose to locate the national headquarters in Indianapolis, Indiana. A core belief of the American Legion and indeed of many Americans in the aftermath of the Great War was that the United States was at risk in the postwar world and would face recurring attacks on its institutions and on "the American way." In the words of Chicago-based Legionnaires, "We still have a fight to be carried to a victorious conclusion here at home."[9] It was hard to know exactly who the enemies were—ethnic and ideological outsiders were prime suspects—but it was clear that the redemption of America required an ongoing battle against them.

The Legion and its members were committed both to the physical protection of the nation and to the rhetorical and ritual recognition of its sanctity. They understood their words, their performances, and their works to be acts of devotion to "God and Country." The Legion was also animated by the belief that no service to nation or to God surpassed soldiering in purity, nobility, and honor. Those who had died in the Great War were a sainted cohort, and those who returned from the war were burdened with the task of shaping a nation and a world of which the fallen would approve. The renowned Presbyterian missionary Robert Speer gave voice to this sentiment when he wrote in 1919, "Their sacrifice is calling to us to finish what they began. . . . The dead ask this of us. They have a right to ask it and to threaten to stir beneath the Flanders poppies if we will not hear."[10] Those who had worn the uniform, whether living or dead, were worthy of veneration for their embodiment of national values and their willingness to suffer and die for the United States.

This connection between the war dead and the returning veteran shaped the Legion's policy agenda, which expressed a combination of benevolent and vicious civil religion. In the name of the fallen, the Legion insisted on benefits and medical care for surviving families and returning veterans. In the name of the fallen, the Legion persecuted those it imagined as disloyal or un-American. Those who ran afoul of the Legion—the IWW, Communists, socialists, anarchists, the Ku Klux Klan, pacifists, Prohibitionists, recent immigrants—had little in common beyond challenging in some way the Legion's vision of America, its history, its present, its future. And though lynchings connected to the Legion were not commonplace, extralegal justice and the suppression of dissent marked their activities throughout the interwar period. The Legion's goal was to cultivate a civil religious orthodoxy and a devout citizenry, uniformly committed to the preservation of the nation, deeply reverent of the nation's mythic past, and moved by civil religious hymns, symbols, and rituals toward belief in the transcendence of America. From this passionately devout people would come men ready and willing to arm themselves and fight the enemy, whenever and wherever he could be met.

Reverend Aaron Allen Heist cut a very different path from the one walked by the American Legion. He was a friend neither of the Legion nor of the industries of mass cultivation and extraction that so dominated the American West during his lifetime. His theological leanings were clearly modernist. His political leanings were distinctly leftward. From a later pastorate, Grace Community Church in Denver, Colorado, he provided both meeting space and spiritual guidance to striking miners in the coal strike of 1927–28. Heist left the ministry in 1931 to work as the secretary of social services for the Columbia Conserve Company in Indianapolis, a cooperatively owned soup canning company. He returned to ministry in the mid-1930s and relocated to California. After thirteen years in the Los Angeles area, during which he preached and protested against the internment of Japanese Americans, he became director of the Southern California branch of the American Civil Liberties Union (ACLU).[11]

In each of these political and geographic contexts—labor organization in Colorado, cooperative industry in Indianapolis (home to the national headquarters of the American Legion), ACLU leadership in Los Angeles—Heist would have found himself in ideological and legal, if not physical, conflict with the Legion. By 1934 his work had earned him a listing in *The Red Network: A "Who's Who" of Radicalism and Handbook for Patriots* published by Elizabeth Dilling, with endorsements from fundamentalist firebrand William Bell Riley; national Americanism director for the American Legion Russell Cook; and Illinois national commiteewoman [sic] of the American Legion Auxiliary Mrs. Melville Mucklestone. Heist represented much of what the American Legion despised in the United States. To be fair, the feelings were mutual.[12]

Ideological differences are only one of many ways that the deadly events of November 11, 1919, and Heist's words of December 25, 1919, diverge. These moments differed also in terms of discourse, practice, institution, and community.[13] Civil religion is not Christianity; a parade is not a sermon; the American Legion is not the Methodist Church. Walter Grimm marched with the Legionnaires before a general public. He and three comrades were shot to death before that same public. Though the lynching of Wesley Everest was carried out by a subgroup of that public—seven cars, perhaps thirty men—its message reached every member of that public and millions more beyond.[14] Reverend Heist preached to a specific and more intentional community. His words were intended for the ears of Astoria's Methodists and for those worshipping with them that day. The sermon lives on today not in newspaper articles from across the country but in a box in a modest library in southern Los Angeles. Even today the very nature of these events makes them seem incomparable. One event was decidedly civic; the other was clearly ecclesiastical.

To leave the analysis here, to accept a rigid separation between the civil and the ecclesiastical, is, however, to ignore not only the combination of the ecclesiastical and the civic in many events in American history before and after 1919, but also much insightful scholarship on civil religion in general and American civil religion in particular. George Mosse's work on the "cult of the fallen soldier" in wartime and interwar Germany finds myriad connections between the "popular piety" of German Christians and the framing of soldierly life and death. Harry S. Stout and Kelly Denton-Borhaug have examined the role of Christian theologies of sacrifice on popular American conceptions of war and service.[15] These writers and many others make clear that there is a more direct route than is immediately apparent from the streets, the jail, and the bridge trestle of Centralia to the pulpit of Astoria's First Methodist Church, and vice versa. This route begins with the realization that the discourses and practices involved in parades and in preaching are more alike than we generally acknowledge. Parades are not sermons, but they can be understood as acts of evangelism. Sermons are not parades, but they travel a moral landscape and often display civic devotion.

The history of public celebrations in America includes numerous examples of civic and religious messages mixing to affirm a community and its particular religious values (the Festa in Italian Harlem), to reject the religion of some members of the community (Protestant Pope's Day observances, anti-Jewish German-American Bund rallies in the 1930s), and to assert violently the limits of "good" religion and "polite" society (New York City's

1834 Fourth of July celebration that became an attack on a church believed to sanction interracial marriage).[16] Parades have religious messages: *our religion cannot be controlled by a church hierarchy; your religion is incompatible with American values; God requires racial separation.* In the Legionnaire's Armistice Day parade through Centralia—in the occasion, the form, even the fracturing—we can see powerfully religious discourses at work. The Legionnaires and their supporters gathered to mark November 11, 1919, as sacred time—a day to be remembered and a day to remember those who had served, suffered, and sacrificed. The day on which the Great War came to an end was the day, in the words of the soldier-authors of the *Stars and Stripes* newspaper, on which "the Prince of Peace [had] at last come into His own."[17] Not all Legionnaires would have used those words, but there can be no question as to their belief in the sanctity of their war and the righteousness of American warriors.

It was not enough, though, for Legionnaires simply to hold these beliefs and remember their fallen friends quietly in their homes. The parade was both a highly public memorial act and an effort at evangelism. *We are remembering Armistice Day*, the parade said, *and so should you. If you can't be a soldier, at least you can support soldiers and acknowledge their service.* Moreover, when the Legionnaires clashed with the IWW in and around the union hall, they were making at least two statements about the makeup of their communities. They were saying first and most clearly that the beliefs and actions of the Wobblies were heretical and that the Legion would not suffer them to corrupt the town. More subtly but no less important, the Legionnaires were claiming a special authority derived from their experiences in war, whatever those experiences had been. Having served America in wartime, they said, we possess a clear understanding of what America is and ought to be. We have the authority to act on that understanding with impunity. We sit at the right hand of the Father.

Sermons, like parades, are often shot through with civic sentiment, bringing the "civil" into direct contact with the obviously "religious." The flow of civic ideas into the pulpit is readily apparent across American history. Lyman Beecher famously issued a "Plea for the West," calling good Protestant men and women to establish a frontier bulwark against an imperial, anti-American Catholicism. The wartime sermons of Union and Confederate clergymen offered sanctifications of union, of secession, and of war in service of both. Billy Graham called his audiences to defend capitalism and democracy against communism. Martin Luther King Jr. preached regularly on civic ideals and unrighteous governmental structures. Reverend Heist's sermon, with its reliance on the analogy between soldier and savior to clarify the Christian understanding of the incarnation, is another example of this steady back-and-forth flow between God and country.

Heist did not map in great detail his perception of the American civic, religious, or cultural landscape. Unlike many in 1919, he took no pains to draw borders around an American community and to insist that some or many or most could never belong. Yet his sermonic map of postwar America, like a great many maps created by nations possessing or aspiring to great power, was rife with judgments about place, privilege, and authority. Though the ground would shift and Heist would eventually find a different vantage point, in 1919 his map of America and of the world had as its axis mundi the American soldier.[18] He not only granted the soldier the status of the "word" of the United States made flesh with the exceedingly powerful historical and essentialist claims that status implies ("In the beginning was the Word. And the Word was with God, and the Word was God."), he also emphasized the enduring reliance of the word on those who embodied it. Heist made clear where and in whom the sacred center of America was found.

In the closing months of 1919, both Heist and the American Legion spoke forcefully about the religious power of soldiering. Believing that they had waged a war "For God and Country," that their friends and brothers and sisters had given their lives "For God and Country," Legionnaires argued in parade and performance that they had a privileged perspective on the proper understanding of "God and Country" and that their will should be done. Though less explicit about the political implications, Heist produced a sermon that must be read as a more sophisticated mapping of the Legion's position. The soldiers who had gone to France to wage war against German tyranny were the word of the United States of America made flesh. As living soldiers, they were "clean flesh." As fallen soldiers, they were "sacred flesh." Is it so improbable that the returning soldier would believe both that the word still dwelled within and that, because of this indwelling, he was empowered to cast out demons real and imagined?

I raise these points about civil and ecclesiastical moments and messages, celebrations and services, parades and sermons, to challenge the rigid boundaries that some would place around these concepts and actions and to argue that civil religion exists across this range of practices and spaces. Moreover, by noting the porousness of categories and the breadth of civil religion as a phenomenon, we can see more easily that veneration of the soldier, worship of the G.I. Messiah, has not been confined to one region of the country, one end of the religio-political spectrum. One would expect the American Legion to portray the violence in Centralia as a clash between orderly, peaceful marchers and malicious, satanic Wobblies. "The Centralia Awakening," an editorial published in the *New York Times* on November 14, 1919, shows that such sentiments circulated well beyond the fraternity of the recently uniformed.

> The word "martyr" is often misused and applied to men who are merely victims. A martyr is one whose death is caused by his support of principles and convictions. The dead soldiers who were marked for slaughter by the I.W.W. because they believed in the American flag were martyrs to that belief, and the blood of the martyrs is the seed of the church. From that scene of their slaughter there has sprung up and spread a national horror and detestation of their slayers which embraces the whole horrible association to which those murderers belong, and it has done more than anything else to solidify the American people against them. Those five lives were not given in vain.[19]

The author wove together the Christian and the American sacred—the age of the martyrs as described by Tertullian and the age of the Civil War described by Lincoln; the church with its cult of the martyrs and the nation with its cult of the fallen soldier; evangelism, awakening, and sacrifice for God, flag veneration, war, and sacrifice for nation. What he found when he stepped back from this tapestry was the makings of a civil religious revival, and soldiers were its epicenter.

Soldiering, Society, and the Sacred

These two moments in the life of the twentieth-century United States—Heist's sermon and the Legion's parade, attack, and lynching—separated by six weeks and one hundred miles, are connected by their attention to and veneration of the American soldier. They imagined the soldier in similar ways and vested in him a similar authority. Evidence of this reverence for the American soldier was and is wide-ranging. Why? Why the veneration of the soldier? Why the particular language—spoken, acted, symbolic—of service, suffering, and sacrifice? To ask these questions is to ask questions also about the relationship between a collective (the nation) and a symbol (the soldier). It is also, necessarily, to ask about the relationship between the nation and the subcommunity (the military) to which the soldier is connected. Indeed, without some sense of how nation, military, and soldier fit together, the answers to questions like those asked above may describe well historical and contextual specifics but miss the forest in their attention to individual trees. For example, one could answer that the American Legion practiced civil religion as it did because of the power that Legionnaires, as former soldiers, derived from the organization's discourses and practices, or that Legion supporters up and down the economic ladder practiced civil religion as they did as cover for common, garden-variety intolerance of ethnic and ideological difference. On this reading, Reverend Heist's words arose from his liberal infatuation with Wilsonian progressivism and the recognition that in the soldier he had found a preacher's best friend: the compelling analogy. One could answer, in short, that soldier veneration and thus civil religion stood in for something else. These answers describe aspects of a moment but fail to account for the enduring appeal of mythologies, traditions, and rituals associated with the military and with soldiering for America. Heist and the Legion looked upon the soldier and saw virtue. Heist praised and the Legion enacted the freedom-defending, world-making power of the soldier. Both brought the imagined, righteous soldier, as civil religious symbol, before the public and argued, in words and in deeds, that he was both *of* them and *apart* from them.

Within two years of the events in Centralia and Astoria, America's leading Protestant clergymen published *Religion among American Men: As Revealed by a Study of Conditions in the Army*. This study, compiled by the Federal Council of Churches of Christ (FCCC), is a third civil religious data point from the Great War era and allows some modest triangulation of key features of American understandings of soldiering and war in the interwar period. The FCCC's Committee on the War and the Religious Outlook (CWRO) undertook the study in order to chart a course for American mainline Protestantism based on soldiers' religious experiences and opinions. Charles Brent, Episcopal bishop and former chief of chaplains, wrote of the urgency of this project in the foreword to the report, "We are worse than fools if we are to learn nothing from the war, and if men did not find their faith all we have a right to expect faith to be when shells are exploding and men dying by the thousands, we need not so much examine our faith itself as the form in which we have been expressing it and teaching it."[20] *Religion among American Men* provides some very clear answers as to how one large group of clergymen imagined soldiering and its significance for them. It also points toward more general answers about the relationship between soldiers and the nation and about the place the soldier occupies in American civil religion.

The Federal Council of Churches of Christ called the CWRO into being in 1917. The generally liberal, modernist leanings of this mainstream Protestant body are clear in the assumptions that guided them. Namely, that Christian leaders must study the momentous and catastrophic events unfolding in the world to discern God's message for the modern church, and that having studied and discerned the lessons, the church should adapt teachings and practices accordingly. In compiling the report, the committee wove its own commentary and analysis together with chaplains' observations, soldiers' responses to questionnaires, and a range of additional reporting. The central assumption of the report (and, not surprisingly, its conclusion) was that Christian churches have a great deal to learn from the military. Using the words of liberal divine Harry Emerson Fosdick, then pastor of New York City's First Presbyterian Church, the CWRO argued for the church to become more like the army. Fosdick had been blunt about the gulf between the two. "There is a fundamental antipathy between [the church's appeal to men] and the spirit in which the whole army is living. The former is thoroughly self-centered. The latter is gloriously self-forgetful" Not one to pull a punch, he continued, "There is a shocking incongruity between an attack at the front—rich and poor, learned and ignorant, prominent and obscure going over the top together—and a congregation in a wealthy metropolitan church singing: 'Onward, Christian Soldiers, Marching as to War.'"[21] *We* are self-satisfied, self-aggrandizing, class-stratified hypocrites, Fosdick argued. *They* are the truly egalitarian, the truly American, the truly Christian. Churches pale in comparison to the army.

A crucial feature of the American Legion's worldview, Reverend Heist's sermon, and *Religion among American Men* is an imagined military, what historian and theologian Philip Sheldrake might describe as a utopia. In *Spaces for the Sacred: Place, Memory, and Identity*, Sheldrake reminds readers that the term "utopia" once had an ambiguity that common usage has removed. "Strictly speaking all imaginary places, *good and bad*, are utopias. To qualify as utopias, imaginary places need to be expressions of human desire—positive or negative."[22] To describe the military this way is to underscore the fact that cultural, political, and civil religious imaginings shape understandings and experiences of the military at least as much as actual encounters with the people, equipment, and institutions that constitute it. The mythic quality of the military, soldiers, and war has been strong and pervasive enough that in encounters with actual soldiers and even in the lives of soldiers themselves, utopian visions play a powerful role in setting the parameters of interpretation. This is true not simply for Civil War battle reenactors or military hardware fetishists. It holds also for those who view the military negatively but have never set foot on a military base. Critical visions of the military have often been informed less by direct encounter and more by over-simple imaginings of vice or virtue, perfidy or heroism.[23]

Americans care about individual soldiers for many personal reasons. Americans care about "the soldier" in general because of the hold of utopian visions of the military upon the American imagination and because of the receptivity of a distant, imagined military to the desires of those doing the imagining. Members of the American Legion, certainly closer to the institution than most, imagined an orderly, harmonious body serving the nation with honor and righteousness; Aaron Allen Heist saw "clean flesh" building a new, more peaceful, more Christian world. Harry Emerson Fosdick saw the military as a model for a reformed church committed to selfless action in the world.

Sheldrake's subsequent discussion of a particular type of utopia suggests a more specific conception of the relationship between America and the military. Writing of monasteries and their meaning as sacred Christian spaces, Sheldrake notes: "Historically the monastic way has expressed the proleptic vision of Christian community in a particularly intensified form. Its specific purpose and power within the Christian community is to be the place that, while socially and culturally 'eccentric,' is paradoxically where people seek to live out the imaginative world of the Kingdom in radical terms."[24] He then weaves his insights regarding utopias into a discussion of the relationship of monasteries (and monasticism) to European society in the medieval period. Monasticism, he writes, was "essentially liminal" and monasteries "examples of utopias—nowhere places that express human aspirations and desires."[25] Sheldrake notes that the relationship between the monastic "utopia" and the broader society was ambivalent. "The question," he writes, "is whether this liminality is intended to underline a kind of utopian vision for redemption of the human city or whether it condemns the city as irredeemable and offers itself as an alternative." Is the monastic community a model to which broader society should aspire or a lifeboat to which broader society should flee?

The list of obvious ways in which the military and monasticism are parallel is long. Members of both groups separate themselves from society and stand more or less apart as long as their affiliation lasts. Their lives apart are born of and reasserted by rituals that dissolve initiates' old identities and bestow new ones; separation is reinforced through distinctive dress, routinized communal living, a life of comparative poverty, and a lived commitment to a higher power. Soldiering and monasticism each can be imagined as a holy community, in which members give their bodies and their lives to an ideal. This exact connection occurred to a contributor to *Religion among American Men* and to a mid-century historian of soldiering for America. The former focused on the fact that both groups exist at society's literal and figurative margins. "The [army] life was abnormal in many ways; men were separated from some of the normal social restraints and stimuli and given a new set of restraints and stimuli. The army was a male community. It was monastic without the religious impulse of monasticism."[26] The monasticism of military life consisted not just in its apartness, but in its maleness, and its replacement of one by another set of "restraints and stimuli" as well. The latter commentator, Samuel Huntington, presented a far more textured account of the military monastic. In 1957 he reflected simultaneously on the United States Military Academy at West Point and on the military's redemptive power for the United States. Describing the West Point campus, he wrote: "The parts do not exist on their own but accept their subordination to the whole. Beauty and utility are merged in gray stone. . . . The post is suffused with the rhythm and harmony which comes when collective will supplants individual whim. . . . Modern man may well find his monastery in the Army."[27] Huntington's utopic gaze settled on communalism, harmony, and the sacrificing of one's "whim" to the greater will. To Huntington's eye, the gray stone buildings surrounding a massive cathedral provided a majestic contrast to the disordered individualism and commercialism of the adjacent town of Highland Falls, New York. But he wasn't writing of the built environment only or even primarily. He was writing of the way that the military took many bodies and made of them one body, ruled by one will, with something religious in the middle.

Huntington could have been echoing another contributor to *Religion among American Men* who, though he did not use the word "monastery," clearly appreciated both the communal and the exemplary quality of military service even as he took note of certain moral blemishes.

Although the abnormal conditions of the military life have created serious moral problems, men have had an opportunity in the army to learn by experience many of the moral lessons the Church is engaged in teaching. The soldiers have been learning subordination of their individual desires to the good of the army. They have been learning a very real lesson in a brotherhood which takes no account of property ownership or class distinction. . . . They have learned intense loyalty to leadership. They have learned the satisfaction of binding their lives to a great purpose, and above all they have learned that the great enthusiasms of life are reserved for those who suffer in a great cause.[28]

In each of these accounts, mythology fuses with firsthand encounters, familiarity fuses with separation, to fuel powerfully utopian imaginings. The military emerges as a civil religious monastery occupied by civil religious adepts who model self-forgetfulness, service, and commitment to the nation. All commentators say in their own way, "Would that we all could live like that."

Probing intersections between military and monastic life helps illuminate the specifically religious dimensions of the relationship between society and the military. For military and monastic institutions are similarly situated toward the societies of which they are, and yet are not, a part. Their members and, more generally, their animating ideals can serve as examples for those not part and, yet, somehow indeed part of the cloistered community. As an American monastery the military distills American civil religion and enacts American communalism in ways that inspire admiration and devotion even as they, as monasteries and convents once did, arouse suspicion. This equation between military and monastery also brings into sharper focus the religious function of military ritual. For the men and women who enter the military and accept the unique commitments of a military lifestyle are not born soldiers. They must be made.

Ritual and the American Soldier

The American military is an exceptionally sophisticated and effective ritual culture. It is religious both because it forges a community and thus trades in one etymological root of the word religion (*religare:* to bind) and because it imparts an orienting ethic of collectivism, order, and sacrifice for a higher good.[29] The military inculcates an ethic of collectivism, sub-ordinating individual identities to collective identity, from the figurative cradle to the literal grave. Beginning in basic training, soldiers are required to embody this ethic: they don uniform clothing, alter their grooming, take their place in the ranks, add titles to their given names. New haircuts, clothes, and names signify new identities moored to a meta-community (the military), a community (the army, the navy, the Marine Corps, the air force), and, eventually, to several nested or overlapping subcommunities (naval aviation maintenance, army combat medic). These are but a few of the myriad instantiations of the collectivist ethic, the valuation of the group over the individual, and the subordination of personal preference, so ad-mired from afar.

The military values order; it teaches and aspires to professional and physical order; it operates on orders. The entirety of the military, from its commander-in-chief, the president, down to its newest seaman, airman, or private is structured in an orderly way. An order given by the commander-in-chief will make its way quickly down to the lowest rung of the collective. Order, orders, and ordering are quite clearly enacted communally when troops engage in the ritual of close-order drill, in which a squad, platoon, or company marches in unison, following the orders of an authority figure. After extensive practice these movements happen without the spacing be-tween soldiers changing and without a single soldier falling out of step. The ethic of order expressed by close-order drill builds on the collectivist ethic but adds to it a prescription for structuring and governing the collective.[30] *Listen to and obey those placed in charge,* the ritual says. *Work together to the ends designated by the commanding officer.*

Military rituals work in subtle and sophisticated ways toward their ulti-mate goal: the creation of a fighting unit the constituent members of which are willing to fight and to kill.[31] The connection between embodied, enacted rituals of military culture and the goal of effectively directed, potentially self-sacrificial violence is, however, less in the ordered marching and the uniform dressing and more in the cultivation and expression through these embodied behaviors of an ethic that elevates the collective and generates respect for authority. Embodied collectivism orients the soldier away from individual costs and toward collective goals. Enacted order encourages both faith in the decisions of those higher up the chain of command and a related sense of control of the situation. The precision of close-order drill, the at-tention to details of uniform dress, and even a concern across the services for physical fitness argue loudly and clearly against the chaos of combat for control of and over bodies. This is the military that parades before crowds: ordered, uniformed, communal; embodying service, enacting communalism. The parading evangelizes civil religion saying to those lining the streets not just that these are ideal, properly devout, properly committed Americans, but that this marching collective is an ideal America. Individuals are present, the formation preaches, but the strength is in the whole.[32]

The ritual culture of the military is directed toward the effective application and "management of violence," but the chaotic reality of violence does not intrude on this ritual life. In fact, military ritual resolutely displaces the variables of combat.[33] Yet the seals between military ritual and the realities of society—away from which it seeks to turn the soldier—and the realities of war—toward which it leads the soldier—are not impermeable. Close-order drill is a ritual with undeniable connections to a broader "cosmos."[34] To take just one example, it meant one thing to be led in close-order drill by an African-American junior officer in 1918 (something quite intolerable to white soldiers) and means something very different (and universally tolerated) today. These meanings were shaped for soldier and society, for military and nation, by the racial dynamics of the cosmos in which the rituals took place.

It is not surprising, then, that in the immediate aftermath of the Great War, the Committee on the War and the Religious Outlook would read the outcomes of military ritual and soldiers' memories of military experiences for clues as to how the churches should march forward through the twentieth century. It is less surprising still, given the muscular Christian culture of the early twentieth century, that the CWRO would believe that the members of the military "monastery" emerged from war service partially evangelized and primed for deeper religious commitments. "Men who have discovered that they belong to their country," one CWRO member wrote, "are better prepared to understand that they belong to God. . . . The brotherhood and democracy of the ranks at its best is a fleeting experience of what the Church seeks in its own fellowship."[35] The churches, he hoped, could turn soldiers' embodiment of devotion to the advantage of Protestantism in America.

Jonathan Z. Smith has argued that ritual is importantly though not exclusively about repetitive action and attention to detail. He writes "[Freud and Levi-Strauss] insist that ritual activities are an exaggeration of everyday activities, but an exaggeration that reduces rather than enlarges, that clarifies by miniaturizing in order to achieve sharp focus. . . . Ritual is primarily

a matter not of nouns and verbs, but of qualifiers—of adjectives and ad-
verbs." He continues, "Ritual precises ambiguities."[36] Through miniatur-
ization, repetition, and attention to detail, military ritual imparts an ethic
and precises ambiguities as to communal structure, authority, and ownership of the soldierly body in preparation for another ritual: war.

From the standpoint of civil religion, war is the nation's most important
ritual.[37] It is important at the national level for the questions it poses and
purports to answer about the extent of embodied commitment to the nation.
Who so loves the nation, war asks, *that he will fight and die for it? Who does not?*
In this communal register war reaffirms the national community to itself,
prescribing roles, dictating actions, determining rhetorics and responses.
War is certainly policy—the commitment of weapons and treasure to the
achievement of a particular geopolitical end, politics by other means—but
it is just as certainly ritual. War is prepared for, enacted, and remembered
in accordance with cultural and religious norms. War authorizes behaviors
that are illicit outside of its framework. War animates speeches and symbols
and invests them with abnormal power. The events that occur during wartime are commonly read as relevant and indeed revelatory well beyond the
period and the location of the conflict.

War is an important ritual at the individual level for the embodied responses it allows to its prescriptions and the validation and cultural authority it can provide for those who serve. From a structural standpoint war
begs to be treated as a classic three-part rite of passage, with individuals
separating from society to become soldiers, soldiers entering the liminal
phase of struggle and *communitas,* and then, finally, returning for reintegration into society either as a veterans or as fatalities.[38] Additionally, one finds
an expected, articulated, and enacted connection in American civil religion
between service in war and social authority. The body, living or dead, of one
who has gone to war testifies that suffering and sacrifice were more than
words, that love of country was more than an idea. A contributor to *Religion
among American Men* argued that soldiers in war, unlike other men, had
truly *lived* Christianity. "Men are actually finding out," he wrote, "what it
means to suffer for others or to have others suffer and die for them. It is not
difficult now to make them see the significance of the Christian teaching of
vicarious sacrifice and atonement."[39]

This is how war as a ritual was and is supposed to work.[40] Yet war fails
as a ritual with sufficient frequency that it poses the interpretive and practical question of how to address and understand this failure. Failures oc-

cur in the combat phase—into which chaos and the unexpected intrude with such violence that performances go awry and soldiers act counter to the ethic they are trained to embody—and in the reintegration phase—in which former soldiers encounter social expectations that remind them of war's horrors and force them, psychologically, to return regularly to combat. Indeed, it seems that these failures are as much the rule of the ritual as they are exceptions to it.

Words as Flesh, Flesh as Words

Sheldrake's discussion of utopias helps illuminate the imaginative patterns associated with the soldier as civil religious symbol, including the collective that defines his soldier-ness (the military) and the activity that sets him and his collective apart from civil society (war). The three objects—soldier, military, war—have quite specific, quite concrete realities. They also have a range of symbolic, mythological, and ritual meanings that exist in continual, low-grade dissonance with those realities, though not completely apart from them. The "reality" of a soldier is not, after all, entirely concrete simply because it is an embodied reality. Cultural conceptions and portrayals of the soldier are not all mistaken merely because they are in some way imagined or general. These realms overlap. Soldiers engage in, are engaged by, and often feed symbolic and mythological discourses; they too embrace the ritual significance of war.

I want to turn now from discourses of harmony and equation to those of dissonance and separation. From Reverend Heist's day to ours, evidence abounds that the pattern of incarnation that he articulated is more complicated as an embodied reality, that the monastery houses souls of all types. Soldiers do not, simply by virtue of being soldiers, carry out the will of the nation or meet the expectations of the citizenry perfectly. At times they run quite far off of the rails. Some resist the demands of soldiering or buckle under their weight. Others use their authority and their uniform in troubling ways. A contributor to *Religion among American Men* issued a caution along these very lines. "The obvious dangers in approaching Christianity through the experiences of the soldier are that too great emphasis be placed on the mere fact of suffering regardless of the character and spirit of the person who suffers, that the Cross of Christ be reduced to the meaning of 'a man laying down his life for friends,' that religion be identified with patriotism, and loyalty to the nation with loyalty to the Kingdom of God."[41] Be careful how you imagine the soldier and what you invest in him, the author warned. Analogies matter. Myths, symbols, and rituals have consequences.

The civil religious moments discussed in this chapter show evidence of the gap between ideal and embodied practices. A brief return to Centralia will allow us to consider not how the word was made flesh in the soldier but rather how former soldiers turned flesh into words. When the American Legion's Centralia post broke from its parade formation and charged the IWW union hall, they, as former soldiers, were embodying what they took to be the word of the nation. They were bringing violence to those they understood to be enemies of life, liberty, and the pursuit of happiness. The vigilante action that followed the initial eruption of violence carried this symbolic and mythological discourse to a more intense level. In Wesley Everest, the man they killed, the mob saw the enemy. And because he was an enemy from within the nation, they sent messages written in his flesh. In pulling Everest from the jail they said that Communists and socialists were unworthy of legal protection. In lynching Everest and allegedly castrating him, they said that Communists and socialists were neither fully white nor fully male. By returning the body to the jail they made certain that Everest's comrades got the message.

Another message is evident in the actions of the mob and the Legion. This message had to do with the interpretation of military service and the application of soldierly authority. Wesley Everest had, in fact, worn a United States Army uniform. His service, brief as it was, would have qualified him for membership in the American Legion. Whether or not the lynch mob knew it, Everest represented a competing evangel. In his life there was no straight line between service to the nation in time of war and antiradical activism on the home front.[42] To the extent that he connected his war service to any kind of postwar action, it was to the aggressive diminution of private enterprise, private capital, and the power of those who controlled both. Everest's body, then, was treated as a symbol of betrayal, of error. Wobblies, the Legion said through his broken body, are antiheroes, anti-soldiers, agents of the anti-Christ. They have earned civil religious damnation.

The Centralia Massacre also demonstrates the possibility of a space between official government words—the word—and the actions and attitudes of the word made flesh. Government agencies arrested and jailed and harassed suspected Communists and were guilty of numerous excesses during the Red Scare. In a moment of trauma, the Legion and its supporters became a mob and sought blood. Though they shared a hostility to communism, these two approaches to dissent were not the same, and the Legion made very clear its deep frustration that the IWW members charged and convicted in the incident escaped with their lives.[43] The actions of Legion members in Centralia and their reactions to the sentences the Wobblies received grew out of a belief that they and only they could solve the problem of Communist infiltration, that the nation and its laws would not do what was necessary, that an enduring awareness of Truth had come of their war service. In their extralegal actions, Reverend Heist might have said, Legion veterans lost touch with the word and became "mere flesh . . . brute force." But the civil religious responses to their display of force and the dying and killing in which they were involved indicate that much of the nation, not just the Legion itself, saw their hands as divinely guided.

Legion vigilantism is not the only evidence from the interwar period of spaces between orthodox narratives of soldiering for the nation and the lived realities of soldiers themselves. One can also find such gaps where men and women who wore the uniform, even wore it heroically, showed themselves uncomfortable with the fit. Though such moments are not characterized by explosive public performance and clear civil religious messages, they nevertheless reveal a great deal about soldiering as civil religious practice.

CHAPTER 2

Symbols Known, Soldiers Unknown

No American soldier before him had been buried with such ceremony. The ship that carried his remains home from France, the U.S.S. *Olympia*, sailed under escort, first by French and then by U.S. destroyers. A military guard stood constant watch over his casket, as if a moment without attention would be an insult to the warrior he had once been. Once *Olympia* was safely across the Atlantic and making her way up the Potomac River to the Washington Navy Yard, military posts rendered salutes with cannon and with guns, "iron throats [that] bade the warrior 'Welcome home!'" His casket was carried from the ship to a caisson drawn by six black horses as Secretary of War John Weeks, Secretary of the Navy Edwin Denby, and General John Pershing looked on. The caisson then began its solemn procession. As horses pulled and wheels began to roll over the rain-damp street, the cavalry band played "Onward, Christian Soldiers."[1]

The final destination for his funeral cortege was Arlington National Cemetery, but in order to allow the American people to pay their respects, his casket lay in state in the Capitol Rotunda for two days. Heroes and dignitaries from other nations joined American politicians and the general public in presenting flowers, wreaths, statues, and other tributes. On November 10, roughly 96,000 Americans moved past his casket in a steady stream for eighteen hours.[2]

At 8:30 a.m. on November 11, 1921, the procession resumed with great ceremony and conspicuously high levels of political participation. President Warren G. Harding and Vice President Calvin Coolidge marched down the

Mall with the cortege. They were joined by Chief Justice William Howard Taft and the rest of the Supreme Court, by cabinet members and congressmen, and by "the war president" Woodrow Wilson, "bent with the cares of those arduous years, himself a wounded soldier, paying tribute to the silent hero." Honorary pallbearers, chosen for their demonstrated heroism, marched as well, each wearing a Congressional Medal of Honor awarded for valor in combat during the Great War. Before being laid to rest in Arlington, the fallen soldier whom they were escorting also received not only the Congressional Medal of Honor, which all agreed he deserved, but also Belgium's Croix de Guerre, England's Victoria Cross, France's Medaille Militaire and Croix de Guerre, Italy's Gold Medal for Bravery, Romania's Virtutea Militara, Poland's Virtuti Militari, and the Czechoslovak War Cross.[3] A quartet from the Metropolitan Opera both sang and led the singing of numerous hymns. Chaplains and the president himself led prayers over the fallen hero. The last man to pay his respects was Chief Plenty Coos of the Crow Nation representing "the Indians of the United States." In a move that had been choreographed by Rodman Wanamaker and the Bureau of Indian Affairs to be "as solemn as the Day of Judgment," Plenty Coos placed his war bonnet and coup stick on the casket, "thus showing that he has left all he has got; he is done with that kind of warfare, and he honors the dead by giving him all he has."[4]

November 11, 1921, was a somber day for the United States. It was a day to recall the human cost of the Great War, which had ended only three years earlier. It was a day of self-conscious ceremonialism and powerful symbolism. And the most remarkable part of the elaborate observance in the nation's capital is that nobody could name the man at its center. Nobody knew where he had come from, how old he was, if he was a brother, father, husband. Nobody knew where he had trained, what rank he had held, how he had fought, if he had fought. Nobody knew whom he had killed, if he had killed, whom he had saved, if he had saved. They knew only that he had lost life, identity, and history—In that order? All at once?—and that his return to and burial in American soil called for every civil religious resource that the nation could muster. He had died in France sometime between November 1917 and November 1918 and was buried there "in honored glory an American soldier known but to God."[5] On Armistice Day 1921 he was born again in Arlington National Cemetery as the Unknown Soldier.

One of the witnesses to this rebirth was Lieutenant Colonel Charles White Whittlesey. Whittlesey was a graduate of Williams College and Harvard Law School, a soft-spoken attorney, bookish to the core. He began his

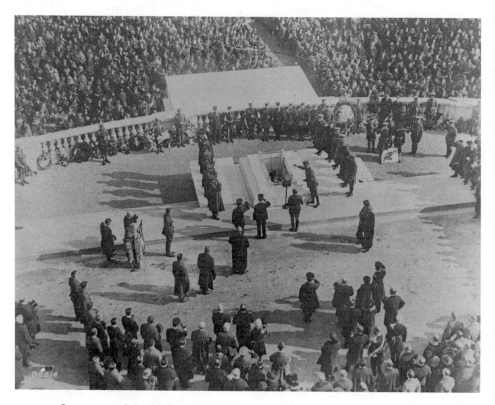

2:1: Interment of the Unknown Soldier, November 11, 1921. (Photo courtesy of National Archives, photo no. 111-SC-80816)

legal career in 1908 at the Manhattan law firm of Murray, Prentice, and Howland but soon went into practice with his close friend John Bayard Pruyn. In the summer of 1916 Whittlesey attended an unofficial military training camp in Plattsburgh, New York, a place where men who wanted to be ready to serve in war could train before war was actually declared.[6] When the United States entered the war in Europe in April 1917, Whittlesey made good on his tacit commitment and returned to Plattsburgh for intensive officer training. After ninety days of being trained, observed, and evaluated, Charles Whittlesey became Captain Whittlesey and was placed in charge of the Headquarters Company, 308th Regiment, Seventy-Seventh Division. He was praised for his firm sense of right and wrong and for his precision in carrying out orders.[7]

Charles Whittlesey was present at the interment of the Unknown Soldier because he had been awarded the Congressional Medal of Honor and was, therefore, a bona fide war hero. The bookish lawyer was, it turns out, a steadfast leader, able to remain remarkably, inspiringly calm under extreme duress. Whittlesey's days of wartime duress began on October 2, 1918, in the early stages of the Meuse-Argonne offensive. He and his men, the soldiers of First Battalion, "A" Company, 308th Regiment, Seventy-Seventh Division, received orders to proceed through thick forest to the site of an old mill. The men did precisely that. But due to rugged terrain, bad luck, and perhaps some undue if also understandable haste, they fell out of contact with their flanking units. As they moved deeper into the Argonne Forest, their experienced and opportunistic German opponents realized what was happening and moved down their flanks and around their rear, completely encircling them. When the German soldiers opened fire there was nowhere for the Americans to run, no durable shelter from the bullets, grenades, and shells. German troops established positions from which to shoot American runners attempting to contact potential reinforcements. They shot men attempting to get water. They advanced on the surrounded men numerous times, nearly overrunning them. The casualties mounted quickly, but Whittlesey directed successful defenses time and again.[8]

Nevertheless, the suffering was extreme. The men of Whittlesey's battalion first ran low on supplies and then ran out. They had nothing to eat, very little to drink, and no medical supplies for the growing number of wounded. To treat these broken, bleeding men they peeled bandages from the bodies that bandages had not saved. Supplies carried in by aircraft and dropped to the desperate soldiers landed on the wrong side of the defensive perimeter. Then, to make matters worse, American artillerymen reckoned the unit's position incorrectly and began dropping shells on them, shredding the men they were trying to save. Again, Whittlesey kept his composure and sent a message via carrier pigeon. "We are along the road parallel 276.4. Our own artillery is dropping a barrage on us. For heavens sake stop it." Torn apart by enemy fire and by American artillery, wracked by hunger, thirst, and exposure, the suffering men held on and looked to Whittlesey for guidance. He kept them calm. He did his best to bury the dead. When the German troops surrounding them suggested that the humane course of action was surrender, he offered no response.[9]

After five full days of siege, suffering, and death in the Argonne Forest, American units finally fought their way through the German lines and reached Whittlesey's "Lost Battalion." Of the roughly 600 men under his command only 194 walked out of the woods. One could argue, as

Whittlesey's commanding general did, that by holding their position, fighting on, and tying up German resources and attention during a critical phase of the war's final offensive the ordeal served a meaningful strategic purpose. From a tactical and a personal perspective, however, it was an unmitigated disaster. Still, Major Charles Whittlesey was held up as the incarnation of American martial prowess and bravery—one of the nation's true war heroes. An immediate promotion to lieutenant colonel was followed by the nation's highest military recognition. His citation focused on the fact that he had maintained his position and "held his command . . . together in the face of superior numbers of the enemy."[10]

It wasn't Whittlesey only but all of the men he commanded—the living and the dead—who were painted with heroic colors. American newspapermen descended on the scene of the siege and on those who survived it to celebrate their trials, their sacrifices, and their martyrdoms. Damon Runyon of Universal News Service and Will Irwin of the *Saturday Evening Post* were among those who led the chorus, with Irwin writing, "Unless some more startling episode has wiped it out before these lines reach America, all the world must know the story of the six lost companies of the Seventy-seventh division."[11] But the *Stars and Stripes'* voice was particularly impassioned. An account of the incident published October 18, 1918, while the war was still raging, followed the blood of these soldier saviors from their once living bodies, into the French soil, and up into the foliage. "Quite suddenly the other day [the Argonne] flung forth its autumn colors. Indeed to those watching from nearby hillsides, it seemed as if it was on that historic October 7 that the Forest of Argonne blazed all at once into russets and golds and purples, and here and there a scarlet tree, as though the roots had drunk deep of young American blood spent freely for an eternal cause once more defended on those hills."[12] The redemptive power of the blood of the American soldier—its power to nourish, to heal, to free—was proclaimed by nature itself.

It is possible that the remains that were carried from France to Arlington by rail, ship, caisson, and hand to become the Unknown Soldier were detached from their identity during the five-day siege of Whittlesey's Lost Battalion. The Unknown Soldier's blood may well have flowed out into the Argonne soil for flora and fauna to assimilate. The remains interred on November 11, 1921, might once have been a man who marched gamely into the French woods following Major Whittlesey. This possibility occurred to Whittlesey. It may have undone him. His friend and fellow Medal of Honor recipient George McMurtry noted later, after Whittlesey himself was gone, that the elaborate funeral had prompted a terse comment from the Lost Battalion's commander: "I should not have come here."[13]

The end of the United States' involvement in the Great War brought numerous celebrations of the martial prowess and sacrificial spirit of the American soldier. It also brought many attempts, institutional and personal, public and private, to reckon with more ambivalent realities. That one of the most enduring of these former—the Tomb of the Unknown Soldier—intersects with a tragic example of the latter is a compelling historical coincidence. Now as then, the attention and affection poured out on one unidentified man is moving. Now as then, Charles White Whittlesey presents a deeply sympathetic figure: an intellectually sophisticated, understated citizen soldier turned in upon himself. These two stories are together here because they were together in a moment, in a place.

These stories are also together here as sites of American civil religion. This chapter takes the historical convergence of a celebrated set of human remains and a hero of the Great War as an opportunity to consider the power of the soldier as a symbol, the connection between that power and the ritual of war, and the tension between civil religious imaginings of heroism and the lives of those imagined as heroes. After a brief discussion of symbols in military and religious contexts and the diverse ways in which they are interpreted, I will consider the construction of both the Unknown Soldier and Charles Whittlesey as symbols of and for the nation. War made each man into something different than he had been before. The nation provided forceful, public interpretations of this transformation, interpretations conceived as honors due them for war-verified heroism. In the case of the Unknown Soldier this interpretation, however problematic, adhered and drew the faithful to him. In the case of Whittlesey, a veteran who lived in postwar America as a recognizable symbol of wartime heroism, public interpretations and presentations were followed by a turn to suicide. This tragedy, in which the Unknown Soldier played a part and which, I will argue, he helps explicate, illuminates both the strains of a life as a G.I. Messiah—strains more widely visible now than then—and one man's ritual challenge to the assumptions at the root of this symbolic existence.

Symbolic Lives

Symbols permeate military and religious cultures. They define the visual culture of places of worship and places of war. Martial and religious symbols—swords, crosses, eagles, banners—appear on uniformed bodies, on buildings and equipment, on everyday items such as mugs and pens, and on intentionally sacred objects such as monuments, altars, and headstones. These symbols make claims. They assert order and belonging. They tell stories and project pride. Military units and religious traditions have symbols, and symbols common to one environment can make their way into the other, but my concern here is with the ways that soldiers themselves become civil religious symbols, images or objects that point and mean rather than people who do and become. Examining this phenomenon from two apparently distinct vantage points—that of the Unknown Soldier and that of Charles Whittlesey—allows us to see more clearly the relationship between soldierly bodies and the power deployed in and through the nation, and to note and analyze the role of religious ritual, narrative, and symbol in that relationship. Additionally, by lingering at these particular sites we can witness competing claims as to the ownership of the soldierly body and the nature of soldierly identity, articulated by a national shrine and a national hero. This competition continues.

The symbolic languages of religions and of the U.S. military mix the ancient and the new, the obvious and the esoteric, the practical and the abstract. They are living languages that express and invigorate their respective cultural systems. The coherence of the military or religious system depends on a certain consistency of meaning in and among its symbols. At the same time, individuals and groups perceive symbols, not to mention entire cultural systems, in very different ways; symbols are, in the words of a student of war monuments and cultural memory, "multifarious" and "ambiguous." There is no reliable way to guarantee stability of symbolic meaning from person to person, group to group, moment to moment.[14] The most familiar religious symbols—from the laughing Buddha to the crucifix—and the most common military symbols—rank insignia, award ribbons, unit emblems—though easily recognizable, have a range of meaning as wide as the experiences of their beholders. Military rank insignia serve the immediate purpose of differentiating individuals in an organization according to experience, responsibility, and authority. But depending on past interactions, past experiences, and thoughts on the gender dynamics of military cultures, a silver eagle that announces a khaki-clad woman as a Navy captain, like a Catholic priest's clerical collar, will say different things to different people. This indeterminacy inheres in symbolic discourse.

Within the realm of civil religion the indeterminacy of a symbol is nowhere more clear than in discussions of the American flag and how it should or should not be treated by Americans. Justifications for laws protecting the flag from desecration are reasoned outward from assumptions of or arguments for its sacred status. Some connect this sacredness to the values the flag represents: freedom, liberty, bravery. Others argue that the blood shed by those who have waged war under the flag makes it sacred.[15] Arguments against protecting the flag from desecration don't necessarily proceed from the assertion that the flag is mundane or profane—just so much colored cloth—nor do they need to come with a list of grievances against the United States. Just as likely is the position that the flag is a sacred symbol but that the principles to which it points are more sacred still and must allow for the destruction of the symbol as an act of protest. This indeterminacy is not the death of symbol or the annihilation of symbolic meanings. Men and women of these three persuasions will pledge allegiance to the flag and feel deep affection for it. Still, what they are "seeing" in the flag is quite different.

America's Unknown Soldier was created with a similar breadth of appeal in mind—with characteristic, though not absolute, indeterminacy. He was one of the 1,300 American war dead who were unidentifiable by the time their remains were recovered. All of these unidentified dead were buried in Europe. There was no reason to transport them across an ocean and parts of two continents. If nobody could claim them, why go to the trouble?[16] The Unknown Soldier became an exception to this policy due both to European precedent—British and French mainly—and to the legislative initiative of Representative Hamilton Fish, a veteran of the Great War and a man with a keen appreciation for the power of civil religion. Writing to then secretary of war John Weeks, Representative Fish described his motivation for introducing Joint Resolution 426 "to bring back the body of an unknown American who was a member of the American Expeditionary Forces in Europe and lost his life in the war, for burial in the Memorial Amphitheater of the National Cemetery at Arlington." Fish led with the obvious purpose "to do honor and pay homage to our unknown dead and to all of their comrades who made the ultimate sacrifice." But he also had other agendas on his mind. His letter to Weeks continues, "It would be appropriate to hold the funeral ceremonies on Memorial Day . . . to develop a stronger interest among the veterans of the World War in Memorial Day and lead to the taking over of the ceremonies from the [Grand Army of the Republic]." Continuing the connection between veterans of the Civil War and of the Great War, he wrote, "It would tend to cement the North and South in one common Memorial Day."[17] It was important to Fish that the "unknown dead" be honored: one directly, 1,299 indirectly. It was also important that honors for the unknown dead revive a civil religious observance—Memorial Day—that could provide a basis for greater national unity. The repatriation and interment were at once about a single unidentified man, his unidentified comrades, and the identity of the nation they died serving.

In accordance with Fish's resolution, the War Department went to great lengths to ensure that before becoming the Unknown Soldier, the remains would be absolutely unknowable. One narrator noted, "So that it would be impossible to ever establish this soldier's identity, the most painstaking care was taken in selecting the body." The army Graves Registration Service (GRS) selected "at random" four graves containing unidentified remains from its four main cemeteries. The remains were removed from their graves and all marks indicating where the caskets had come from and where the remains had been found were "obliterated or removed." The four identical caskets were then transported to Chalons-sur-Marne in eastern France and placed in the town hall where Sergeant Edward Younger of Chicago, a soldier who "fitly represented the spirit of the American Army . . . having been decorated for bravery by both French and American Governments" was handed a bouquet of white roses to place on one of the four coffins.[18] Younger's choice, the third casket from the left, became the Unknown Soldier and began the journey home. "From that moment," one author wrote, "[the casket] became sanctified in the eyes of man and its precious contents were never left unguarded." The other three returned to unnoticed anonymity in the American cemetery outside of the French village of Romagne.[19]

This process of shuffling the unidentified dead was necessary because GRS cemeteries (both temporary and permanent) were often highly regionally specific, which is to say that quite a few unknowns could be ruled out as *the* Unknown if the point of origin of the unidentified remains became known. The possibility that one identity could be attached more plausibly than another to the chosen body would be particularly antithetical to the purpose of "paying tribute to all the unknown soldiers" and would undermine a symbol meant to be "truly representative of all."[20] By foreclosing even a general identification of the soldier, the U.S. government radically expanded opportunities to identify with him as son, brother, husband, or comrade. The Unknown Soldier became all unknowns and every unknown, plausibly general and intensely particular. Poet John F. Brandon's thoughts on the Unknown appeared in the *Providence Journal* the day of the interment.

He is all brothers dead, all lovers lost
All sons and comrades resting over there
The symbol of the knightly, fallen host
The sacred pledge of burdens yet to bear.
Mangled and torn, for whom we pray today
Whose soul rose grandly to God's peaceful Throne
Leaving to us this quiet, shattered clay.
Silent and unnamed, but not Unknown.

The ceremony on Armistice Day 1921 took this broken blank of a soldier, this "shattered clay," and began rebuilding and reimagining him. According to one observer, mourners' imaginations were already at work as the caisson rolled past. "The thousands who lined the way gathered from all parts of the country to pay honor to the Unknown, symbolic to many of some dear relative or friend, to everyone of the spirit of the nation."[21]

Charles White Whittlesey did not lose his life or his name in the Great War. Rather, the nation found these things of his and made of them symbols of American heroism. In the process, Whittlesey lost his prewar life as he had known it and, eventually, the sense that his life as Charles White Whittlesey was meaningful as such. The finding and the losing were, thus, of a piece. The story of the Lost Battalion's exploits in the Argonne Forest very quickly became martial legend, and Whittlesey, quite naturally, became a hero. The suffering that he and his men had endured were treated as a stage in the ritual of war, a trial that both enriched those who passed through it and showed that American soldiers, living and dead, could still wage and endure the savage violence of the imagined frontier.[22] For the qualities that he demonstrated amidst the fires and trials of combat, Whittlesey became a symbol of the American experience of the war and was asked again and again to present himself in public as that symbol.

Barely two months removed from the Argonne Forest, Whittlesey faced a crowd gathered at the Sixty-Ninth Regiment Armory in Manhattan to celebrate victory in the war. Six of New York City's Episcopal churches had organized the event for the evening of December 15, 1918, which featured Whittlesey and Secretary of the Treasury William McAdoo as speakers. The evening began when "surpliced choirs of these [Episcopal] churches entered singing 'Onward, Christian Soldiers.'" Secretary McAdoo then introduced Whittlesey as the epitome of the American, Christian soldier, showering praise on him for what he had done nine weeks earlier. "That

2:2: Lieutenant Colonel Charles White Whittlesey wearing his Congressional Medal of Honor. (Photo by Underwood and Underwood, 1918)

was a splendid American defiance. It is one of those records of valor that will live forever in American history. I take my hat off to Whittlesey. There in France he gave new history to the Stars and Stripes." Whittlesey then spoke in a predictable idiom of the valor of his men and their strength in the face of "hardship and suffering." He singled out Father Halligan, an "intrepid" chaplain in the 308th, who had risked life and limb to bury the soldier dead. Whittlesey departed from the script when he turned to a discussion of his men's attitudes. He informed the audience that there was a noticeable lack of hatred in the trenches. "Our men who have been facing and fighting the Germans won't come back hating them. Why, they might even share their cigarettes with the Kaiser himself if they met him on the road." An observer from the *Outlook* noted, "Silence greeted this portion of the speaker's address, a contrast to the vigorous applause which punctuated the rest." The *Outlook* could strain and see the virtue in a veteran who was "incredibly tolerant" of the vanquished enemy. The audience, it seems, could not.[23]

Ten days later, on the day before Christmas, Whittlesey stood with his mother, father, one brother, and "thousands" of shivering Bostonians on Boston Common to receive the Congressional Medal of Honor. The *Boston Daily Globe* had announced the event in the morning paper, reminding readers that the "Pittsfield man" to be celebrated that morning had authored acts of "conspicuous gallantry and intrepidity" in the cauldron of war. The announcement appears to have worked. A photo in the Christmas Day edition shows a smiling Whittlesey flanked by General Clarence Edwards and his parents with a sizable crowd behind them. Many more people read in the paper of Whittlesey's history-making leadership. "Down through the years will ring the exploits of Lieut. Col. Whittlesey leading his brave boys of the 308th Infantry who, when apparently trapped in the Argonne forest, and ordered to surrender by the Germans replied, 'Go to hell,' and fought doggedly on."[24] Whittlesey had not told the Germans to go to hell, but the phrase made for good copy.

In the three years between his mostly triumphant return from war and his involvement in the interment of the Unknown Soldier, Whittlesey's star shone brightly in spite of his inclination toward a low profile. The hero was asked to play himself in a silent film based on the experiences of the Lost Battalion and gave his image to that legend-making apparatus. In other venues, however, Whittlesey was more guarded, regularly resisting calls to discuss "what it was like" during those five days in the Argonne. He did not want to augment the legend, to polish the symbol that he had become. Perhaps he sensed that in spite of being alive, in possession of his name, and being known around the country, he too was an unknown soldier.

What came more naturally to Whittlesey than symbolic life was lending a hand to his former brothers-in-arms. He was asked again and again to be a source of strength and support for his comparatively unknown men and their families. These former soldiers made regular appearances at his law office. They came asking for work, for money, and for advice. Whittlesey did what he could for the men in whose suffering he had played such a significant part. He became involved with the American Legion, with relief efforts for fellow veterans, with all manner of charitable organizations. On one occasion he helped the Polish stowaway cousin of one of his soldiers avoid immediate deportation.[25] That the men who had served under him were having trouble reintegrating into society demonstrated that something was out of joint. Symbols could be called on to speak; they could be presented as heroes and held up as exemplary, but what of intensely particular men?

Whittlesey the soldier-symbol was not without his own problems. He was haunted by memories of the men he had led. He dreamt of the dead, dreamt he was sleeping next to them. He knew, standing at the Memorial Amphitheater at Arlington National Cemetery, that the burial of the Unknown Soldier would uncover for him once-known soldiers now three years gone. He told his friend George McMurtry, "I shall have nightmares tonight and hear the wounded screaming once again."[26] There can be no doubt that those who created the Unknown Soldier did not intend Charles Whittlesey or any other observer to look with dread upon the rituals of the interment and the symbol at their center. Their intent was to console, to honor, to unify. Many who attended the ceremony on Armistice Day 1921 saw their nation honoring an unknown soldier who had sacrificed everything for them. They felt united in gratitude, sadness, and awe.

Charles Whittlesey saw it differently.

The Rituals of Symbols

As veterans of the Great War and fellow soldier-symbols, the Unknown Soldier and Charles Whittlesey followed very similar ritual paths. Both endured rituals of initiation, rituals of indoctrination, preparation for the ritual of war, and movement into the trials of combat. Both also looked forward, it is safe to assume, to rituals of reintegration. The Unknown Soldier's progress along this path slowed considerably when he died, even more when he became decoupled from his name, but the path did not change and the end of the rite—reintegration—remained clear. We can imagine myriad differences between Whittlesey and his unidentifiable comrade, but the rituals that shaped their lives should not be one of them.

To think in these terms is simply to recognize that war as a rite of passage is capacious enough to account for most, if not all, personal outcomes: death, injury, survival; duties performed, duties shirked; embodiments of bravery, cowardice, things in between. To note that tragic outcomes are part of the ritual is also to begin to acknowledge a connection between the possibility of tragedy and the enhanced status of the combat veteran.[27] In other words, the hero becomes the hero through a direct encounter with death in combat. Having endured the ritual of war, living soldier-symbols testify to its redemptive power. Having given their lives in war, fallen soldier-symbols, though voiceless, testify to the sanctity of the nation and the cause.[28] Finally, as the stories of the Unknown Soldier and Charles Whittlesey demonstrate, war as a rite of passage is not over until the soldier is reintegrated into society or returned to his or her loved ones. The tone of a victory parade is very different from the tone of a funeral for a fallen soldier. They follow different ritual patterns and can employ different symbolic languages. But the work that they do of completing a cycle—bringing units, people, and bodies back, announcing praise and bestowing honor, giving thanks to God, asking God for comfort—is the same.

What set the unidentified remains of a Great War soldier apart *ritually*, at least momentarily, was that they had no identity. Identity is a central concern of any rite of passage. A rite of passage, be it adult baptism or the hajj, can make no claim to transformative power, no claim to enhance identity, status, or authority if the pre-ritual identity is obliterated. If the "before" vanishes completely, so too does the ritual significance of the "after." The rituals that created, repatriated, and celebrated the Unknown Soldier must be understood, then, as directed at addressing and remedying his lack of identity and giving the remains of the man a plausible persona. The ritual did this by making visible and audible the religio-cultural core of American understandings of soldiering and by theologizing in no uncertain terms the effects of war as ritual.

Inside the amphitheater on that November day, the voices of a quartet from the Metropolitan Opera sang portraits of a faithful Christian soldier who, like Christ before him, had sacrificed life, brought salvation to the world, and entered heaven. Soprano Rosa Ponselle and contralto Jeanne Gordon, both at the beginning of national opera careers, were joined by tenor Morgan Kingston, whose son John had been wounded fighting for the British, and bass William Gustafson in John Arkwright's and Cuthbert Harris's hymn "The Supreme Sacrifice." Also known as "O Valiant Hearts," the hymn was written during the war and sung at the interment of Britain's Unknown Warrior.[29]

> Proudly you gathered, rank on rank to war
> As who had heard God's message from afar
> All you had hoped for, all you had, you gave
> To save mankind—yourselves you scorned to save.

Asserting the interlocking nobility of war and warrior, nation and soldier, the lyrics went on to imagine the Unknown Soldier's death as a gift given to all. A gift, the hymn continues, with a divine pedigree. "While in the frailty of our human clay; Christ, our Redeemer, passed the selfsame way."

And though the unidentified soldier and all fallen soldiers had suffered on "lesser calvaries" (and from exponentially greater destructive power) they were no less recognizable as American examples of *imitatio Christi*.

> These were his servants, in His steps they trod
> Following through death the martyred Son of God
> Victor he rose; victorious too shall rise
> Those who have drunk His cup of sacrifice.

The unidentified remains celebrated and honored that day were not those of Jesus of Nazareth. They were, however, his modern martial embodiment.

Any questions as to the Unknown Soldier's religious identity and the strength of his moral fiber were chased from Arlington by Christian hymn after Christian hymn, Christian prayer after Christian prayer. Following President Harding's delivery of the Lord's Prayer, the operatic quartet led the assembled mourners in "O God, Our Help in Ages Past," Rosa Ponselle performed "I Know That My Redeemer Liveth," and all sang together "Nearer My God to Thee." Scripture readings came from two former American Expeditionary Force chaplains, one Christian, one Jewish. But a single Jewish voice—Rabbi Morris Lazaron—could hardly counter the Christian tone of the ritual and the Christian theology directed at the one "known but to God."[30] According to the narrative of the service, he was a modern-day Christ whose sufferings were short and whose glory was eternal. This elaborate ritual reintegrated a fallen soldier into the nation he vowed to serve. It was an expression of gratitude, presented in a powerfully Christian idiom, for a death imagined as selfless sacrifice. He had balanced commitment to the nation and commitment to God perfectly, treating them as one and the same. The U.S. government filled him with a Christian particularity and a militant heroism, imagining *him*, to be sure, but in the process imaging itself as well.

Charles Whittlesey truly was a Christian by birth though the faith seems to have lost its hold on him. His sensibilities regarding ritual must have been shaped by the Presbyterian Church of his youth but were also cultivated by military life and by other expressions of American civil religion.[31] As he took part in the Unknown Soldier's ritual of reintegration, aspects of the process must have felt troublingly familiar. Since his ill-fated but heroic venture in the Argonne Forest, who Charles Whittlesey was and who he had been mattered less to those who venerated him than what war had made him. The interment ceremony thus ran parallel to his own experience in that a narrative was forced upon the man in inexact relation to his experiences of or attitudes toward the war. In the case of the Unknown Soldier there was no story to get wrong, no words or actions to misrepresent. The Unknown Soldier could not resist this process. Even the living, breathing Whittlesey found contesting it to be difficult. The solution that he saw was to join the Unknown Soldier in no longer living, no longer breathing.

We cannot know with certainty that Charles Whittlesey's actions after the ceremony at Arlington were a direct response to what he saw there. But his approach to suicide—his precision, timing, even his chosen location—indicate that the day and its symbolism loomed large. With the interment accomplished, the shrine properly sanctified, and the Thanksgiving holiday approaching, Whittlesey set to planning his own end. Over dinner with his friend John Pruyn and Pruyn's wife and child, he talked of spending the preholiday weekend with his parents in Pittsfield. His parents were not expecting him. Earlier in the week he had told them that he would be staying in Manhattan. Pruyn later recalled that during the evening Whittlesey had seemed like his prewar self. He was happy and at ease. He spent a long time playing with the baby.[32]

On November 20, 1921, with his tracks well covered, the war hero boarded the United Fruit Company's steamship S.S. *Toloa* bound for Havana, Cuba. The ship's captain recognized him and invited him to dinner. He was, by the captain's account, in good spirits at the meal but then excused himself for the evening. Nobody saw Whittlesey the following day. After thirty-six hours the crew opened his stateroom and found his packed luggage, guidance as to where to send it, and the wording of a wireless message to his family. They also found nine sealed envelopes each with a personal farewell to a family member or a friend. The note to John Pruyn read in part, "Just a note to say goodbye. I am a misfit by nature and by training and there's an end of it. I'm sorry to wish upon you the job of executor; but there is very little to do." According to friend and law partner R. Forsyth Little, Whittlesey's desk at the law offices of White and Case was clean and organized. Instructions regarding the twelve cases assigned to him were left in the upper left-hand drawer. He had also drawn up a new will. He left his Congressional Medal of Honor to his mother.

A Soldier and His Rituals

We do not struggle as students of religion or as observers of American public life to see civil religion at work in a postwar funeral procession, a presidential prayer, or the presentation of a Congressional Medal of Honor. A veterans' organization marching through a town, rioting with "subversive elements," and lynching a man registers as civil religion as well. What I would like to suggest is that the private actions of the men and women who, as soldiers, so routinely become symbols of civil religion have civil religious significance also. Moreover, attempting to interpret these actions as expressions of or reactions to civic faith is one possible way of seeing beyond the symbol and moving from the unknown to the not-unknown soldier. We should, however, proceed cautiously in interpreting Whittlesey's actions. In the end only he knew (if he knew) why he jumped. But the clues are myriad. They begin with the forethought and precision that marked his actions from November 11–21, 1921, which seem to displace and to contest the sudden, random deaths wrought by war and the uses to which the war dead are put.

Whittlesey prepared for his suicide. He took great care to ensure that he could complete the act. This care is of a piece with the care invested in the repatriation and celebration of the Unknown Soldier, and it presents us with another legible civil religious ritual. Witness a man who followed orders in the midst of war and led his men to deaths sudden, excruciating, and largely unnecessary, a man who watched as his government built and sanctified a Christian hero out of blank remains. He chooses death and decides to control its every detail. He pays his rent, he explains his case load, he buys his tickets, he packs his bags.[33] He pens personal farewells to those he loves and writes orders to the ship's captain as to how those letters and his bags should be handled. He packs his bags again. And finally, at a moment of his choosing, he jumps. The majority of the war dead known to Whittlesey had been killed in combat in France—surprised by death, hauled off to the afterlife by bullet, bomb, or bayonet. As combat fatalities, their bodies and their memories became part of the symbolic lexicon of American civil religion, holy in themselves but subject to interpretation and reinterpretation in terms that further sanctify the nation. Whittlesey seems to be saying through the ritual of his death: *I did not die that way, but I do not want to live this way.*

It is noteworthy also that Whittlesey killed himself in a way that placed his body beyond the reach of all. One can interpret this decision as a counter-ritual to at least three troubling moments in his life as a soldier. First, having spent five days in the company of dead and dying men, pinned down to a landscape that allowed no refuge from the gore and decomposition of dead bodies, Whittlesey may well have chosen his particular death as a kind of courtesy. By jumping from the S.S. *Toloa*, he ensured that no one would have to tend to or even see *his* dead, decomposing body. Second, Whittlesey had been terribly affected when he looked upon the casket of the Unknown Soldier, a casket that held a body without a name. Whittlesey chose a death that inverted this haunting anonymity. He chose to discard his body and to become *only* a name, to withdraw in the most permanent way possible from the symbol into which he had been imagined. Finally, at a somewhat grander level, we can read Whittlesey's suicide as directed against war as imagined by those who encountered him as a symbol. *War does not redeem*, his ritual proclaims, *war injures and degrades. Through its absence, my body will tell a different story.*

Whittlesey's actions in the final days of his life seem to have been directed toward throwing off the symbolism that he had been living and toward establishing and defending his particularity. Of course, by choosing suicide Whittlesey rendered himself forever powerless to contest the rituals of reintegration employed by his nation. By rejecting symbolic existence, he also embraced it forever. This sad irony is evidenced clearly in the memorial address delivered on December 4, 1921, by Nelson K. Averill, commander of the 308th Regiment. Averill's eulogy was a typical recounting of a soldier-symbol's virtues ("outstanding character," "absolute lack of fear," "stern and strict conscience," "always sure of the right") and reached a predictable denouement: "No man as a soldier can stand higher in the history of the republic and no man is more entitled to the nation's gratitude." Averill did recognize the tortured state of betwixt and between in which Whittlesey moved for three years after the war, but in the end he asked mourners to forget all that. "While we were at first stunned and could hardly credit the news, yet the more I think his case over the more firmly I am convinced that his death was in reality a battle casualty and that he met his end as much in the line of duty as if he had fallen by a German bullet on the Vesle or in the Argonne."[34] Thus did Colonel Averill make of Whittlesey another symbol of soldierly sacrifice in war.

In his own civil religious ritual, Charles Whittlesey controlled death and directed it to himself. The counter-ritual that was his suicide stands as starkly against the uncontrolled, public, gory, no-time-to-say-good-bye deaths of war as any death possibly can. To reintegrate Whittlesey as another casualty of war is to forget that Charles White Whittlesey served, survived, and then served some more and that, finally, it was he who chose the ocean.

The Known and the Unknown

Benedict Anderson begins his classic study of nationalism, *Imagined Communities,* with a discussion of tombs of unknown soldiers: "arresting emblems," he writes, "of the modern culture of nationalism."[35] Tombs of unknown soldiers interest Anderson because they provide such strong evidence of shared terrain among nations and religious traditions—"death and immortality"—and because they are one place where a nation imagines itself. Such tombs, he writes "are . . . saturated with ghostly imaginings," imaginings of the heroic, the self-sacrificial, the essence of the nation. They are, in short, symbols. But they are symbols of a peculiar sort. For, at the risk of being vulgar, there is nothing especially noble or ennobling about a body so torn by combat, so decomposed, that nobody can determine who it once was. The nation must imagine the ghost of the soldier. It must clothe the dead man once again in flesh, dress him again in uniform, fill him again with the blood that poured out of him, and then imagine the tearing of the clothes and the flesh, the shedding of that blood, and the soldier's willingness to die. Because of this need to imagine a soldier, a death, and, through them, a nation, the tombs involve themselves in a disingenuous nomenclature and a subtly circular epistemology.[36] Their names proclaim the soldier unknown at the same time that the tombs fashion him as partially known. The tombs foster familiarity and knowing through invocations of the soldierly ideal, through the forging of a religious identity, and through a highly intentional receptivity to the imaginings of mourners.

The creation of a national shrine to the Unknown Soldier made an argument that went beyond the obvious statement of the importance of remembering and honoring those erased by war, beyond the necessary construction of a ghostly persona. The argument it made, and continues to make, is that unknown soldiers are those whom we can no longer name, that identifying and knowing are synonymous. The tomb subtly but surely juxtaposes the known soldier and the Unknown Soldier. One has a name, a family, a home. The other has none of this, only an imagined history of heroism. But the shrine and the interment ceremony and the regular public presentation of American soldiers make clear that unknown/known is, in fact, an inaccurate dichotomy. With respect to soldiering, war, and American civil religion, the better classification is between the unknown and the partially known or, forgoing strong epistemological claims altogether, the unidentified and the identified. All soldiers as public symbols are, at best, identified and partially known.

There is more to this illusion of known and unknown than the usually mysterious contours of individual identities and interpersonal relationships; there is more to it than the general inscrutability of people. The symbol of the soldier in American civil religion facilitates a false knowing of the unknown, a too-rapid forging of an identity possibility. This knowing process is, in the end, what the elaborate interment ritual for the Unknown Soldier was all about. The Christian and martial themes of American civil religion were channeled to fill the vacuum of identity that war had created and that government had preserved. At the same time, though, the symbol of the soldier and the soldier as symbol facilitate a "not knowing" of the soldier who is identified and partially known, a hiding of the visible body, a forgetting of the remembered personality. To the extent that individuals involve themselves in the mytho-symbolic discourse of soldiering and the rituals through which that discourse reaches the nation, they become simultaneously unknown and known, symbol and person. If the known vanishes leaving only the unknown, as was the case with the "Unknown Soldier-to-be," the nation can intervene and rebuild a known hero.[37] If the known persists, as it did in the case of Charles Whittlesey, it must still interact with the ritual processes by which the nation attempts to reduce the unknown. This struggle is not combat, but it can swallow a person whole.

In the years following Charles Whittlesey's suicide, the Pittsfield Cemetery surely saw its share of visitors. Family, friends, and perhaps even fellow soldiers who wanted to demonstrate their gratitude, could travel to that tiny piece of Massachusetts and the small marker bearing Whittlesey's name to be in the presence not of his body but, as far as they could construct it, his memory. Whittlesey's share of visitors surely paled in comparison to the stream of pilgrims to the Tomb of the Unknown Soldier. The "Pittsfield Man" with his complexities, his reluctance, his ghosts, could not match the "Mystery Hero" as a symbol of soldiering for the nation.[38]

Some of those who looked upon the Unknown Soldier's tomb came to Arlington National Cemetery to wander among the diverse headstones of once-prominent generals and, eventually, make their way to the tomb and the Memorial Amphitheater. There were some, too, who visited the tomb to be in the presence of a dead son, husband, brother, or father whose remains had never been identified. In a twist worthy of Schrödinger, he was both there and not there. There were also those who came as participants in a "pilgrimage" program orchestrated by the American Legion in the 1920s and 1930s. State Legions had sponsored their own pilgrimages to the tomb since the Unknown Soldier's interment, but at the national convention in 1929, Mary Frances Hall, a former worker with the Knights of Columbus and a member of the American Legion Women's Auxiliary, offered a proposal for the nationalization of pilgrimage activities. Hall's plan was simple. Each of the forty-eight state Legions would be assigned a "pilgrimage week" and would travel, assisted by reduced fares and chartered trains, to Washington, D.C., and Arlington National Cemetery. This steady flow of traffic would be a sign that the Unknown Soldier and the soldiers he symbolized had not been and would not be forgotten. It being "desirable to develop such a movement to the fullest extent in order that the sacrifices symbolized by the Unknown Soldier can best be impressed upon the consciousness of the American people," the Legion established a National Pilgrimage Committee and charged it with "arrang[ing] the Washington details of these Department pilgrimages, with special reference to contact with the War Department for proper ceremonies, the notification of press correspondents and press photographers, the securing of a wreath to be placed on the Tomb, the notification of senators and representatives from each particular State, and such other special meetings . . . as shall be desired."[39]

The New York Legion made its first pilgrimage under the new program in a single day, Sunday, September 28, 1930, using a special train to carry 225 legionnaires on the round-trip.[40] The pilgrims visited numerous sites around Washington, D.C., took lunch at the National Press Club, and provided musical entertainment for their wounded comrades at Walter Reed Hospital. Between 4:00 and 4:30 p.m., they were on the "hallowed grounds" of Arlington National Cemetery observing a "Ceremony at the Tomb of the Unknown Soldier" and visiting the graves of veterans from New York. Legion Departments in Washington State, California, New Mexico, Colorado, Mississippi, and Alabama followed suit. The National Pilgrimage Committee took care of the arrangements for these and subsequent pilgrimages, adding to the itinerary visits to Woodrow Wilson's tomb, "the Smithsonian Institution where may be seen the original Star Spangled Banner," and "the Library of Congress which holds the original of the Declaration of Independence and the Constitution."[41]

The National Pilgrimage Committee was thrilled by the growth of the program and began to envision great things. The Pilgrimage Committee chairman, H. Edmund Bullis, wrote to James F. Barton, national adjutant of the Legion: "I feel that the Pilgrimage idea is something which over a period of years can be built up as an important part of the Americanization Program of the Legion. I can visualize tens of thousands of school children coming annually to the Tomb of the Unknown Soldier under the auspices of American Legion Posts."[42] This national symbol of complete sacrifice would strengthen young boys and girls in their civil religious devotion.

What was it about the symbol of the Unknown Soldier that evoked such emotional, memorial interest? Why did a woman from Brooklyn conceive of a plan to maintain nearly constant demonstrations of respect for this one set of remains? Was it the remarkable extent of the damage war wrought on the soldier's body? Was it pathos, the imagined loneliness of the unknown? Did legionnaires embrace the pilgrimage plan with such enthusiasm because of the extraordinary otherness of the remains? In a recent essay on the Vietnam War Memorial, historian Levi Smith notes that part of that memorial's genius is that it can function both as a "window" and as a "mirror." The names engraved on the monument act as a window. They encourage visitors to attempt to see those who fought the war and died and to try to make sense of tragedies personal and national. The polished marble surface is the mirror. It reminds the visitor that she is always present in the viewing, always implicated if not in the actual lives of the fallen and the events of their day, at least in their memory and interpretation. The reflection of the viewer, Smith notes, is ever present.[43]

The materials and the layout of the Tomb of the Unknown Soldier offered no such viewing experience. Nevertheless, for soldiers who approached it as pilgrims in the interwar period it undoubtedly served as both window and mirror. Many saw it as a "window" onto the experience of war—a way to look at what war had meant, to recall what they had done, and to see the dead, albeit dimly, once again. To the extent that these pilgrims saw the tomb as a mirror, many surely saw reflected back at them a suffering, sacrificing servant: a valiant warrior for the right, the very embodiment of what it meant to be an American. And just as surely as the Unknown Soldier brought comfort to some and comfort's opposite to others, there were also pilgrims who saw things in and through the tomb that ran counter to official narratives. This is the indeterminate nature of the symbol. As history moved forward, the interpretations of the events and the deaths visible in the window, never uniform to begin with, changed.

Writing for the *American Legion Monthly* in April 1937, Frederick Palmer imagined the Unknown Soldier alive, "walking the streets of his home town," catching up on the state of the Great War as a cultural, political, and religious memory. "He would find," Palmer wrote, "that our effort in 1917–18 has been belittled. The Allies have helped us belittle it. Because they have forgotten how they prayed to us for salvation and how they flattered us to get into the war and to keep us fighting." Through a *window* that once looked out on civic performances of unity and fidelity, one could now see division and apostasy. What Palmer saw reflected in the *mirror* was a mix of forcefully restated orthodoxy: "The story of the American soldier in tin hat . . . is immortal history. He had part in the greatest crusade of all time" and a less roseate assessment of soldiering in the age of industrial violence. Palmer wrote again of the revivified Unknown, "He would know, too, out of fresh memory, that all wounds in war are not of the flesh. He would be aware of the unseen scars—the mental scars—of men who subjected body and mind to the intensive drill and the harness of discipline . . . in answer to the call of Allied disasters to make haste or the war would be lost."[44] These unseen scars, evidence of wounds that had no place in the symbolic discourse of soldiering, are an unexpected point of connection among known soldiers and the Unknown Soldier, a point of connection derived not from imbuing the unknown with Christian American familiarity but from a frank acknowledgment that wars add layers of the unknown to those who wage them. Some level of unknown-ness is inherent in the uniform and in the civil religious rituals in which the known soldier participates. This unknown-ness is deepened relentlessly, often invisibly, by war.

CHAPTER 3

In Honored Glory, Known but to God

In the second century of Christian history, Felicitas, a slave woman and Christian catechumen, was killed by Roman authorities in a North African amphitheater. Felicitas is something of a shadow figure in the history of Christianity. We know of her death and life because the bright-shining, visionary Perpetua, daughter of a wealthy family, met her end with Felicitas and because somebody, perhaps Tertullian, saw fit to record or redact the events. In contrast to the vivid transgendering visions and intrafamilial drama that swirl around Perpetua, Felicitas's narrative is impoverished. When the tale begins she is pregnant, but the fervent prayers of her cohort lead to an early delivery. Mocked by a prison guard for her reaction to the pain of childbirth, she rebukes him and states that she will not suffer the torments of martyrdom alone: "another will be inside me who will suffer for me." "Crushed to the ground" by a mad heifer during her execution, Felicitas regains her feet with the help of Perpetua. The death of Felicitas never stands as an event in itself. Instead of a description of the death instrument or Felicitas's reaction to it, we have the narrator's voice proclaiming: "Ah, most valiant and blessed martyrs! . . . Any man who exalts, honors, and worships [Christ's] glory should read for the consolation of the Church these new deeds of heroism which are no less significant than the tales of old. For these new manifestations of virtue will bear witness to one and the same Spirit who still operates, and to God the Father almighty, to his Son Jesus Christ our Lord."[1] Felicitas suffered in her own body and died a death that was her own, but in the surviving account she is a set piece demonstrating the power of prayer, the perfidy of Roman rule, the compassion of Perpetua, and the enduring power of the Spirit. Thus was the death of a North African slave dislocated from an ancient, suffering body and incorporated into the narrative of an ongoing cosmic struggle.

In the second century of United States history, an army nurse named Felicita died in a hospital in France. We know about this modern Felicita because, like the ancient African martyr whose name she shares, she too was an actor in a cosmic struggle: the Great War. Felicita Hecht was born in Pittsylvania County, Virginia. She was a Catholic and trained in nursing at St. Vincent DePaul Hospital in Norfolk. Hecht was a mother and a widow when, in 1917, she shifted from private nursing in and around Norfolk to the Army Nursing Corps. She placed her children in the care of Sister Olympia at St. Mary's Academy in downtown Norfolk and went off to work in training camps up and down the Eastern Seaboard: Camp Sheridan, Camp Lee, Camp Upton. Through 1918 she helped care for the wounded and the rising number of victims of the influenza pandemic. While working with influenza patients at Camp Upton she contracted the illness herself and was "greatly impaired," but she survived and sailed for France on November 14, 1918, three days after the armistice.[2]

For six weeks after her departure from New York Hecht falls out of historical view, but she was likely working with her unit, Base Hospital 105 outside of Brest, France.[3] It is also likely that she, like many of her fellow nurses, felt depleted by the emotionally fraught, physically demanding work of nursing seriously wounded and often dying men. Perhaps she wondered about persistent pains in her chest and lungs. She may have believed them to be the lingering effects of the flu.

Felicita Hecht reappears on January 3, 1919, when Maude Parson, chief nurse of the hospital center in Kerhuon, France, wrote a letter to Sister Olympia at St. Mary's Academy, in whose care Nurse Hecht had left her children. Nurse Parson, it seems, had written messages to the children on behalf of their mother, conveying news of her illness, but had not told them the whole story. She clarified the situation to Sister Olympia: "You will see by the enclosed letter that I have not told them that their mother is not expected to live." Felicita Hecht had escaped the deadly grasp of the flu, but the enemy she faced now was more tenacious. "The diagnosis given by attending physicians," Parson explained, "is 'Metastisis of both lungs and meninges, secondary to malignant tumor, right breast.'" She was dying of breast cancer. Felicita was under good care, Nurse Parsons assured

Sister Olympia, adding, "She doesn't seem to suffer very much."[4] One can imagine, though, that as Felicita approached death with her soon-to-be orphaned children an ocean away, her suffering was indeed great. Felicita Wootlow Hecht died in France on February 8, 1919.

The remains of Felicita Hecht are buried in Grave 22, Row 31, in Plot D of the Oise-Aisne American Cemetery in Fere-en-Tardenois, France. She lies in that Great War cemetery with 6,011 other Americans who died from injuries or illness in the war.[5] Oise-Aisne American Cemetery is a beautiful place. Mature trees surround a meticulously kept graves area, subdivided by walkways into four plots. Filled with row upon row of white marble crosses and an occasional Star of David, the cemetery slopes gently upward toward a Romanesque chapel and memorial designed by Ralph Adams Cram of the Boston-based firm Cram and Ferguson. Jacques Gréber, a French landscape architect, designed the grounds.[6] The cross over Felicita Hecht's grave is indistinguishable from the cross over the grave of famed American poet and Catholic convert Joyce Kilmer (Grave 15, Row 9, Plot B), is indistinguishable from the cross over the grave of Vinton Dearing, son of Baptist missionaries (Grave 22, Row 33, Plot D), is indistinguishable from the grave of *New York Evening Sun* editorialist Quincy Sharpe Mills (Grave 19, Row 20, Plot B), is indistinguishable from the grave of native Oregonian Lambert Wood (Grave 9, Row 39, Plot D). If noticed at all, Felicita, like Felicitas, is meant to be contemplated as a saint surrounded by saints; her story is subordinate to and shaped by a more powerful narrative of divine action and ideal human interaction

The stories of these two barely visible women—Felicitas and Felicita—both mothers, both martyrs, demonstrate the intentionality of history. We know the stories we know from the past because someone has taken the time to tell them. More to the point, the stories that we know—those held in scripture and other genres of ancient literature, those conveyed as elements of national histories, those that are part of local and family lore—are the results of purposeful processes of narration and preservation that reflect the interests of an individual or a communal author. The stories of Felicitas and Felicita point deeper into this rather basic point about history to the peculiar place of the heroic dead in history and to specific shared dynamics in the construction of their memories. Working in service of communities calling for loyalty and devotion, the authors of martyrologies and hagiographies call readers to veneration, even imitation, of their subjects. In their narratives the details of individuality matter insofar as they confirm

3:1: Oise-Aisne American Cemetery, near Fére-en-Tardenois, France, holds the remains of 6,011 Americans who died during or immediately after the Great War.

the embodiment of transcendent virtues. For the author of *The Martyrdom of Saints Perpetua and Felicitas* and for the "author" of Oise-Aisne American Cemetery, the blood of the martyrs is clearly the seed of "the church," but that blood flows not from the veins of a woman, a nurse, a mother. Rather, it is blood shared by the devout, blood shed with minimal suffering, blood that flows forward through history from the Cross.

This chapter examines the American overseas cemeteries where Felicita Hecht and 125,162 other American soldiers and war workers are buried, treating them as both sacred texts and sacred spaces.[7] It describes the process that led to their construction and the theology of soldiering and war that they narrate. America's overseas military cemeteries were crucial sites for working out this theology, for giving it material expression, and for connecting it to the dead bodies of Americans. As these cemeteries comfort the mourning and honor the fallen, they also argue for the righteousness and the redemptive power of American war-making in the Great War and in World War II, for the Christlikeness of the American soldier, and for the salvific power of death in combat for the United States.[8]

America's involvement in two world wars between 1917 and 1945 left more than 500,000 American soldiers and war workers dead. That number is small next to the totals for the major European combatants, but one can be forgiven for finding it staggering nonetheless: 100,000 dead for each year of combat; 8,000 dead for every month. America's landscape avoided the ravages of war. America's human landscape did not. Because these wars were waged in other countries on other continents, these half million dead and the idea of their deaths presented the federal government and the military with two closely related problems, one logistical, one ideological. The logistical problem was what to do in 1918 with 80,000 dead and then, in 1945, with nearly 300,000 more. What is a nation to do with soldiers who die thousands of miles and vast oceans away from those who might mourn them? The ideological problem was how to justify such loss of life in wars geographically distant from the United States. What interest was worth the lives of so many young men and women? How could the nation justify death on such a scale?

The American Battle Monuments Commission (ABMC) and the twenty-three overseas military cemeteries that it superintends are at the center of the official solution to these problems. It was the ABMC that developed the architectural and artistic idiom for narrating soldierly death in the world wars, that moved against other attempts to narrate those deaths, and that maintains the resulting "hallowed grounds" as pristine though remote sites of American civil religion.[9] To understand ABMC cemeteries and the relationship they describe between the individual "fallen soldier," the nation, and the divine requires sensitivity to religious constructions of individuality and collectivity, and awareness of the symbolic and narrative appropriations of divinity pertaining to war and death. It requires, additionally, a willingness to examine simultaneously religiously charged memories of individuals and the connection between memorial spaces and a national collective.[10] It requires students to read memorial landscapes, to study these spaces for the civil religious messages written into them with flora, with stone, and with sacred word and symbol.

The ABMC cemeteries have an air of inevitability about them that can obscure the fact that they emerged from deliberative processes and reflected the desires of military leaders, politicians, artists, veterans' organizations, and families of the fallen. Because they present the war dead so effectively, it is difficult to either imagine that the cemeteries could have been any other way or to notice the sanctifying work that they perform. Scholars of religion regularly read stories like that of the Christian martyr Felicitas and see the shaping hand of a narrator. One aim of this chapter is to describe similar narrative processes at work in the memorialization of the American nurse Felicita among over a hundred thousand others. Another aim is to argue that ABMC cemeteries accomplish on a large and admittedly beautiful scale—and with a population that cannot resist—the task that American civil religion regularly performs with the living soldier, to wit, the construction of the American soldier as a G.I. Messiah.

In making this argument I will make frequent use of the term "hagiography," which is a useful if imperfect way to describe the cemeteries' depictions of the fallen soldiers and the relationship of soldiers to the nation in whose service they died. Hagiography is a genre of "literary portraiture" common among the world's religions. Hagiographies describe historical instances of holy living—the lives of saints and other religious adepts—and fashion models of holiness to be admired and, perhaps, emulated. Within the Christian tradition hagiography has long been a way of connecting the divine and human realms in the life and body of a specific individual.[11] The hagiographer—the man or woman committed to telling the life of a saint— approaches her subject with a reverent eye and a didactic purpose. Long or short, formulaic or surprising, hagiographies aim to describe Christian lives par excellence and to cultivate appreciation of them. ABMC cemeteries are as short on life details as any hagiography would dare be, but they are intensely hagiographical in their construction of a particular model of holiness connected to service and sacrifice for the nation and in their assertion that the men and women buried within their walls lived and died that holy model. The symbols, structures, burial patterns, and the words etched into cemetery chapel walls argue quite clearly that a particular set of Christian and American virtues are especially saintly and that those buried within the cemetery walls embodied these virtues.

The ubiquitous white crosses and occasional Stars of David that mark ABMC graves narrate this uniform embodiment but do not describe or detail individual holiness. Grave markers bear the name, rank, hometown, and death date of the interred but divulge no other details: no dates of birth, no descriptions of place and cause of death, no histories, and, with the exception of seven headstones in Suresnes American Cemetery, no epitaphs.[12]

It is, then, an implied hagiography. As the story of Felicita Hecht demonstrates, the ABMC's memorial approach begins with the dissolution of the individual and "his" refashioning into a national saint. ABMC cemeteries strongly encourage visitors to embrace this memorial elision.[13]

These cemeteries serve multiple purposes for the nation. They are not just places where the war dead are buried and where people can go to mourn and to remember. They promote as virtuous a particular model of citizenship and a particular vision of the nation.[14] ABMC cemeteries have long served as venues for speeches and ceremonies during which representatives of the nation articulate American values and describe visions of America's role in the world. They are ideal venues for such civil religious moments and their simultaneous sanctification of the nation, the cause being described, and the soldier dead. At the same time, ABMC cemeteries allow for multiple interpretations and reinterpretations of this ideal. In other words, while they manifest an intentional and often quite overt combination of the practical and the ideological in service of a civil religious orthodoxy, the meaning of these cemeteries is neither incontestable nor perfectly stable.[15]

Remembering the Soldier Dead

The American Battle Monuments Commission was established in 1923 by Public Law 534 of the Sixty-Seventh Congress and remains an arm of the executive branch of the U.S. government, answerable directly to the president. Today the ABMC administers and maintains twenty-three cemeteries in France, Belgium, England, Luxembourg, the Netherlands, Italy, Tunisia, and the Philippines. Although ABMC cemeteries reflect trends in the handling and burial of American dead dating to the early nineteenth century, the years 1919 through 1937 most shaped the ABMC's policy vis-à-vis the soldier dead and the artistic and theological idiom it uses in memorializing them. Details of expression vary from cemetery to cemetery and from one world war to another. The spaces themselves are not uniform. But the core theology of soldiering, the work of fashioning and generalizing a saintly model of American citizenship, and the connection of both to the exercise of American power in a violent world have been present from the very beginning.[16]

As noted above, ABMC cemeteries came into being in answer to two deceptively simple questions raised by the Great War. The first question was mostly practical: What was the U.S. government to do with nearly

80,000 dead bodies an ocean away from those who loved and mourned them?[17] The second was more ideological: How did the United States want its involvement in the Great War and those who died in the effort to be remembered? By far the simplest answer to the first question would have been to require, as the British did, permanent overseas burial. But early in the war the War Department stated that families could have their loved one's remains repatriated if they so desired. The War Department stuck to this promise, though it was no simple matter. A report sent to Secretary of War Newton Baker in May 1920 by his assistant Ralph Hayes outlined the significant logistical, hygienic, and political obstacles that lay in the way of a large-scale repatriation. As Hayes pointed out, Congress and the War Department were but two of the three parties whose support was needed to bring remains home. French authorities also had a say and did not like the idea of using the precious resources of their war-devastated country to unearth and transport decomposing Americans. Would the process overwhelm the rail system? What risks did the movement of dead bodies pose to the physical and mental health of the French people? After extensive negotiations in the late spring of 1920, exhumation and repatriation began. Families representing approximately 43,000 soldiers chose to bring their loved one's remains home.[18]

Even before repatriation began, the United States had to decide what to do with the dead who would remain in France. The first task, as the *Stars and Stripes* announced on February 28, 1919, was to gather them, "that in death they may be as they were in life—in serried ranks, shoulder to shoulder, comrades." There were several practical reasons for this ingathering. First, American dead were buried in roughly 1,700 separate locations, many of them makeshift and subject to regular disturbances. Hayes wrote, "Battle burials, unhappily, were made often under conditions unavoidably terrible. . . . These places were subject to constant inundation, which made highly desirable the removal of American dead to more suitable locations." Second, some of the war dead were buried well enough but reposed in farmland or public spaces that would soon return to their prewar functions. The physical integrity of their actual burial sites might be secure, but the spaces would hardly be sacred. Third and most important, geographically dispersed graves would make care of the graves sites and visits by mourning families exceedingly difficult. Hayes explained, "Grouped graves permit of care and attention being bestowed upon them which would be quite impracticable were they left in the far separated spots where they happened first to be."[19] Practical, sanitary, and funerary reasons figured prominently in the postwar plans for America's war dead.

The official answer to the question of how America's role in the war would be remembered and connected to the war dead began to be articulated in earnest with the organization of the ABMC in 1923. But in the five years that passed between the armistice and the establishment of the commission, other parties had stepped in to preserve memories of war and of the fallen. General Thomas North, who served as secretary of the ABMC from its establishment until his retirement in 1968, understood this memorial impulse but sought to limit its expression. The democratization of war memorials would, he feared, also be their debasement. North wrote, "Some of the troop units were already building monuments which bore inexact relation to the scope of the achievements they were commemorating; the accuracy of some of the inscriptions was open to question; the markers for the most part were poorly designed, poorly built, and lacked title to their sites and provision for their maintenance. The record of many fine units was not monumented [sic] at all."[20] Left unchecked, this memorial impulse might fill the French countryside with obelisks and plaques that told a history that was fragmentary, bombastic, and subject to rapid deterioration.

The Lafayette Escadrille Monument expresses this nongovernmental memorial impulse in a grand way while also pointing to the hazards of a democratized memorial process. Built with private funds on land donated by the French government, the Lafayette Escadrille Monument memorializes the wartime contributions of a small group of cosmopolitan Americans who stepped outside the nation to fight in the French Air Force prior to America's entry into the war. Their monument, a half-scale reproduction of the Arc d'Triomphe, stands atop a crypt, which holds the remains of sixty-one members of the Lafayette Escadrille. General North might be forgiven for thinking that such a grand monument to the memory of a small band of extranational warriors bore "inexact relation to the scope of the achievements" commemorated. Moreover, his concerns about quality of construction and provisions for maintenance have been borne out completely in the eighty years since the monument's dedication. Designers of the monument did not account for a local water table that is far too high for a structure of such weight and depth. This major oversight has led to chronic water infiltration problems in the crypt and the partial compromise of the structure's integrity. Making matters worse, the endowment established to fund maintenance of the site was ravaged when the stock market crashed a mere

3:2: Lafayette Escadrille Memorial, Parc St. Cloud, Marnes-la-Coquette, France.

sixteen months after the dedication ceremony in 1928. The monument still stands at the far western end of the Parc St. Cloud outside of Paris, but the messages of American sacrifice and French–American cooperation it was meant to convey must compete with messages of neglect and marginality forced upon it by nature and by history.

The Memorial Battle Cloisters of the American Cathedral in Paris, demonstrate the validity of concerns about a democratized memorial impulse from another angle. The cloisters are a reminder of the competing claims to ownership of the memories of America's war dead and the differing ideas as to the ends to which those memories might be directed. Dedicated two months after the ABMC came into being, the Memorial Battle Cloisters aspired to honor all of America's war dead and boasted top-shelf designer Bertram Goodhue and renowned American sculptor Mahonri Young, youngest grandson of Brigham Young. This memorial was conceived by Reverend Frederick Beekman, who took over as dean of the Church of the Holy Trinity in Paris when his predecessor resigned due to war exhaustion.[21] Dean Beekman was not at all exhausted by the war and saw to it that Holy Trinity became a hub of wartime and postwar worship. In the wake of the war he

3:3: Battle Memorial Cloisters, American Cathedral in Paris.

sought to parlay these experiences into the recognition of his church as the "National Memorial Church in Europe"—a gathering point for mourners seeking information about their fallen sons, brothers, and friends and a pilgrimage site for those interested in seeing the pews that once had been filled with soldiers who "came from death and went to death."[22]

The cloisters that Beekman commissioned occupy four and a half bays along the north wall of an open courtyard in the cathedral complex. Four full bays are decorated with the insignia of each American division that fought in the Great War. Below each insignia are listed the areas in which its men fought and the numbers of combat deaths they suffered, broken down by "officers" and "men." The half bay orients the visitor to the meaning of the display. It features Mahonri Young's sculpture *Columbia Sheathing Her Sword*, bas-relief representations of key battles, and a large plaque inscribed in English and French:

To the Memory of Our Dead
The Americans who during the Great War of 1914–1918
came overseas with their comrades two million strong
and gave their lives fighting beside their allies, for

3:4: Battle Memorial Cloisters, American Cathedral in Paris. The sculpture is *Columbia Sheathing Her Sword*. Mahonri Young, sculptor.

country, for humanity, for God. These cloister memorials
are dedicated in gratitude and pride.
They loved not their lives unto death. Let light perpetual shine upon them.

In contrast to the triumphal arch that memorializes the Lafayette Escadrille and holds the bodies of its dead, the cloister is impersonal, numerical. It narrates the war effort not in terms of ideals and cooperation but in terms of units that fought in regions and lost numbers. This spreadsheet of war's human costs bears a close if unintentional relationship to Dean Beekman's broader memorial program in that he hoped to convince each of the forty-eight states to endow the pews of Holy Trinity permanently and thus to lift the burden of debt from his outpost of expatriate Episcopalianism. Beekman undertook two fund-raising tours of the United States and encouraged fellow Episcopalian divines to generate enthusiasm for the plan by soliciting testimony from members of the American Legion and appeals from Gold Star families.[23]

Beekman's campaign began to falter as early as 1920 when he failed to generate significant interest in pew endowments beyond New York, Washington, D.C., and Pennsylvania. When his highest profile endorsee, General John Pershing, assumed the chairmanship of the American Battle Monuments Commission a mere two months before the dedication of the Memorial Cloisters, any lingering hopes that Holy Trinity would be known beyond the masthead of its own bulletins as "the Church of Memorials of the American Dead of the Great War" vanished. Nevertheless, the Battle Memorial Cloisters of the American Cathedral were dedicated on Memorial Day 1923. Bishop Charles Brent, former chief of chaplains of the American Expeditionary Force, attended and prayed, "In the name of our God, who by the glorious example of the crucified one taught us that in the midst of death we are in life, we do now unveil and dedicate this memorial battle cloister in honor of those, who in the cause of freedom were careless of their lives even unto death, and, having made the supreme sacrifice now rest with him."[24]

In spite of having played an active role in the religious lives of some American soldiers, in spite of an inspired and artistically respectable attempt to memorialize the fallen, in spite of a deep and mostly ingenuous desire to accommodate the mourning and to assist in the sacred practice of civil religious pilgrimage, Holy Trinity would not own the sacrifices of American soldiers and war workers. Those bodies and the civil religious power associated with them belonged to the federal government.

The initial charge to the ABMC ensured that efforts such as those undertaken by veterans and families of the Lafayette Escadrille and by Reverend Beekman and his vestry would be difficult to see through to completion. In addition to their role in "select[ing] sites for . . . memorials to mark and commemorate the services of the American forces in Europe" and "erect[ing] works of art and architecture in the American cemeteries," the ABMC became a monumental gatekeeper. As ABMC Secretary North recalled, the commission was to "cooperate with American citizens, States, municipalities, or associations desiring to build war memorials in Europe *as the Commission may determine* with the proviso that all agencies of the U.S. Government were prohibited from aiding any such project unless it had received the Commission's approval and that of the Fine Arts Commission."[25] Without the support of a generally unsupportive body, individual American citizens or communities would be left to their own memorial devices. In the meantime, the ABMC could turn to its own program of conceptualization, design, and construction.

"Monumenting" the G.I. Messiah

From very early on, ABMC planners and designers, and American political leaders wanted to create monumental cemeteries for the war dead, cemeteries that not only held the gathered dead and testified to American contributions to the war effort but were impressive and expressive of American values. Ralph Hayes wrote in 1920, "Following the determination upon the permanent sites of the American Fields of Honor overseas, the work of beautifying them may be pushed forward speedily, in order that they may serve alike as a symbol of a Nation's gratitude to its departed sons and a demonstration to all peoples for all time of America's response to a great threat." Landscape architect and Commission on Fine Arts chairman Charles Moore put a finer point on it in 1921: "Unless we [make] those cemeteries 'little Arlington[s]' no one will know that American troops fought in France. We must have something more than a patch of white"[26]

The ABMC designers drew on several of Arlington's stylistic elements, including a generous apportionment of space per grave, the principle that each body should have its own plot and headstone, and a policy prescribing acceptable grave markers. But the artists and architects employed by the ABMC used these concepts to create memorial environments very different from Arlington or any other domestic veterans' cemetery. In short, because ABMC designers were working with a fixed population, they were free to treat soldiers' bodies as elements in their landscape constructions. Closed communities of the dead allowed designers to space and distribute evenly, arrange symmetrically, and thus emphasize equality and order to a far greater degree than the sprawling grounds and multiple, conflicting memorial idioms of Arlington allow. They exhumed and reburied the fallen, rearranging their ranks in pursuit of an artistic and monumental vision. Additionally, because families ceded control of their loved ones' bodies to the government, decisions regarding how to memorialize the individual became a matter of official policy, not family preference. This level of control over the memorial landscape interacted well with the Beaux Arts principles of "geometry, hierarchical order, and symmetry" that dominated the ABMC throughout the planning and construction phases of the Great War cemeteries. The result was a system of cemeteries with "a sense of monumentality and common purpose . . . clearly intended to impress both European and American visitors."[27]

General Pershing and the ABMC—in consultation with the Commission on Fine Arts and architect Paul Cret—also brought an emphasis on

3:5: St. Mihiel American Cemetery, near Thiaucourt, France. U.S. and German forces clashed near here in September 1918. The cemetery, shown circa 1935, holds 4,153 Americans. The sculpture in the foreground depicts an American officer standing in front of a cross. The inscription below him reads, "Blessed are they that have the home longing, for they shall go home." Paul Manship, sculptor. (Photo courtesy of the National Archives, photo no. 117-MC-28[4])

sacred symbol and structure to the cemeteries. At the most basic and striking level, the ABMC chose as permanent headstones religious symbols—the Latin cross or the Star of David—cut from white marble. Charles Moore, who was involved in the American Graves Registration Service's initial cemetery construction efforts, originally "planned to replace the [temporary] wooden crosses with permanent markers similar to those used in the Civil War enlisted men's section of Arlington." (Short, rounded headstones, "inconspicuous in themselves" in Moore's words.) This plan, once made public, elicited an outcry from congressmen, veterans, and Gold Star mothers who insisted, along with General Pershing, "that the permanent markers be crosses."[28] The aesthetic effect of this decision, ABMC brochures note, is to reinforce the cemeteries-wide principles of symmetry and order and to provide a contrast between the verdant lawns and the brilliant white markers. The theological effect is to assert at the ground level the sacredness of the space and the uniformity, even the Christ-like-ness of those buried beneath the crosses and stars.[29] Stars of David, present in far fewer numbers than Latin crosses, mark out a difference in religious identity but not a departure from a hagiographic vision that is at once American and overwhelmingly Christian.[30] This becomes most obvious in the chapels erected by the ABMC at each of the Great War cemeteries.[31] The cemetery chapels vary in design from neoclassical, to Romanesque, to neo-Gothic but employ strongly Christian imagery to sanctify the dead and the cause for which they fought. Death in war becomes the highest expression of American patriotism and Christian living. Jewish symbols, to the extent that they exists in the chapels, are generally quite small and occupy places of lower visibility. While these cemeteries clearly construct the fallen Jewish soldier

3:6: Interior of the memorial chapel at Oise-Aisne American Cemetery. The inscription on the altar reads, "With God is their reward." The chapel was designed by Ralph Adams Cram of Cram and Ferguson, Boston.

as fully American—a painfully elusive status for American Jews in the first five decades of the twentieth century—the Christian-dominated chapels and the overwhelmingly Christianized memorial environment speak simultaneously of Jews who have been saved in spite of their Judaism. It is as if their Christ-like sufferings in war or their deep devotion to the United States disrupted their Jewish identity just enough to accomplish something like a saving conversion. Indeed, while the ABMC marked the graves of unknown Great War soldiers with Latin crosses or Stars of David in proportion to the rates of service of Christians and Jews, the graves of *all* unknown World War II soldiers—with a single exception in Manila—are marked with Latin crosses.

Eight ABMC cemeteries were dedicated in 1937—a full two decades after American entry into the Great War. Monumental in themselves, these memorial landscapes presented consistently hagiographical messages to families of the fallen, to American pilgrims, and to anyone—French, English, Belgian, German—who might think the American war effort unimpressive. Aesthetically they emphasize order and symmetry, uniformity and equality. Theologically they sanctify the fallen, the war, and the nation.

Meuse-Argonne American Cemetery

In the fall of 1918, American, French, and British forces launched the final offensive of the Great War against an exhausted but well-entrenched and experienced German opponent. As described briefly in chapter 2, the fighting in the Argonne Forest was chaotic and costly. It involved attacks on and through heavily forested, hilly terrain against systems of trenches that German forces had been developing for almost four years. Soldiers of the American Expeditionary Force (AEF) were fresher, more eager to fight, and more willing to take casualties. Death came in many forms to those who fought there. Bullets and bayonets, shells and gas, grenades and mines. Many also died of disease—Spanish flu was especially deadly. As the AEF began to absorb these losses it did what most armies do: it buried the dead where they fell or not far from the site and moved on.[32] When the armistice halted combat operations on November 11, 1918, the United States had nearly eighty thousand dead soldiers and war workers to account for and, if enough of a body could be found, to bury.

By Memorial Day of 1919, two cemeteries, though far from finished, were ready enough to host dedication ceremonies. General John Pershing,

commander-in-chief of the AEF, spoke to a group of soldiers and dignitaries gathered at the site that would become Meuse-Argonne American
Cemetery near the small town of Romagne-sous-Montfaucon. He moved
directly into a hagiographic register, describing the fallen men (he did not
mention women) as exemplary and worthy of contemplation if not imitation. His words, recorded in the *Stars and Stripes* on June 6, 1919, described
a tight connection between the space the dead occupied and a vision of
American society. "Through their sacrifices we have gained a more lofty
conception of liberty and a distinct vision of a better world. . . . To the
memory of these heroes, this sacred plot is consecrated as a shrine, where
future generations of men who love liberty may come to do homage. . . . It
is up to us to uphold that for which they died. It is for the living to carry
forward their purpose." Pershing articulated the core of the civil religious
orthodoxy that each cemetery would narrate: the sainted dead buried here
died for the righteous cause of liberty; "this sacred plot" calls to us to pay
homage and to continue their work.[33]

Today the Meuse-Argonne American Cemetery at Romagne-sous-
Montfaucon is the largest ABMC cemetery in Europe. Laid out on 130
acres of land, Meuse-Argonne holds the remains of 14,246 American dead,
including 486 unknowns, 4 chaplains, at least 7 women, and 3 infants.[34] The
key features of the cemetery are its eight rectangular graves areas, a narrow
grass mall that functions as a central axis, and the memorial chapel. In sharp
contrast to the daily brutality and regular chaos that characterized the final
months of the Great War, the Meuse-Argonne cemetery is a place of peace
and order. Jacques Gréber's landscape design emphasizes peace by cloister-
ing the entire cemetery with trees that have grown to make the brick walls
around the perimeter redundant. The space achieves a high degree of order
by using linden trees to divide the graves area into two rectangular sections
and those two main sections into four rectangular subsections. This is a
world of right angles and clean lines. Moreover, the eight "formations" of
the war dead, separated from each other by walls of mature, box-pruned
lindens, are themselves devoid of trees, shrubs, or any vegetation save the
impossibly green grass and a rare dandelion. Each section is thus dominated
by white marble crosses arranged in rows and columns. ABMC regulations
dictate that no grave marker can deviate from the row or column line, level
or plumb, by more than five millimeters. To achieve and preserve this degree of order, construction crews buried concrete beams twenty inches below the ground and anchored the crosses to them. These beams run the
length of each row and guarantee that crosses will neither sink nor lean.

3:7: Meuse-Argonne American Cemetery, the largest ABMC cemetery in Europe, holds 14,246 Great War dead. (Photo courtesy of the American Battle Monuments Commission)

The graves area at the Meuse-Argonne cemetery slopes upward toward a "memorial chapel" designed by Louis Ayers of the New York firm York and Sawyer. It is a modest Romanesque structure with open loggias extending to either side of an enclosed chapel. The exterior tells in prose and maps the story of the righteous battle waged by these American saints. The interior of the chapel features an apse in which hangs a Christian cross, encircled by the flags of the allied nations. A small stone representing the Decalogue sits on the floor to one side of the altar. With pews, marble floors, and stained glass, the chapel was clearly designed as a place of Christian prayer and reflection, a place to bring one's sadness and sense of loss and to seek meaning. The inscriptions in the chapel's interior are particularly directive in this task. The first, penned by General John Pershing, states the chapel's civil religious purpose, "This chapel is erected by the United States of America as a sacred rendezvous of a grateful people with its immortal dead." Three others draw on biblical and liturgical language to answer questions about the eternal fates of those "immortal dead." The phrase "God hath taken them unto himself" adapts scriptural passages regarding choseness (Psalm 135:4) and forgiveness (2 Cor. 5:19), and inscriptions reading "Peaceful is their sleep in God" and "Perpetual light upon them shines" transform the petitions of a requiem mass ("Grant them everlasting rest" and "Let perpetual light shine upon them") into statements of settled law.[35] In short, the chapel inscriptions proclaim in Christian idiom that the suffering, exertion, pain, violence, and darkness of war have resolved themselves into divine relief, peace, rest, and light eternal for the fallen.

The Meuse-Argonne American Cemetery is a memorial world as separate from the world around it as it could possibly be. It holds the dead and is thus separate from most spaces for the living, but the way that it holds the dead also separates it from other spaces for the dead. The cloistered feel, the ramrod straight, brilliantly white crosses, the level of attention to grounds keeping and maintenance, not to mention the chapel's inscriptions, speak loudly and clearly the message that these are exemplary Americans who, through noble service and heroic sacrifice, have achieved salvation.

Normandy American Cemetery

Little more than two years after the dedication of the completed Meuse-Argonne American Cemetery in 1937, there was war again in Europe, North Africa, and Asia. World War II involved American soldiers for far longer than World War I (December 1941–August 1945; April 1917–November 1918) and cost far more military personnel their lives (405,399; 116,516). The United States entered the war in December 1941 and soon faced problems of death and burial similar to those faced in the aftermath of the Great War. This time, however, the United States had a policy in place, a precedent. Grieving families could repatriate remains at government expense or choose permanent overseas burial for their fallen soldier. The design and construction of fifteen cemeteries took place over the decade and a half following World War II. The two largest of these are Manila American Cemetery in the Philippines (17,202 war dead) and Lorraine American Cemetery (10,489). The most famous is Normandy.

Normandy American Cemetery is situated on a bluff that rises above a stretch of coastline where on the morning of June 6, 1944, U.S. Army troops came ashore as part of Operation Overlord. The purpose of the invasion was to establish an Allied foothold in northern France from which to carry out an effective ground war against the German Army. On that morning, U.S. soldiers landed at beaches code-named Omaha and Utah; British soldiers landed at Sword and Gold; Canadian forces took Juno. This was the largest amphibious assault in history, and by all accounts it was a spectacular success. When the sun set on the first day of the invasion, 144,000 Allied troops were on French soil. Total dead among all Allied forces numbered 3,000. Roughly 2,000 of those were American dead, most of whom were killed at Omaha Beach.[36]

Not long after Allied landing craft hit the beach in front of German coastal defense installations, the Normandy coast became a burial ground. The transformation of that burial ground into a memorial landscape, however, took twelve years. Dead soldiers whose families requested repatriation were exhumed and sent home. Soldiers who had been killed and buried farther inland, sometimes side by side with German soldiers, were exhumed and brought to St. Laurent, as the Normandy cemetery was then known. The ABMC contacted sculptors, architects and landscape designers who developed proposals, negotiated revisions, and, finally, began work.[37] But this work took time. Edith Morton Eustis who traveled to St. Laurent cemetery on July 22, 1952, to visit her son's grave wrote to ABMC chairman General George Marshall venting her frustration that in the three years since her last visit no apparent improvements had been made. "When one thinks of the 8 years that have passed since D-Day, the 7 years since peace—one cannot avoid a feeling of shame that the richest country in the world has so neglected and overlooked the soldiers who died for her." Four years later, the ABMC dedicated the Normandy American Cemetery with great fanfare. *National Geographic* described Normandy and the other six cemeteries dedicated that summer as evidence of "A Faith Kept."[38]

Normandy American Cemetery at Colleville-sur-Mer is every bit as committed as Meuse-Argonne to portraying the men buried there as saints. The hagiography of Normandy is strongly Christian and is resolute in its assertion of salvation for the war dead. Just as at Meuse-Argonne, white crosses dominate the landscape of Normandy. But because the crosses at Normandy are presented without rigid separation by landscaping elements, the scale of the cemetery is amplified. Moreover, in laying out the cemetery, designer Markley Stevenson brought the main walkways together to form an enormous Latin cross, visible only from the air, with the cemetery chapel marking the intersection of the horizontal and vertical elements (see figure Intro:3) As at Meuse-Argonne, the chapel and memorial narrate Christian American heroism. The chapel contains a large cross above an altar and, on the floor to one side of the altar, a representation of the Decalogue. On opposite sides of the chapel are two engraved statements: "Through the gate of death they pass to their joyful resurrection" and "Think not only upon their passing. Remember the glory of their spirit." Over the former is an engraved Latin cross; over the latter, a Star of David. Across the eastern section of the graves area (walking from the chapel down the long board of the cross's vertical section) is a memorial that centers on a statue, *The Spirit of American Youth Rising from the Waves*, by Donald De Lue.[39] The inscription at the base of the statue situates that "spirit" firmly within the register of American martial Christianity. It is the opening lyric of Julia Ward Howe's famous "Battle Hymn of the Republic": "Mine eyes have seen the glory of the coming of the Lord." The full text of Howe's hymn weaves Christ thoroughly into the martial world both as agent, "Let the savior born of woman crush the serpent with His heel," and as exemplar, "As he died to make men holy, let us die to make men free."

Like Meuse-Argonne, Normandy uses land and nature to convey a message about a world war and the men who died waging it. Normandy is, however, more sophisticated in its narration. Normandy American Cemetery is not a battlefield cemetery in the spirit of Gettysburg, Shiloh, or the ABMC cemeteries at St. Mihiel and Aisne-Marne in France. It is a campaign cemetery placed at the site of a dramatic, historic battle. It gathers dead Americans on ground made famous for the daring and heroism of a particular fight on a particular day, though less than 10 percent of the 9,387 buried there died on D-Day. A small sampling of the crosses—which mention the date but not the location of a death—bears this out. Robert A. Price, June 6, 1944 (D-Day); Merlin J. Rosenberger, July 8, 1944; Melvin Rosenbaum, July 29, 1944; Samuel H. J. Cohen, August 1, 1944, Dolores M. Browne, July 13, 1945. The diverse circumstances under which those buried in the Normandy cemetery died are thus in subtle tension with the narrative of uniformity presented by the headstones and the mythic landscape on which the cemetery is situated. The location and the tales—real and imagined—of D-Day heroism allow, even encourage, visitors to efface these differences and to imagine that *these* dead sacrificed their lives to secure *this* strip of land.

The cemetery at Normandy offers another answer to the architectural and religious questions that ABMC planners first faced when designing the Great War cemeteries. To wit: What kind of cemetery and memorial "over there" will tell an appropriately sacred and, to quote from post–Great War correspondence, "impressive" story of the American contribution to the war? The Christian imagery and language of Normandy American Cem-

3:8: Headstone of Sergeant Dolores M. Browne, Normandy American Cemetery. There are 9,387 American soldiers buried at Normandy. Roughly 900 of these died on D-Day, June 6, 1944. Sergeant Browne, an African-American woman, died from injuries she suffered in a jeep accident. A brief summary of her war service is available at www.findagrave.com. (Photo by Kate LeMay)

etery encourage visitors to contemplate the glory of the fallen. The land it occupies engages the American mytho-religious imagination while subtly reconfiguring the history of the space. Large numbers of bodies were arranged by the ABMC at the site of the most famous "American" battle of the war in Europe, a site that places each dead man on the beach below, or scaling a bluff, or attacking a machine gun emplacement. The civil religious potential is powerful indeed. One can easily "see" the heroism that was required, wonder at the bravery and selflessness, and evaluate oneself and the nation, *our* luxuries and securities, in light of *their* sacrifices and all that their losses secured for *us*. Normandy constructs a sacred that encourages comparison to the holy dead, awe at their sacrifices, and thankfulness that, as a fallen soldier's daughter says in a film shown at the visitors' center, "They gave their future so that we could enjoy ours." Entries in the Normandy American Cemetery guest register indicate that this sacred space remains potent: "Beautiful"; "Thank you"; "Merci"; "Grazie."[40]

Suresnes American Cemetery

Among ABMC cemeteries Suresnes is unique in that it has been dedicated three times by major figures of American internationalism: President Woodrow Wilson in 1919; the American ambassador to France, William C. Bullitt, in 1937; and General of the Army and Nobel laureate George C. Marshall in 1952. Suresnes has required three dedications to mark three stages in its life as a place of noble death; at each stage an authoritative voice characterized anew the war dead (see figure Intro:1). When President Wilson spoke on Memorial Day 1919, he channeled "the voice" of America's Great War dead saying, according to the June 6, 1919, edition of the *Stars and Stripes:* "We command you in the name of those who, like ourselves, have died to bring the councils of men together, and we remind you what America said she was born for. She was born . . . to show mankind the way to liberty. She was born to make this great gift a common gift." Wilson looked out that day on a field of graves arranged head-to-head and marked by temporary wooden crosses and Stars of David. He also saw a large audience of the living and, the cemetery being unfinished, a great deal of mud. On Memorial Day 1937, Ambassador Bullitt spoke of the dead as if they were living, proclaiming that they had "won their fight" and, as the *New York Times* reported the next day, "received here their discharge."[41] Suresnes looked different that day than it had eighteen years earlier. Thick green grass covered the ground. White marble crosses and Stars of David replaced the wooden markers. The graves and the bodies in them had been spaced out and reoriented to face one direction—east—with a view of Paris. A chapel had been added as well; the neoclassical building designed by Charles Platt featured a gray marble altar bearing a gold cross and an adaptation of Jesus's words in the Gospel of John: "I give unto them eternal life and they shall never perish."[42]

General George Marshall spoke at Suresnes on September 13, 1952, as chairman of the ABMC. Marshall's address from the steps of a newly expanded memorial chapel conveyed with minor alteration words provided by David Bruce, the State Department's public affairs officer. Marshall offered the dead as models for the living, saying, "I hope they are deaf to the [Communist] propaganda that demands that we living Americans [Yankees] go home and leave Europe to the mercy of ruthless aggression. . . . The dead cannot go home. And we will not go home until our friends here feel that our presence here is no longer essential to their security, and when we can leave a land free of terrors . . . a land where . . . a feeling of good faith dominates life."[43] Marshall was in Europe to monitor progress on cemeteries being constructed for the American dead of World War II and to dedicate, at Suresnes, what he termed a "shrine" to the American dead of both world wars. Plans for this shrine, drafted under General Pershing, involved the addition of two loggias to the original cemetery chapel and, as General Robert Woodside reported in August 1949, the disinterment and movement within the cemetery of some of the Great War dead.[44] The ABMC disturbed these graves to make room for twenty-four unknown World War II dead brought in from temporary cemeteries across Europe. The presence of these new dead gave the "shrine" an especially powerful Christian appearance. For rather than arrange these twenty-four soldiers in the traditional row-on-row pattern, the ABMC arranged their plots, and thus their headstones, in the shape of a Latin cross (see figure Intro:2).

Three features of this "revision" demonstrate the hagiographic dynamic at work at Suresnes and, more subtly, across the network of ABMC cemeteries. First, the 1952 revision did little to alter Suresnes's character as a Great War cemetery. Twenty-four sets of unknown remains from World War II were unlikely to draw next-of-kin who wanted to imagine themselves in the presence of a beloved soldier whose remains had never been identified. (One purpose of the Tomb of the Unknowns in Arlington National Cemetery was to provide a comparatively accessible place of mourning for families of the missing and the unidentified dead.) Whatever minor funerary purpose the relocation and rearrangement may have served was overwhelmed by the political, ideological, and theological purpose of creating a venue that allowed speakers and visitors contact with the American dead of both wars. Second, the arrangement of the twenty-four unknown dead in the shape of a Latin cross was a remarkably intentional act in the already highly intentional world of the ABMC. This explicit use of remains as landscaping elements is a clear expression of the ABMC's hagiographical presentation of "the American soldier." *Not only did these men die to save you,* the cross of dead soldiers proclaims, *they themselves are saved.* Their individual qualities—virtues, vices, beliefs, doubts, the specifics of humanity—are unknown, unknowable, and, quite simply, irrelevant. By virtue of having served the United States and having died in service, they became American saviors.

Third, the loggias added to the memorial chapel offer guidance to Americans as to how best to "remember" and carry the gospel of the war dead to the world. The south loggia is dedicated to the Great War; the north commemorates World War II. Defying the asymmetrical place of these wars in American memory, the loggias are of the same size and contain the same elements: engraved plaques, bas-relief depictions of soldiers carrying an empty stretcher, and at the far end of each loggia, a single memorial room dominated by a solitary white statue. In the Great War memorial room stands John Gregory's *Memory;* the World War II memorial room holds Louis Iselin's *Remembrance*.[45] These statues depict female figures bearing somber expressions. *Memory* (the Great War) evokes Mary. Her eyes are closed. Her hands are raised, brought together in prayer. From the features of her face and the position of her hands to the straight, simple lines of her dress, *Memory* projects quietude and passivity, if not quite serenity. *Remembrance*, located opposite *Memory*, is not prayerful. Her eyes are wide open, her hands folded left over right beneath her right breast. Her gar-

3:9: *Memory*. John Gregory, sculptor. Suresnes American Cemetery.

3:10: *Remembrance.* Louis Iselin, sculptor. Suresnes American Cemetery.

ments are wrinkled and flowing. Her head, uncovered to show hair worn off the neck, and her almost gaunt face speak of activity, engagement, vigilance. Her gaze, though pained, is vivid and lively and fixed on something above and beyond her visitors. *Remembrance* is in the room but not of the room. She is defined by a purpose that is "out there," beyond the sacred ground of Suresnes.

Memory and *Remembrance,* devotion and vigilance, prayerfulness and watchfulness. These statues are an enduring expression of both the hagiographic vision of the ABMC cemeteries and the civil religious messages of men like Wilson, Pershing, and Marshall. This place, they say, is inward directing and outward directing, a space for self-evaluation and for contemplation of the "true" nature of the world beyond the trees and grass and marble crosses. At Suresnes, the only cemetery where the ABMC attempted the uncomfortable task of interpreting two wars to save the world in light of each other, the civil religious orthodoxy of the entire cemetery system is most clear. We must guard our memories of these G.I. Messiahs and contemplate their sacrificial deaths. We must honor their collective memory and continue their redeeming work in a dangerous world.

Ideals, Bodies, and the National Sacred

The ABMC understands its cemeteries to be *sacred* spaces, "hallowed ground," plots of American soil in foreign lands that make possible a "sacred rendezvous . . . with the immortal dead." At one level these claims are unremarkable, bordering on civil religious cant. Veneration of the fallen warrior is older than Homer; connections between sacred space and the "holy dead" in Western traditions date at least to late antiquity.[46] Yet there is more going on in ABMC cemeteries than the burial and sequestration of the war dead, on one hand, and the reflexive perpetuation of civil religious clichés, on the other. These spaces narrate an ideal of American citizenship. They encourage pilgrims to imagine an ideal soldier, an ideal army, an ideal America. Every element of these works of architectural hagiography—the chapels, the ubiquitous white crosses, the cross of crosses at Suresnes—validates the pattern: service, sacrifice, salvation. The cemeteries themselves and the American officials who have interpreted them juxtapose this narrative and these ideals to the less pristine, less ordered realities of America and the world to the end of cultivating reverence and emulation. Moreover, the hagiographies attempt to shape thinking about American soldiers and the wars they have waged, allowing little space for questions about the morals of either. Service to the nation, they say, dissolves all earthly difference and, like perfect service to God, covers and cleanses all manner of sins.

The ABMC cemeteries weave sacred narrative into landscape and, at Normandy, use sacred landscape to sustain a narrative. These are common elements of a "sense of place."[47] But narratives and spaces are devilish things. Implied hagiographies and civil religious orthodoxies can be challenged by the very bodies in the very ground to which they are tied. As Philip Sheldrake writes: "Every place has an excess of meaning beyond what can be seen or understood at any one time. This excess persistently overflows any attempt at final definition. A place can never be subordinated to a single valuation, one person's prejudices, or the assumptions of a single group." We fail to understand the religio-political "texts" that these cemeteries are if we do not see their design and their Christian symbolism working to contain "overflows of meaning" in favor of an intensely civil religious "final definition."[48] ABMC cemeteries use burial patterns quite consciously to represent the "American" ideals of equality and democracy. War heroes lie buried next to cooks, nurses, and those who never got close to the battlefield. The dead are arranged without regard to class, race, creed, or national origin, presenting to the pilgrim a vision of American society not realized in the lifetimes of the soldiers. These cemeteries also contest the individualism of American cultural practices in general and American cemetery design in particular. Whether the scion of a New England family, the working mother of two children, the grandson of slaves, or the child of recent immigrants, each body lies in a grave of its own and is marked by a standard white marble headstone. Finally, ABMC cemeteries employ an inversion classic in both Christian and American memorial practice by which the dead, not the living, are truly empowered. Their deaths—described at almost every turn as "sacrifices"—are meant to place a claim on the living, to require those who walk among the crosses and the Stars of David to pursue "the ideals" for which these men and women are said to have died. ABMC cemeteries gather together what historian Drew Gilpin Faust has named the "constituency of the slain" to inspire or to convict the pilgrim.[49] The words of Dwight D. Eisenhower, inscribed at Normandy American Cemetery, spell it out clearly: "To these we owe the high resolve that the cause for which they died shall live."

We also fail to understand ABMC cemeteries by ignoring the counternarratives not quite erased by the crosses, the chapels, and the green grass. For beneath the multitude of hagiographic devices lie more complicated personal stories and moral realities. Felicita Hecht is buried in Oise-Aisne. Suresnes holds the remains of the Cromwell twins, Gladys and Dorothy, who, exhausted by their work with the wounded and dying, threw themselves from the ship carrying them back to New York and drowned.[50] Dolores Browne and two other female, African-American soldiers, killed in a jeep accident, are buried at Normandy. Throughout ABMC cemeteries one can find the white marble crosses marking the remains of African-American soldiers, mistreated by the U.S. Army from beginning to end. A hidden plot at Oise-Aisne holds ninety-six Americans executed for rape and murder during World War II. The visible elements of ABMC cemeteries make them obvious civil religious shrines. The buried realities help us understand the work being done on and above the surface. These realities can also remind those who are attentive to them that the narrative of service, suffering, and salvation rests imperfectly over the bodies on which it depends.

ABMC cemeteries transform injury and death and brokenness and lone-liness and suffering into beauty—and not beauty only but beauty tended by the nation on a scale achievable only by a nation, and a victorious nation at that. This is fitting. It echoes the fact that only the nation is capable in victory or defeat of actions that generate such great suffering, injury, and brokenness. Men and women who became instruments of national power in life receive in these cemeteries a small measure of that power in return every day. Groundskeepers scrub their crosses and stars regularly and mow the grass around their plots, and as of fifteen years ago or so, "Taps" has sounded every evening on a donated carillon. Those family members who are still alive visit only rarely, but these dead—or at least these spaces of death—are not forgotten.

The ABMC's acts of devotion have transformed burial grounds into compelling narratives and potentially accusing beauty. This is not, how-ever, a one-way relationship. At ABMC cemeteries, narratives and beauty also sustain the power. Within the well-defined walls of the ABMC cem-etery, the diverse narratives of American war and American religion are forged into a nationalist theology in which the redeemer nation acts through its incarnate sons, sacrifices some of them for the good of the world, and then keeps them alive in memory as citizens draw near to contemplate the glory. The Christian substructures of this theology are visible throughout each cemetery. Christian language and symbol explain the United States' place in the world and encourage devotion to the G.I. Messiah.

For those who recognize the power of war memories but resist reading them solely as expressions of civil religious orthodoxy, ABMC cemeteries offer something more than testimony to the saving power of soldierly sacri-fice. These American sacred spaces with their seamless presentation of the martial, the national, and the Christian provide an opportunity to reflect on and analyze the ways in which the United States refashions and theologizes the human cost of war.[51] Their architectural hagiography portrays again and again heroism and saintliness, but the graves hold the bodies of particular people whose own narratives of war may or may not validate this saintly narrative. ABMC cemeteries thus offer more than a chance to "remember" the fallen within an official framework. They offer a chance to stand "on hallowed ground" and from that point of privilege to turn myths of war in on themselves, to record voices and experiences long obscured, to add narrative-altering layers to the hagiography, to discover levels of meaning long hidden.[52] Few people have taken this opportunity and few ever will.

The cemeteries recede steadily from public consciousness, and contrary to the motto of the ABMC, time indeed dims the "glory of their deeds." But because the deeds themselves are always both imagined, in that their realities are inaccessible to visitors, and generalized, in that not all of the dead encountered the same realities, it is not the dimming of the deeds as much as the dimming of the theology that is of civil religious consequence. And the theology, I believe, is as vigorous as it has ever been.

Having written sacred narratives of heroism with the bodies of its martyrs, having imagined and built them into a unity of spirit, a unity of virtue, having proclaimed them saved, we should not be surprised that *the nation*—the federal government and "the people"—expected that sacrificial spirit to be carried forward into a dangerous world by a Christ-like soldiery. Indeed, as the United States moved from a four-year war with Nazi Germany, Fascist Italy, and Imperial Japan into a decades-long struggle against global communisms and other objectionable forms of government, both citizens and soldiers projected the G.I. Messiah forward using mythic memory to shape expectations of American responses to uses of unrighteous power.

In the midst of an operation designed to bring omniscience to the American nation, one man fell to earth. His story demonstrates some of the challenges of giving flesh to the word of the nation at the same time that it demonstrates the degree of devotion some Americans felt to the G.I. Messiah. His story also allows us to consider the religious dimensions of one man's struggle with a catastrophic fall from the heavens and to analyze the ritual process undertaken by the nation to make sense of the savior who wasn't.

CHAPTER 4

Saint Francis the Fallen

The lynched and mutilated body of a serviceman turned Wobbly. Four bodies of Great War veterans, members of an American Legion parade. The unidentifiable body of an American soldier. A war hero's body, missing from a ship in the Atlantic. The buried bodies of over 120,000 American soldiers and war workers. These have been some of the sources for this book so far. Soldiers' bodies are central elements of American civil religion. Their bodies are also the means by which American soldiers engage with and practice this religion. As a society and as observers of society, we do not have to work hard to note and to analyze the public, visible actions of these soldierly bodies and to connect them to civil religion.

The limits of reading only the public actions of such sources are, however, worth noting. First, because civil religion in general and American civil religion in particular rely so heavily on the visible, the symbolic, the publicly ritualistic, it is precisely in these public arenas that one encounters and is most easily overwhelmed by civil religious orthodoxy.[1] To study civil religion within what are, in effect, vertical boundaries (the walls that separate public from private) and horizontal boundaries (the earth that separates the visible from the buried) is to stack the deck in favor of consensus, leaving little space for counternarratives and counter-rituals. In so doing we fail to take the full measure of civil religion and we do not use our theoretical and analytical capacities to their fullest. Second, by thinking about and reading only the public actions of soldiers' bodies we impose a boundary that soldiers themselves do not and often cannot observe. The bodies on display in public moments of civil religion are the same bodies that cross thresholds into barracks, apartments, and houses when the ceremonies end and the crowds go home. Uniforms come off, but they hang as reminders in closets. Soldiers' bodies in private spaces are abled and disabled, groomed and tattooed, much as they are in public spaces. Moreover, if one myth of warfare has been ripped to shreds by the past century, it is the myth of a soldier's ability to leave war completely behind, to, as it were, get it out of her or his body. Civil religion moves back and forth between public and private on and in the bodies of soldiers. To ignore private civil religious moments because they are not obviously connected to the *civitas* is akin to turning from the domestic religious practices of Hinduism or Catholicism. It is to paint a picture of civil religion as all state, all public, all orthodox, and to miss not only devotional, meaning-making practices but also sites of resistance to and reinvention of myth, symbol, ritual, and tradition.[2]

The story at the center of this chapter makes this point about boundaries and claims and bodies in both direct and roundabout ways. It is the story of Francis Gary Powers, trained by the air force, employed by the CIA, knocked from the sky by a Soviet missile while piloting a U-2. It is the story of things done and things left undone, words spoken and not spoken that, because of expectations set by martial mythology and by the ritual environment, raised questions about Powers's faith in the nation. This story demonstrates quite directly the remarkable extent of public and official claims to the body of the American soldier. Voices external to the government and, I will argue, voices internal to it as well insisted that Powers's body belonged to the nation and that he should have destroyed it before it fell into enemy hands. Powers, though a devoted practitioner of American civil religion, did not surrender his body to the nation and did not overtly resist the enemy that held him. He survived and, at trial, he apologized. Survival, self-preservation, and apology are not commonly thought of as controversial. Yet because of the geopolitical backdrop, war's status as civil religious ritual, and perceived challenges to American mythologies of soldiering, they became the stuff not only of controversy but of crisis.

On a somewhat grander scale, the U-2 incident forces us to confront the fact that though it is the civil religious ritual par excellence, war is an inherently unstable ritual, a ritual that regularly undermines itself and troubles its own mythology. Francis Gary Powers deserves our attention because his conduct in two distinct ritual environments so clearly constituted a ritual failure. That is, his actions and his words fell far short of what civil religious mythology prescribed for a soldier facing an enemy in war. As an interpretive problem such ritual failures are a boon. One scholar of ritual writes, "Failed ritual directs our attention to 'what really matters' to performers and participants and others in one way or another involved in the ritual."[3] When rituals fail, the cosmos to which they are related comes more clearly into view, the whispered mythologies on which they rely must be stated and restated, loudly, publicly. Twice in the summer of 1960 a soldierly body provided an improper ritual performance when facing the enemy. The combined force of these failures led American observers to say out loud that a soldier's body is not his, that a soldier's words are not his, and that by acting in ways that argued the contrary, Francis Gary Powers had revealed himself as unfit to be called an American soldier.

As a human problem, war's ritual failures regularly transform themselves into tragedy. These tragedies lodge most permanently in the bodies of soldiers and radiate outward into families and communities. The work of American civil religion, especially its mythological and public performative aspects, is not so much to hide these tragedies as it is to render them meaningful, even sacred. Ritual failures exert a peculiar kind of pressure on soldiering as an embodied practice, but American civil religion has ample resources from which to draw forceful, affective responses. In the case of Francis Gary Powers, the Senate Armed Services Committee offered public redemption and reintegration. The committee's proceedings created a ritual bridge back to America, and Powers crossed it. But having originated with and been, at bottom, about Powers's body, the crisis stayed with him long after he came down from Capitol Hill. Performed forgiveness could not cleanse Powers of his embodied infidelity.

The Man. The Myth.

Before there was Francis Gary Powers the pilot, the prisoner, the accused infidel, there was Powers the boy. Before there were Peshawar, Sverdlovsk, Moscow, and Vladimir Prison, the places in and over which Powers's drama played out, there were the impoverished landscapes of Appalachian coal country. Before there was outrage at his actions and inactions and a tell-all memoir published by his ex-wife, there were wartime and postwar cultures that shaped the actor and adapted the mythology of the G.I. Messiah to a rapidly changing world.

Francis Gary Powers was born in 1929, the year the creeping poverty rural America had known since the end of the Great War found its way to

Wall Street. The Powers family lived in the coal country of eastern Kentucky and western Virginia, far from the stock markets but close to some of the resources that inflated them. Powers's parents were not wealthy, almost no one in that corner of America was. The Great Depression diminished what little the family had and also set them on a peripatetic course. They moved from one mining community to another in Appalachia—Burdine, Kentucky; Harmon, Grundy, and Pound, Virginia. In 1945 the family moved north to Detroit so that Oliver Powers, Francis's father, could work in the booming defense industry. But the end of World War II found them back in coal country, older and not a great deal richer, hoping that Oliver's shoe repair business could support the family. The elder Powers did not like this life of poverty, instability, and dislocation. He did not like it for himself. He liked it less for his son. Oliver Powers dreamed that Francis would escape the mines by way of college and, God willing, medical school. Dr. Francis Gary Powers would be his family's salvation.[4]

Like so many fathers' dreams for their daughters and sons, his was realized only partially. Francis did leave the rugged hills, but he never made it to medical school. It was not that he was incapable of completing the pre-med curriculum at Milligan College, but the learning did not come easily to him and he found it harder and harder to invest energy in an endeavor so far from his passions. Those passions had been sparked unwittingly by his father and then stoked by the winds of war. The spark came in 1943, when Oliver and Francis came upon a county fair and the elder Powers paid for his son to ride in an airplane. The fourteen-year-old boy had always loved the view from high places, especially the cliffs of the Cumberland Mountains around the family home, but the experience of flight was truly intoxicating. When the female pilot brought the plane back to earth after twice the allotted time, she could have told Oliver that his son was hooked. Francis had begged her to keep him aloft.[5]

Powers was too young to join the war effort in Europe or the Pacific, but in those moments of flight perhaps he imagined himself a gunner, a bombardier, or a fighter pilot. Perhaps, too, he looked toward the horizon and thought about the war going on out there. Writers and directors in Hollywood were looking to and over that same horizon and finding in the wars they imagined validation of American martial prowess and proof that the nation and its soldiers were righteous. These films took for granted that war was a ritual that transformed men, bound them together, brought them closer to truth. They described the religious lives of the soldiers as models for America: happily ecumenical but religiously profound. They asked audiences to witness soldiers' actions and to hear their words. They filled screens with stories of the sacrificial work of soldiering and the barely hidden Christian spirit of America's G.I. Messiahs. Four films from the decade before Powers entered the air force—*Guadalcanal Diary* (1943), *God Is My Copilot* (1945), *The Best Years of Our Lives* (1946), and *Battleground* (1949)—show the subtle and the not-so-subtle ways that such myths of soldiering conveyed civil religious orthodoxy and the power of mythology to shape actions and reactions, to shape civil religion as imagined and civil religion as embodied and practiced.

In 1943, the year that Francis Gary Powers first climbed into an airplane, the war film *Guadalcanal Diary* played in theaters across the United States. Based on the book by journalist Richard Tregaskis, the film follows U.S. Marines as they fight the Japanese for control of Guadalcanal. As one would expect of a wartime release, *Guadalcanal Diary* is an expression of civil religious orthodoxy. In line with filmic conventions of the day it depicts combat but shows no gore. American soldiers kill and are killed in many scenes, but no bodies are turned inside-out. There is no blood. There are only uniformed men rolling over as if to sleep—unblemished sacrifices to the cause of freedom. Over the course of the film, those who do not die in combat grow and mature, learning the ways of war, putting aside childish things. This transformation is most clear in the film's final scene, in which veterans of the battle—purposeful, wise, transformed—march past a formation of jaunty, wise-cracking replacement troops.

In *Guadalcanal Diary*, war also transforms religion from a dividing to a uniting force, from mediated by institutions to revealed directly by war. The ecumenical spirit fostered by war flourishes in the film under the watchful eye of the marine unit's chaplain, Father Donnelly, "Notre Dame, Class of 1917, all-American fullback for two years." At the beginning of the film Chaplain Donnelly (Preston Foster) is leading a worship service aboard the troop transport ship. A large gathering of marines surrounds him and sings the popular Protestant hymn "Rock of Ages." Among the singers is at least one Jewish soldier who receives a compliment on his voice, "Say, Sammy, your voice is okay!" to which he replies, "Why not? My father was a cantor in the synagogue." Religious differences exist among the soldiers— Protestant, Catholic, Jew—but these differences, the film tells us, are and ought to be meaningless.

Later, in the midst of a long and punishing Japanese naval artillery attack, Chaplain Donnelly witnesses and validates an expression of soldierly faith tailored by and to war. Taxi (William Bendix), a generally jovial marine who is a New York taxi driver in civilian life, is shaken by the constant shell explosions and finally begins to speak. His monologue is actually a prayer, the prologue to which accounts for the nontraditional form. ("I ain't much for this prayin' business. . . . My old lady always took care of that.") As Taxi proceeds, he weaves together insights about soldiering, the divine, the nation, and the ideal relationship among the three. He begins with a statement of powerlessness brought on by the bombs. "I'm telling you, this thing is over my head. It's going to take someone bigger than me to handle it." He then moves to a confession that situates him as typical, normal, and for audiences, normative. "I'm no hero, I'm just a guy. I came out here because somebody had to come. I don't want no medals. I just want to get this thing over with and go back home. I'm just like everyone else and I'm telling you I don't like it. Except maybe I guess there's nothing I can do about it. I can't tell them bombs to hit somewhere else. Like I said before, it's up to someone bigger than me, bigger than anybody. What I mean is, I guess it's up to God." Taxi's situation, like that of the United States, is not of his own making, yet war is making him more aware of a higher power and leading him toward a better self. One of the lessons that Taxi is learning in war is that a special relationship exists between the American soldier and God. The soldier's God understands and forgives soldiers in light of the struggles and sufferings they endure. He explains:

> And I'm not kidding when I say I sure hope He knows how I feel. I'm not going to say I'm sorry for everything I've done. Maybe I am and maybe I'm not. When you're scared like this the first thing you do is start trying to square things. If I get out of this alive I'll probably go out and do the same things all over again so what's the use in kidding myself. The only thing I know is I . . . I didn't ask to get in this spot and if I get it, it sure looks that way now, well then I only hope He figures we've done the best we could and lets it go at that. Maybe this is a funny kind of prayin' to you guys, but it's what I'm thinkin' and prayin'.

A soldier works out salvation, Taxi argues, by putting his fate in God's hands and doing the best he can. When the prayer concludes, Father Donnelly adds his "Amen." Two other men in the dugout follow suit.

Taxi's prayer reaffirms the righteousness of American soldiers and America before God. Indeed, the prayer connects the three so tightly that the spaces between them all but vanish. Taxi and America are fighting because "someone" had to do it. God and America are grateful for the soldiers' service. Soldiers demonstrate their devotion to America and to God by "coming out here," and "getting this thing over." America and God demonstrate their love for the men by forgiving them their petty sins. A soldier's willingness to die, his surrender of body to nation and God, earn him merit without end. Soldiers, however "homely," are America's civil religious adepts.[6]

The messages of *Guadalcanal Diary* were replayed two years later for those who, like Francis Gary Powers, aspired to fight in the air, and for the parents, wives, and siblings who loved them. *God Is My Co-Pilot* (1945) was also adapted from a firsthand account of the war in the Pacific written by Colonel Robert Lee Scott, Jr. Like *Guadalcanal Diary, God Is My Co-Pilot* bears witness to the transformative and evangelical powers of war and argues that fighting men express their faith with their bodies as much as with their words. The film also uses a wise and likeable Catholic priest, Michael "Big Mike" Harrigan (Alan Hale) to witness, interpret, and validate soldierly faith. Big Mike is a mission priest, not a chaplain, but his twenty-four years of service in China have brought him into regular contact with soldiers and pilots.

In his conversations with the film's main character, American pilot Robert Lee Scott (Dennis Morgan), Big Mike speaks from experience about what fighting men are really like and how their faith looks in practice. In the first extended conversation between Colonel Scott and Big Mike—in the cockpit of Scott's transport plane—Scott notes that the priest sounds "more like a soldier than a missionary." Big Mike responds: "Oh, I guess there's not much difference. Only in the weapons maybe. We both fight the forces of evil. Take the same chances." This is a new and surprising insight to Scott, who quickly confesses that he is "not exactly a religious guy." Big Mike disagrees, countering that he has "yet to meet a flier who didn't have some faith or religious code of his own." This initial encounter sets the parameters for the relationship between Scott and Big Mike throughout the film. Scott uses his flying skills to help Big Mike with his missionary work. Big Mike interprets Colonel Scott back to himself, finding a vibrant, lived Christianity where others—Scott included—might see a uniformed man who is "not exactly a religious guy."

Later, Colonel Scott and Big Mike are together in another cockpit, this time caught in a storm over a Chinese mountain range. Big Mike uses the occasion to gently press Scott on his understanding of the forces that sustain him in times of trial. Scott remains reticent, uncomfortable speaking in overtly Christian terms about faith. But Big Mike is more than happy to suggest that Scott and all pilots have a deeper religiosity than they confess. After narrowly missing a mountaintop, Big Mike asks, "Do you still feel you're flying on your own Scotty?" "No," Scott replies, "that was pure luck." Big Mike nudges Scott further. "You know, I knew another pilot. An RAF boy down Burma way. . . . He's dead now, but before he checked out Scotty, he put into words, simple, beautiful words, something you and every man who flies should feel. Would you like to hear it?" "Scotty" consents and Big Mike continues. "They who scorned the thought of any strength but their own, learned at length how fear can sabotage the bravest heart, and human weakness answering to the prod of terror calls 'Help us, o God.' Then silence lets the silent voice be heard bringing its message like the spoken word: Believe! Believe in me! Cast out your fear. Oh I'm not up there beyond the sky, but here, right here in your heart. I am the strength you seek. Believe! And they believed." As Big Mike concludes his recitation, the storm breaks and sun shines around them. Colonel Scott never voices his acceptance of the sentiments expressed by Big Mike—the film makes clear that explicit theologizing is the job of the priest—but the changing weather suggests the truth of Big Mike's explication. God is not "up there," he is in the pilot's body. Whatever Scott and other pilots feel or say, their actions demonstrate "belief."

The civil religious mythology of a righteous nation and its righteous soldiers faced significant challenges in the aftermath of World War II.[7] It was no small task to reintegrate ten million servicemen and women into postwar society, to assimilate their experiences, to comfort those who were grieving, to heal those grievously injured. At the same time, the nation and its politicians had to make sense of a changing international landscape and an America that had revealed itself again as capable of world-altering violence and life-altering domestic policy. Moreover, the United States and Great Britain were forced to come to terms with unsavory truths about the wartime alliance that made victory over Nazi Germany possible. Namely, the righteous alliance had involved Josef Stalin, one of history's truly unrighteous personalities. From 1942 to 1945 Stalin's armies had bled Hitler's armies from the east, eventually causing them to stagger and fall. But Stalin's facility with killing was not directed only at external and demonic enemies. Stalin killed internally, prodigiously. He killed 19 million of his own citizens, the vast majority of whom posed no threat to him or to his government. The Good War, in other words, had been won because of an alliance with a man every bit as perverse and morally impoverished as the vanquished Hitler. Now Stalin and his ideology of oppression, exploitation, and state violence stood ready and able to extend their influence into an exhausted world.[8]

The postwar period, thus, posed two major challenges to American civil religion as practiced and imagined through soldiers. The first of these was how to make sense of soldiers' fates in war. Simply put, had the death, injury, and displacement been worth it? The second challenge was how to gird the nation for possible war with a country that had recently been an indispensable ally. What did the rise of a global Soviet threat say about soldierly sacrifices past and future? As described in chapter 3, the nation had crafted answers to these questions in its overseas military cemeteries, but Americans like Francis Gary Powers did not have to travel beyond the local theater to learn of the righteousness of American soldiers or to experience the redirection of those sacrifices toward a new enemy. Two critically acclaimed films illustrate sophisticated and textured but still quite orthodox attempts to reckon with these personal and global challenges. *The Best Years of Our Lives* (1946) and *Battleground* (1949) built upon the assumptions that structured *Guadalcanal Diary* and *God Is My Co-Pilot* but redirected those assumptions and their orienting mythology against apparent ruptures and ritual failures. These films and dozens like them did not create civil religious orthodoxy on the question of soldiering and war. Rather, they presented that orthodoxy with minor refinements again and again. To borrow from historian John Bodnar, they took a war that brought suffering and loss to hundreds of thousands of American households (and tens of millions more in Europe and Asia) and made it into a good, a complex good, but a good nonetheless.[9]

The most famous of these films addressed and ultimately defended America's faith in war as a rite of passage through a closer look at the reintegration phase of the ritual. *The Best Years of Our Lives* (1946), which won seven Oscars, including Best Picture, Best Director (William Wyland), Best Actor (Fredric March), and Best Supporting Actor (Harold Russell), put on screen many of the struggles soldiers faced when returning from war.[10] The film focuses on three veterans—Fred Derry, Homer Parrish, and Al Stevenson—who return to their hometown of Boone City from three distinct war experiences, Derry as a pilot, Parrish as a sailor, and Stevenson as a soldier. Interactions among the three men as they travel home from the war demonstrate the bonds that service forms among men. When the uniforms come off and civilian clothes go on, though, signs of the old divisions of society appear. The three men had emerged from and must now return to different socioeconomic positions. Fred Derry, a highly decorated pilot, returns to desperately poor parents and a fast-living wife who married him for his uniform; Homer Parrish, who lost both hands in the war, returns to a middle-class home and his high school sweetheart; Al Stevenson, a sergeant in the army, returns to wealth, his old job as a banker, a devoted wife, and two grown children.

The three men must navigate the challenges of placing war-altered bodies and lives back into a society where, the film argues, understanding and respect can be scarce. No one has greater struggles than the physically disabled Homer Parrish. While in the service, he tells the others, he was given training and support in the use of the hooks that now serve as his hands. No such support is apparent to him among the civilian population. He sees, sometimes accurately, sometimes not, family members, friends, and strangers who are filled with pity, curiosity, and horror. Homer finds his status as a tragically damaged body emotionally, if not physically, paralyzing. The status that Fred Derry once enjoyed as a pilot is meaningless, he finds, in a town that knows little and cares less about his martial exploits. The only work that he can find is in the drug store where he worked before the war. When he finally accepts that job in order to provide for his wife, he faces the double indignity of working for a mouse-like clerk who did not serve in the war and living with a woman who belittles him regularly. Al Stevenson's postwar situation is the most comfortable in terms of his physical and financial condition, but he is frustrated by bank executives who doubt his ability—proven in war—to evaluate the character of men. These differences in postwar circumstances serve at once to point up the injustices of postwar America as compared to the meritocratic, more authentically American military and to argue the virtues of those who gave flesh to the will of the nation.

The Best Years of Our Lives looks beyond public civil religious observances, moments of easy orthodoxy, to more private acts of civil religious devotion, where the faith is worked out body by body. And while it presents the messiness of soldiers' lives on the home front, it pins blame for the mess not on soldiering, the military, or war—each of which is treated in full accordance with its respective mythologies—but on a society that is too slow to acknowledge the saviors in its midst. Fittingly, given Gospel precedents, those most ready to embrace these returning G.I. Messiahs, to see in them the promise of redemption, are American women. Each of the three story lines features a devoted woman (Fred's new love, Homer's devoted girlfriend, Al's patient wife) whose love is a necessary part of the soldiers' reintegration. The struggles and disappointments veterans find on the home front will be blunted and perhaps made right, the film argues, by patient and loving wives. In spite of the presentation of postwar difficulties, all three stories and the movie itself point to the validity of civil religious mythology and ritual readings of war, adding a call to women to do their duty as domestic healers and "beautiful souls."[11]

Three years after *The Best Years of Our Lives*, during Powers's final year at Milligan College, another war film, *Battleground* (1949), won multiple Oscars for its portrayal of American soldiers' trials during the Battle of the Bulge. Like the marines of *Guadalcanal Diary*, the soldiers of the 101st Airborne, on whom the film focuses, are a diverse group whose differences melt away in the fires of war. The opening scene of the film makes no overt reference to religion but nevertheless shows that American soldiers are of one ritual mind and one communal purpose. While two new replacement troops look on in admiration, the tobacco-spitting Sergeant Kinnie (James Whitmore) leads the veteran men through an elaborate round of close-order drill. This embodied demonstration of unified will and responsiveness to orders is followed quickly by another demonstration that is far more grave. The morning after the impressive display on the drill field, Sergeant Kinnie announces the cancelation of an upcoming leave in Paris. The unit, he explains, has been ordered into combat to help counter a German breach of Allied lines.

The picture of war in *Battleground* is less roseate than it was in *Guadalcanal Diary*. There is more vivid dying and more open questioning of the meaning of the war. Still, the answers provided by the film remain orthodox in civil religious terms. Suffering is ennobling. The cause is just. The American soldier is righteous. These lessons hit the viewer with particular force at the point in the narrative when hope for the American soldiers, besieged and in danger of being overrun, is at a low ebb. The marching and waiting, the killing and dying have transformed Private Jim Layton (Marshall Thompson) from a fresh-faced, romantic young soldier into a gritty, sarcastic, supposedly clear-eyed veteran. Layton voices his frustration with the realities of war as lived when, with German troops closing in, he learns that a chaplain is preparing a Christmas service for the men.

"We've got nothing to worry about," he says rolling his eyes, "Holy Joe is going to pray for us at the Christmas service." Layton then recites Isaiah 40:31 from memory but tempers the prophet's message of hope with commentary based on his discordant war experiences. "They that wait upon the Lord shall renew their strength. Shall mount up with wings of eagles, *if the fog lifts*. They shall run and not be weary, *unless they have frozen feet*. And they shall walk and not faint, *if they don't lose too much blood before the medics come*." As he concludes, German propaganda falls from the sky, reminding the soldiers that they are surrounded and outnumbered and that their loved ones are worried about them. "Hot chow and safety are just 300 yards away," the leaflets say.

Cold, exhausted, hungry, and nearly hopeless, the soldiers in Layton's platoon resist German temptation and join the rest of their company (and a single African-American soldier placed front and center) for an open-air Christmas service led by a straight-talking chaplain. The chaplain begins by asking if any in the group are from Ohio. A handful of them are, as is he. He asks next how many are Lutherans. A similar number speak up. He then describes a doctrine of soldierly ecumenism that sounds a great deal like the ecumenism preformed during Chaplain Donnelly's shipboard service in the opening scene of *Guadalcanal Diary*. "These services aren't just for Lutherans any more than they're just for men from Ohio," he explains, "All of us Holy Joe's are switch hitters." To demonstrate his true ecumenism, the chaplain tells the gathered soldiers that he led a Hanukkah service in Holland just a few weeks ago, then asks one of the soldiers present, "How'd I do Levenstein?" Levenstein proclaims amidst a chorus of laughter that the chaplain was "pretty good for a beginner!" Religious differences, like differences in home state, are irrelevant in the midst of war, when all become one.[12]

Having established the ecumenical framework, the Lutheran chaplain from Chillicothe turns to the content of his sermon. His focus is not on what soldiers ought to confess about the Incarnation, he makes no mention of Jesus as infant or Jesus as man. "The sixty-four-dollar question," he says, "is 'Was this trip necessary?'" The faces of the soldiers gathered with him reflect a seriousness tied to their narrative present. *Is it necessary to fight and die against Nazi Germany?* Audiences in 1949 surely heard the question asked of the nation's recent martial past. *Was it necessary to lose so many sons in World War II?* The chaplain addresses both audiences simultaneously. "Nobody wanted this war but the Nazis," he says, "Millions have died for no other reason than the Nazis wanted 'em dead." This reminder opens the door to interpretations of the geopolitical present facing the film audience. "There's a great lesson in this and those of us who've learned it the hard way aren't going to forget it. We must never again let any force dedicated to a super race or a super idea or a super anything become strong enough to impose itself upon a free world. We must be smart enough and tough enough in the beginning to put out the fire before it starts spreading. So my answer to the sixty-four-dollar question is yes, this trip was necessary. As the years go by, a lot of people are going to forget, but you won't and don't let anybody tell you you were a sucker to fight in the war against fascism." In other words, World War II was one chapter of a larger, longer struggle pitting the United States and its allies against those "dedicated to . . . a super anything." Soldiers know this, he says, and "aren't going to forget it." As the chaplain concludes his brief (re)interpretation, German artillery grows so loud that he asks each soldier to "pray in his own way to his own God." Somewhat taken aback that his more experienced comrades are bowing their heads and kneeling, Private Layton slowly bows his head as well. The hard-bitten warriors who have been leading him, Layton learns, are also men of faith.

Shortly after the service, as Layton and his fellow soldiers are digging in and preparing for a self-sacrificial struggle, war washes the cynicism from Layton's earlier adaptation of Isaiah. The fog that has left the American ground forces without air support finally lifts, allowing American planes to bring destruction to God's enemies and succor to the righteous. As American bombers pound the German positions and drop desperately needed supplies, Layton returns to Isaiah and recites the opening lines of the same passage with joyful vigor, "They that wait upon the Lord shall renew their strength! Shall mount up with wings of eagles!" In the film's final scene, Layton and his comrades march off of the front line having endured and been strengthened by their trials. Those who fell have given their lives to redeem the world. Those who survived are wiser, tougher, and more clear-eyed about their place and America's place in the world. In future wars, which, as the chaplain indicated, may pit the United States against its former Soviet ally, the fight will be the same, God will take a similar view, and soldiers will express their profound and enduring faith with their bodies. It did not take long for that future to arrive. One year after the release of *Battleground,* American soldiers—some only five years removed from service in World War II—were called back to war.

On June 25, 1950, North Korean armies attacked South Korea, initiating three years of war, privation, and brutality on the peninsula. Communist forces from the north were backed by China and the Soviet Union; putatively democratic forces from the south were backed by the United Nations and, most fully, the United States. In a television and radio address on July 19, 1950, President Harry Truman told Americans that this was not an internecine battle being fought in an Asian backwater. "This attack has made clear," he proclaimed, "that the international Communist movement is willing to use armed invasion to conquer independent nations." Contemptuous as they were of "basic moral principles," the Communists (not only the North Koreans) had to be confronted and stopped. He continued, "The free nations have now made clear that lawless aggression will be met with force. The free nations have learned the fateful lesson of the 1930s. That lesson is that aggression must be met firmly."[13] This was foreign policy and national politics, not film, but Truman's message matched that of *Battleground*'s chaplain from Chilicothe exactly.

There were clear continuities between the experiences of war in Korea and combat in Western Europe. Private Layton's pessimistic riff on Isaiah, though scripted, captured some of the realities that connected the Battle of the Bulge and the back-and-forth of the Korean War—bad weather, frozen feet, blood. Other realities of the Korean War had not been presaged in the stories and films about World War II. Foremost among these were the psychological and ideological manipulations American soldiers often faced as prisoners of the North Koreans and the Chinese. Over 7,190 American soldiers were taken prisoner in the course of the war. Some of these were murdered immediately. Others were held for a time and then murdered. Some were merely brutalized—beaten, starved, exposed to the elements, deprived of any medical attention. All suffered from deprivations of varying degrees; 4,428 survived.[14] These were not new experiences. However, along with the extremes of mistreatment, many soldiers were also subjected to reeducation campaigns aimed at "converting" them to Communism and winning their sympathy and support for North Korea and China. A recent history of soldiering in the Korean War describes the civil religious crisis brought on by American soldiers' actions in captivity. "Rumors began to circulate that through indoctrination or 'brainwashing' the Chinese had successfully 'turned' many Americans in their care, if not favorably disposing them to Communism, at least leading them to commit various acts of treason and collaboration." The extent of the problem was unclear, but

"Army psychiatrist William Mayer . . . claimed that one-third of American POWs had 'yielded to brainwashing' in North Korea." These findings led to army investigations and significant public concern about the fitness of the men who had served, "everyone wanted to know what made this generation of soldier behave differently in captivity than Americans captured in previous wars."[15]

Observers described the crisis in terms connected to the mythology of soldiering for America: "The behavior of too many of our soldiers in prison fell far short of the historical standards of honor, character, loyalty, courage, and personal integrity." These standards had, presumably, girded captured soldiers in the Great War and World War II against ideological infidelity.[16] In light of the disturbing developments in Korea, it was hard to escape concern that America's civil religious devout were softening in their faith. In response, an advisory committee on prisoners of war met for two months in the summer of 1955 to develop a new creed for American soldiers at risk of becoming POWs. The *Code of Conduct,* drafted by the committee and established by President Eisenhower's Executive Order 10631 in August of 1955, addressed the problem of apostasy by making clear to American soldiers that war against an ideological enemy did not stop when the bullets ran out. It reads in part,

> I am an American fighting man. I serve in the forces which guard my country and our way of life. I am prepared to give my life in their defense.
>
> If I am captured, I will continue to resist by all means available. I will make every effort to escape and aid others to escape. I will accept neither parole nor special favors from the enemy.
>
> I will never forget that I am an American fighting man, responsible for my actions, and dedicated to the principles which made my country free. I will trust in my God and in the United States of America.[17]

The *Code of Conduct* sought to counter future attacks on the identity of American soldiers (and on America itself) by extending the realm of embodied civil religious practice beyond beachheads, cockpits, and battlegrounds into death march formations, unsheltered confinement pens, and vermin-infested holes. Resistance to and in captivity became an important measure of the dedication and sacrificial spirit that characterized the "American fighting man."[18]

Fallen Angel

When Francis Gary Powers donned an air force uniform and took off in a training jet, he flew right into the thick of American civil religious mythology and the expectations connected to it. Powers did so eagerly. While an undergraduate at Milligan College he had walked among scores of veterans who embodied his dreams of flying and fighting for America. Powers was "keenly disappointed to have missed World War II," a feeling that was compounded as, day after day, he interacted with men whom he "knew" had something he did not: experiences of battle, chances at true heroism, war-verified manhood. His experience "in the shadow of the greatest generation" was not unique by any stretch.[19] Powers was one among many hundreds of thousands who had watched with envy as older siblings and friends marched off to do their duty in World War II. He wanted to be part of a similar struggle.

Powers graduated from Milligan in 1950 and immediately enlisted in the U.S. Air Force. After his initial two-year enlistment, he signed on again, this time to become an officer and a pilot. By this point the Korean War had become a morbid, stalemated reminder of the Great War (indeed, one of the popular war films of the period was James Cagney's remake of the 1920's classic *What Price Glory?*, an homage to Marine Corps culture set in Great War-era France), but it nevertheless promised Powers the proving ground he desired. Powers was a quick study as a pilot and was nearly combat ready, but appendicitis slowed him down and then, much to his chagrin, an armistice ended the fighting in Korea. "Again," he wrote, "I'd lost my chance to fight, to prove myself."[20] He would not soon follow Hollywood pilots Colonel Robert Lee Scott or Fred Derry into aerial combat. He would not have the opportunity to forge bonds with veterans of Guadalcanal, Bastogne, or Inchon. Personal involvement in the myths and rituals of war remained just beyond Powers's reach.

Powers was, however, an exceptionally talented pilot and those around him took notice. In 1955, not long after he had committed to indefinite service flying the F-84G and to a life as the husband of Barbara Gay Moore, the Central Intelligence Agency approached Powers.[21] Would he be interested, CIA recruiters asked, in a program designed to keep the United States aware of developments deep within the Soviet Union? A new plane had been built. It could fly higher than anyone had thought possible. With some hesitation Powers agreed to enter the program and to join Operation

4:1: Francis Gary Powers posing with a U-2. He is wearing his pressure suit, required because of the altitudes at which the U-2 flew. (AP Photo/Allied Museum)

Overflight. The work sounded exciting. The pay was six times his air force salary.[22] He would be away from his young wife and would be very restricted in what he could tell her, but these were the costs of service. These were the sacrifices of war.

The film *Battleground* used the theatrical device of a sermon to call American audiences to vigilant, intelligent, and muscular resistance not to the German army and Nazism (that enemy had been vanquished for four years when the film debuted) but to Stalinist Communism. Powers answered this call, but he found himself stationed on an unlikely front. After completing training in the U-2, he moved to Incirlik, Turkey, with a squadron known as "Second Weather Observational Squadron (Provisional)" or, more informally, "Detachment 10-10." From airbases located in Turkey and Pakistan, the pilots involved in Operation Overflight flew many types of surveillance missions, some deep into Soviet airspace. Sophisticated cameras on board the aircraft took hours of film of military and industrial installations. The U-2 was slow, clumsy, and quite difficult to fly, but it operated at altitudes so high that neither Soviet fighter planes nor any known surface-to-air missiles could reach it. This was as close to omniscience as the U.S. government could get. Soviet leaders knew about the program and tried to conceal their activities from it, but for nearly four years they said nothing. They were too proud to protest what they were powerless to stop.[23]

Francis Gary Powers entered the air force as an individual. He chose the path that led him across the front lines of the Cold War. In making these choices he chose also to practice and embody American civil religion. And as a soldier, he bore the weight of a nation's expectations. Powers learned this when, one morning in 1960, he fell farther than any man had before. Literally. Powers took off from Peshawar, Pakistan, at dawn on May 1, 1960. His destination that day was Bodo, Norway. His points of departure and arrival were not nearly as important as his route, which called for him to fly over the Soviet Union from south to north, filming and photographing. "I wondered how the Russians felt," he wrote later, "knowing I was up here, unable to do anything about it. I could make a pretty good guess." Three hours into the flight, the Russians removed all doubt as to their feelings. High above the industrial city of Sverdlovsk, a bright orange flash filled Powers' vision and the U-2 that he was piloting began spinning and tumbling earthward. "My God," he remembered thinking, "I've had it now."[24]

The plane was equipped with explosives powerful enough to destroy the reconnaissance equipment, if not the entire aircraft. In the event of a mishap, pilots were expected to activate a timing device attached to the explosives and then to get clear of the plane using an ejection seat. If the seat failed, the pilot had seventy seconds to extricate himself before he was blown apart with the U-2. But as Powers's plane fell, he judged that he could not eject without severing his legs and therefore did not activate the explosives.[25] Instead, he forced the canopy open manually, pulled himself out of the seat, and tried to reach the activation device from his new position. He tried repeatedly to reach the mechanism, but it was beyond his grasp. Finally, with the ground coming closer and closer, Powers let go of the crippled plane and fell.

Among the items Powers carried with him on his flight was a hollowed-out silver dollar coin provided by the CIA. Inside the coin was a sheath that contained a needle tipped with curare, a deadly asphyxiant. One prick of the needle would kill him within two minutes. He was also carrying a .22 caliber pistol and over two hundred rounds of ammunition. A single shot to the head from the pistol would do the trick as well. Though he "seriously considered it" out of fear of being lynched by a Russian mob, Powers used neither the needle nor the gun to take his own life.[26] Instead, he landed safely in a field outside of Sverdlovsk and eventually found himself face-to-face with a gathering of perplexed Russian farmers. The police arrived soon after to take him into custody. At the jail in Sverdlovsk, the KGB took over.

The only thing that the American ground crew in Bodo knew was that something had gone wrong with the mission. When it became clear that Powers would not arrive at the airfield on Norway's isolated western coast, they sent word to CIA headquarters and then to President Dwight D. Eisenhower. The pilot, they lied, had reported engine trouble. Given the amount of fuel on board it was impossible that he was still airborne. On the morning of May 2, 1960, Brigadier General Andrew Goodpaster confirmed the bad news that he had outlined for Eisenhower the previous afternoon. A U-2 was lost. The consensus from the ground crew on up to the White House was that Powers had given his life in service. To be fair, those Americans who knew of Operation Overflight never suspected that a pilot could survive the chain of events that unfolded around Powers that fateful morning. Nobody was supposed to survive a high-altitude mishap in the U-2, let alone the disabling of the aircraft by a surface-to-air missile. If the missile explosion itself didn't kill the pilot, the rapid decompression of the cockpit at altitudes well in excess of 68,000 feet would be hard to survive. Chances were also slim that Powers could extricate himself from the tumbling aircraft and live through the remaining fall to earth.[27] If the explosion, the decompression, the exit, and the fall didn't kill him, crowds of angry Russians—devotees of a "super idea"—would surely have their way. Supposing that Powers, a Cold War Houdini, somehow made it through this narrow and hellish gauntlet, he would certainly face torture at the hands of the KGB. The remedy for this situation was concealed inside of a hollowed-out silver dollar.

Upon confirming that a U-2 was indeed missing, U.S. officials focused their energies on explaining the violation of sovereign airspace reported by the Soviet Union. Officials had always maintained that the U-2 was a research plane designed to observe weather patterns and collect data on high-altitude air currents. The CIA stuck to this story. On May 5 the State Department released a statement reporting that an unarmed weather plane was missing and that its pilot had reported problems with his oxygen system. It was "entirely possible," the statement continued, that he had lost consciousness, flown off course, and crashed somewhere in southern Russia.[28] The plausibility of this diplomatic performance depended on two conditions that nobody in the United States could verify but which seemed reasonable to assume: a destroyed plane and a dead pilot. Nikita Khrushchev ruptured this performance before the world on May 7 when he presented not only large sections of the U-2, its reconnaissance equipment intact, but also, alive and in good health, Francis Gary Powers.

Ritual Failure, Cold-War Style

May 1, 1960, began a long period of personal trial for Powers. He suffered physically and psychologically from his fall, interrogation, and imprisonment. By mid-May, however, American voices were registering the crisis as something that far exceeded the limits of Powers's physical frame. And, in fact, it did. Powers was part of an operation that for four years systematically violated the airspace of the Soviet Union. Caught red-handed, the CIA, the State Department, and President Eisenhower felt immediate fallout at home and abroad. Premier Khrushchev canceled a summit meeting with Eisenhower, signaling a substantial cooling of relations. Newspapers across the United States critiqued the Eisenhower administration for engaging in espionage at all, for mishandling the aftermath of the incident, and for being bullied, not to mention outwitted, by Khrushchev.[29] An editorialist for the *Cincinnati Enquirer* looked at the crisis and saw a time of national trial. He published "Stand Firm America" on May 12, 1960. "The courage and the loyalty of the American people are being weighed this instant in the Kremlin. Make no mistake about it. Nikita Khrushchev, possibly with some tougher Communists pushing him on, is probing public and official opinion in this country to see just how soft we are. If he determines that we are divided, hesitant, afraid, he and his cohorts will determine that the time is ripe to confront the free world with impossible ultimatums. . . . Herein, at this hour, again lies the greatest danger of a world holocaust. We pray that the American people will stand behind their President, united and unafraid." The nation was facing a test like the tests fictive American soldiers faced in *Guadalcanal Diary, God Is My Co-Pilot,* and *Battleground.* The enemy was strong and persistent, but Americans could be stronger, and if they learned from the problems encountered in Korea and stood together, America could triumph.[30]

In this drama Francis Gary Powers was not simply an unfortunate man in a flight suit. He was a proxy for America in the war against Stalinist Communism. As such, he was supposed to be an exemplary practitioner of American civil religion, to resist demonic enemies as the marines had in *Guadalcanal Diary,* to steel himself against enemy propaganda as the soldiers had in *Battleground.* He was supposed to do better than the American servicemen in Korea who had "lacked the right stuff," let down their guard, and become unwitting pawns of the Communists. Powers certainly had the means at his disposal to resist, choose the last full measure of devotion, or both. As an American soldier in the age of the *Code of Conduct* he ostensibly had the mettle to stand firm in the face of all odds. But his story played out differently in Moscow than it would have in postwar Hollywood. In moments of extreme ritual significance—the shoot-down and the trial— Powers delivered performances that diverged sharply from the expectations cultivated by creed and mythology.

The first ritual moment that Powers encountered was the downing of the plane itself. It was the moment when combat reached up, grabbed, and tested him, when the Cold War flashed hot and became, suddenly, simply war. At such moments, according to mythology, American soldiers show their devotion with their bodies. Powers had clear orders regarding the disposition of a crippled aircraft—activate a timer on an explosive pack that will destroy the U-2's cameras, most of the U-2, and perhaps yourself. Yet he and the other pilots had three sets of orders regarding their bodies. His official orders, though quite specific, were rather odd. If evasion and escape were impossible, the orders said, cooperate with your captors. "Conduct yourself with dignity . . . maintain a respectful attitude toward . . . superiors" and make "no attempt to deny the nature of the mission."[31] In short, when the gig is up, the gig is up. *That smoking heap over there,* one can hear the obedient, downed pilot saying, *is an American reconnaissance plane. I am its pilot. Any questions?* A second set of orders, these derived from the *Code of Conduct,* were directly contradictory. These orders demanded resistance with all available means and the divulgence of minimal information: name, rank, and serial number. Both culturally and militarily promulgated, these orders tied his status as "an American fighting man" to his willingness to use that .22, that needle, or both. Still another set of orders came from the intelligence officer in Powers's unit after Powers asked what a pilot should do in the event of a crash. "What if something happens and one of us goes down over Russia? . . . A plane goes down and a pilot is captured. What story should he use? Exactly how much should he tell?" The intelligence officer's response paralleled the first set of orders initially—"you may as well tell them everything"—but then took an ominous turn: "because they're going to get it out of you anyway."[32] Put differently and more darkly, if you hope to keep anything at all from the Russians, you had better be dead.

Throughout his interactions with Russian civilians, the KGB, and various Soviet attorneys and officials, Powers acted in accordance with the first set of orders. He protected classified information to the best of his ability, but because a U-2 aircraft and all of his papers were in Russian hands, he deemed basic facts about his mission not worth concealing. He did not let the Soviets have their way with him, but neither did he mount a spirited resistance to their questions, their legal proceedings, or their system of government. He did not fire his pistol at the farmers or poke a Russian police officer with his pin. He did not treat capture or the threat of capture as cause for self-destruction. Instead, Powers calibrated his ritual performances in the shoot-down and its immediate aftermath to avoid both unnecessary suffering and confrontation for confrontation's sake.

An early indication that Powers's performance in this first ritual moment diverged from expectations came during the second ritual moment, his August 1960 trial in Moscow's Hall of Columns.[33] Powers sat through three long days of questioning and testimony, none of it friendly or even obliquely exculpatory. He answered the hostile questions from the state's procurator general, Roman Rudenko, and the slightly less hostile questions from his defense attorney Mikhail Grinev. His responses were polite and thorough. On the third day both men summed up their cases. Rudenko made clear that this case was not primarily about Powers. "Thus having bought Francis Powers with dollars, having made him an accomplice in its foul crimes, the American intelligence service considered in advance the possibility of the failure of its agent and, striving to avoid exposure, tried to convince him of the inevitability of suicide should he find himself alive on Soviet territory. . . . Here we have the bestial, misanthropic morality of [CIA director] Mr. [Allen] Dulles and company which for the sake of that yellow devil, the dollar, disregards human life."[34] Rudenko was convinced that in exchange for a high salary the United States government expected pilots of stricken U-2s to sacrifice themselves rather than become Soviet prisoners. Mikhail Grinev's rendering of the case differed only slightly. He enjoined the judges to "take into account" that by not destroying the plane and himself the American spy had disobeyed the orders of his senior U.S. officers and given embodied assistance to the Soviet Union.[35] Powers's third set of orders, those involving the coin, the needle, the poison, bulked large in the Soviet courtroom.

4:2: Francis Gary Powers on trial in Moscow's Hall of Commons, August 17, 1960. His defense attorney, Mikhail Grinev, is seated at left. (AP Photo)

Powers had an opportunity to respond just before the court adjourned to decide his fate. His statement, in which he countered the notion that he was an embodiment of the nation he served, provided cause for civil religious concern back home. With the whole world watching, Powers reminded the court that the trial was not only about the world's superpowers, territorial integrity, and espionage, it was also about *his* body. "I plead to the court to judge me not as an enemy but as a human being who is not a personal enemy of the Russian people, who has never had any charges brought against him in any court, and who is deeply repentant and profoundly sorry for what he has done. Thanks." Powers appeared to be making a separate, personal peace with the Soviet Union and to be admitting that what he had done was wrong. He not only apologized, he said he was "repentant." These words of contrition capped a toxically improper ritual performance for this American soldier.[36]

When the judges returned with a sentence, Powers was relieved to learn that he would not be executed. But the sentence he received—ten years in prison—was no great consolation. Soviet authorities allowed him some time with his parents and wife, who had traveled to Moscow to attend the trial. His mother gave him a New Testament. He and Barbara made love repeatedly when a sympathetic guard left them alone.[37] Powers was then packed off to Vladimir Prison, 150 miles east of Moscow. He wrote to Barbara on September 5, 1960: "The way I feel now, I would much rather have stayed with the airplane and died there than spend any time in prison. . . . To take away one's freedom is worse than to take one's life."[38] From the perspective of many of his countrymen, these self-sacrificial impulses were too little, too late.

On the same day that Powers wrote his lament to Barbara, Holmes Alexander published an editorial in the *Los Angeles Times*, "Shameful Conduct of Powers Tarnishes a Heroic Tradition." More than six thousand miles from the site of the shoot-down and the trial, Alexander played judge, jury, and executioner. He excoriated the man from Appalachia for "not mak[ing] a heroic figure of himself or his country." Alexander continued: "Powers flubbed his duty first and last. . . . Hundreds of pilots have bailed out of aircraft. It is clear from the testimony that Powers panicked when his plane was disabled. His nerve and his training deserted him. He did not execute the ejection cleanly. He did not destroy his plane and equipment. He did not take his own life. He was at no time a man to choose death before dishonor."[39] Alexander saw the orders and the ritual environment in precisely the terms that Rudenko and Grinev had. Powers's duty had been not only to destroy the equipment but to destroy himself as well. Both belonged to the nation. Neither should have been allowed to fall into enemy hands.

Alexander was not alone. In a speech before the twentieth annual convention of the Federation of Insurance Counsel, Philadelphia mayor Richardson Dilworth, a veteran of both the Great War and World War II, labeled Powers's conduct in the trial, "a disgraceful performance" and a "terrible example to the entire world." The fact that Powers had survived the incident and then, in Dilworth's view, sought first to save himself indicated that a crisis was brewing. The New York Times News Service reported that Dilworth believed a third world war to be avoidable only if "we . . . believe in one thing strong enough to die for it, and that thing ought to be our nation."[40] Mrs. Samuel Sonenfield of Westlake, Ohio was so upset that she wrote to CIA director Allen Dulles. Her original letter does not survive, but Dulles's response indicates that she judged Powers to be a self-serving mercenary. In reply, Dulles subtly referenced the experience of American POWs in Korea, "At this point all I would add is that you should take into account the fact that Powers was over a hundred days in solitary confinement without access to family, friends, his own legal advisers, or any U.S. Embassy representative . . . [and] that undoubtedly the Soviets had drummed into his mind what they wished to come out at the trial." No true American soldier, he implied, would have acted or spoken in such a way.

Dulles also assured Mrs. Sonnenfield that U-2 pilots were interested in more than money: "No one went out into the open market to try to lure candidates by the pay scale, which, I may add, is about equivalent to that which a chief pilot on one of our airlines receives today."[41] Holmes Alexander cast the economic motive in terms of the recent global war and the not-so-recent Passion narrative: "Powers [is] a collaborator, in the despicable World War II meaning—a person who sells his country, buys himself comfort and safety, by working with the enemy. . . . He took the silver of betrayal." One who did not choose death over capture was, on Alexander's account, as craven as Judas, selling his loyalty for silver pieces. One who did not resist the forces of evil with every inch of his being, one who let the cup pass from him, could not be a G.I. Messiah. Unfounded stories that Powers was going to be released from prison and had decided to remain in Moscow gave credence to the claim that the onetime messiah had turned Judas.[42]

Powers's critics claimed that he had, unlike the soldiers of American myth, reacted to crisis by serving his own interests rather than those of his country. His disordered individualism in the midst of the ritual of war revealed not only flaws in his true nature and confusion in his true loyalties but the likelihood that similar problems lurked within America. His apologetic closing statement before a Russian judge and jury made all the more clear that rather than save the nation or the world he had chosen to save himself.

Performing Reintegration, Living Liminality

On February 10, 1962, less than two years after his capture, Powers walked onto Berlin's Glienicker Brücke from the East German side. Approaching him from the western edge of West Berlin was Soviet master spy Rudolf Ivanovich Abel. Abel had been sentenced to thirty years in prison in 1957 for directing a massive espionage ring inside the United States.[43] Abel's freedom purchased Powers's and vice versa. The two walked past each other at the bridge's midpoint, but Abel's shadow followed Powers home.

American commentators found the exchange offensive. The assistant U.S. attorney general who had put Rudolph Abel behind bars said, "It's like trading Mickey Mantle for an average ballplayer. We gave them an extremely valuable man and got back an airplane driver." A representative of the American Legion, John Wickers, said, "I view the exchange with astonishment and disgust. Powers was a cowardly American who evidently valued his own skin far more than the welfare of the nation that was paying him so handsomely." Taking stock of the story as its antihero returned to the United States, the *New York Herald Tribune* asked the questions they believed to be on the minds of Americans: "Why, knowing that neither he nor the U-2 should fall into unfriendly hands, didn't he blow himself up, and the plane? Why didn't Powers use the poison needle he had on hand? Or the pistol he had with him?" Others chimed in: "tower of jelly," "more mercenary than patriot," "he was hired to do a job, and he flopped at that job."[44] What does it mean, commentators asked, if their Cold War soldiers are more willing to die than ours? Is our truth really true if our soldiers will no longer confess with the flesh as the martyrs once did? Where have you gone, Nathan Hale? Had Powers only recognized the ritual moment for what it was, performed properly, and scratched his forearm with that pin or stared down the Soviet judges and called their system—their "super idea"—a mockery, so much trouble would have been avoided.

Instead, on March 6, 1962, barely a month after his release, Powers was asked to take part in a remedial ritual designed to undo the damage done to him and the nation in Moscow. He appeared, lawyer by his side, before the Senate Armed Services Committee for hearings on the incident. The purposes of this ritual response to the "public trial in Moscow" were at least two. First, in light of harsh criticism of his conduct, the committee sought to rehabilitate Powers as a devout practitioner of American civil religion, to demonstrate that in spite of it all, he was a faithful American, an American fighting man. Second, because Powers was not simply a man but a soldier, and not simply a soldier but a soldier whose status as a proxy for his nation had been placed in full view of the global public, the committee had to respond to Soviet charges that U-2 pilots operated under a suicide order and, more damning still, that an American soldier, in the heat of a Cold War confrontation, had chosen to live. A simple confession of faith from an embodied practitioner of American civil religion would not suffice to answer these charges. Instead, the committee had to work its way through Powers's survival of the May Day shoot-down, his nonuse of the poison needle, and the absence of any outward signs of resistance.[45]

Powers raised the topic of non-sacrifice first. He told the committee of the struggle to extricate himself from the stricken aircraft and while describing his descent by parachute stated, "I . . . thought of the coin with the poison pin in it. This had been given to me just prior to the flight, and it was my option whether to take it or not, and I chose to take it."[46] Concerned that, if captured, someone would find and take the coin, Powers removed the pin, placed it in his pocket, and tossed the hollow coin away. The ploy worked until finally, during a full examination at the police headquarters in Sverdlovsk, someone discovered the sheathed pin. Chairman Richard B. Russell asked for clarification. "You say they didn't find this needle until about the third time they examined you. . . . Where was the needle hidden?" It was, Powers reminded Russell, loose in his pocket. The senator moved on. "I wish you would clear up the matter of the needle, Mr. Powers. Were you under any obligation to destroy yourself if you were captured?" "Oh no," Powers replied, "It was entirely a pilot's choice to carry the needle." Later, with the chairman's prompting, Powers read into the record the official orders to pilots involved in mishaps over hostile territory. As noted above, they included the words "cooperate," "dignity," "respect," and "make no attempt to deny the nature of [the] mission."[47] Observers could now see both that official orders did not call for suicide and that Powers, a good soldier, had followed the letter of his orders.

In the hearing's concluding phase, the senators worked to foreground these orders, to make absolutely clear that suicide before capture was not mandatory, and to show that Powers was, indeed, a good soldier. He may not have risen to the heights of heroism, observers could conclude, but at least he had, as Taxi proclaimed in *Guadalcanal Diary*, done the best he could. Senator Leverett Saltonstall used this very standard in his final evaluation. "Mr. Powers, I will just say this: After listening to [CIA Director James] McCone and after listening to you, I commend you as a courageous, fine young American citizen who lived up to your instructions and who *did the best you could* under very difficult circumstances." Senator Prescott Bush of Connecticut concurred, "I am satisfied he has conducted himself in exemplary fashion and in accordance with the highest traditions of service to one's country." The most revealing and affective exchange took place between Powers and Senator John Stennis of Mississippi. Stennis acknowledged that some had found Powers's conduct troubling, but he continued,

"It is with satisfaction to me that I learn that you have been fully exoner-
ated by the men who most know how to judge what you did . . . they found
that you have discharged all of your obligations to your country, and it is
with satisfaction to us here and I think to the American people to learn
that, to know it is true. I know it makes you feel mighty good."[48] Powers, at
last responding properly to a ritual requirement, replied, "There was one
thing that I always remembered while I was there and that was that I am an
American." This led Stennis to the heart of the matter:

> Senator Stennis: You are an American.
> Mr. Powers: Right.
> Senator Stennis. And proud of it?
> Mr. Powers. Right.
> Senator Stennis. That is fine. [Applause] You felt that the American
> flag would finally find you and follow through and do what was good
> for you?
> Mr. Powers. Yes I did.[49]

This was no coward, no Communist initiate. This was an American fighting
man, a man who had "done the best he could" in a difficult circumstance and
had never forgotten, ritual performances notwithstanding, that America—
indeed an heroic and oddly ambulatory American flag—would seek him out
and "do what was good" for him. It was indeed "fine" to hear one accused of
imperfectly incarnating the word of the nation confess his faith that the nation would save him. Of course, it would have been far easier to reintegrate
a man martyred in the cause of freedom, but faced with a living, breathing
soldier of the Cold War, the senators too "did the best they could."

In a 1962 interview with newsman Eric Sevareid, Allen Dulles, who
had recently left the directorship of the CIA, described the U-2 incident
in terms similar to those established by the Armed Services Committee.
Dulles also supported Powers's account of his orders and endorsed the notion that Powers had done the best he could. He told Sevareid, "On the
whole he handled himself properly." By way of explanation Dulles offered,
"He was an aviator. . . . He had a very difficult assignment merely on the
aviation-navigation side, and to expect him—to make him a great un-
dercover agent was impossible." Sevareid probed further, moving to Powers's non-sacrifice, his improper performance. "Mr. Dulles, some people
said that the pilot, Mr. Powers, should have taken his own life. Is there any
way you can have a man sign a contract to commit suicide?" Dulles was

emphatic. "No—no, no, you couldn't—first place, it would be ineffective. In the second place, I think it would be immoral, and we just didn't do it." He explained the curare on the needle in the coin in much the way Powers did. "We said, 'Here, you have this. If you get into a situation where you think death is better than what awaits you, use it.'"[50]

At the time of the incident, Francis Gary Powers did not think that death was better than what awaited him, but his decision to live generated both short-term pain and long-term frustration. In the short term, living meant not knowing whether his parents, his wife, or his fellow pilots knew if he was alive and how he had been captured. It meant being forced to watch and listen in silence as stories, no less damning for their falsehood, filled the vacuum of information. In the medium term, living meant learning of a rift that had developed between Barbara and his parents and then enduring her long, slow turn away from him. Living also meant nineteen months in Vladimir Prison and, once released, encountering a powerful narrative that he, Francis Gary Powers, was a stain. A *Dallas Morning News* editorial built a typical case against Powers based on ritual expectations and false information. "It has been reported that at least two U-2 pilots blew themselves and their planes up when they ran into trouble. These are the real U-2 heroes, and Powers should not be allowed to join them until he has given a good explanation of why he failed to do the same."[51]

In the long term, living through the shoot-down and its aftermath meant being pushed to the margins of the military, the community to which he had turned to become a man. The United States Air Force, from which Powers was on loan to the CIA and to which he hoped to return, refused to count his service to the CIA toward a military retirement as they had promised, telling him, in effect, to go away. In recognition of exceptional service, the CIA presented its highest honor, the Intelligence Star, to all pilots attached to Power's U-2 squadron. They did not invite Powers. "I was to be the scapegoat," he wrote in his memoir, "And there was absolutely nothing I could do about it." Powers finally received his Intelligence Star two years later. The CIA kept the ceremony secret.[52]

To Kill the Bear: Lessons from the Russian Ritual Realm

Writing of bear hunting rituals among indigenous tribes of Siberia, J. Z. Smith has described a disjunction between how the hunt is imagined and described, and how it is actually executed. The former realm, in which the hunt is imagined, is the realm of ritual; the latter realm, in which the hunt is carried out, is the realm of doing what needs to be done to kill a bear. In the former we find myriad proscriptions, "strict rules of etiquette" such as "the animal may be killed only while running toward the hunter." In the latter realm, Smith observes, nobody actually hunts this way. To carry ritual proscriptions into the realm of the hunt is to invite starvation. He writes, "Not only ought we not to believe many of the elements in the description of the hunt as usually presented, but we ought not to believe that the hunters, from whom these descriptions were collected, believe it either." These rituals draw our attention to the incongruence between "ought" and "is" or, perhaps more precisely, "ought" and "must be . . . if we want to eat."[53] At the same time these rituals argue the dogged persistence, the cosmic and social importance, of the ritually and mythologically propagated "ought" in the face of a widely known "is."

In American civil religion as embodied and practiced by soldiers there is a similar disjunction between war as imagined—the realm of ritual—and war as waged—the realm of the hunt. The films described in this chapter, not to mention close-order drill, the parades, eulogies, and military cemeteries described elsewhere in this book belong more to the former realm than to the latter. The explosion, the struggle, the disorientation, and the fall that Powers experienced on May Day 1960 belong more to the latter realm than to the former. But we must not draw too sharp a distinction between these realms in the case of soldiering and American civil religion. Not only the ethic of collectivism and order described in chapter 1 but also the myths of soldierly righteousness discussed throughout this book move into and out of combat in and on the bodies of soldiers. And the soldiers themselves, the heroic and the not, the strengthened and the broken, return home to worlds dominated by rituals and ritual mentalities. They know these rituals, both those performed for the civilian public and those directed at the military subcommunity. They participate in them. They shape them.

Francis Gary Powers's story is, on the one hand, a classic case of American confusion between the civil religious "ought" described in mythology and ritual and the embodied "must be" practiced by American soldiers at war. The commentators cited above insisted that a single soldier in a singular situation should have conducted himself in accordance with ritual proscriptions painted on the silver screen and etched into American martial mythology. They asked from their distant news desks and well-worn Barcaloungers why, with God on his side, Powers did not deny the Soviet bear access to either his plane or his body; why he did not openly dismiss the legal proceedings as a travesty; why he did not prick himself into oblivion or force the Russians to spill his blood for him. Why, in sum, did he not resist?

Powers's story also places a more analytically challenging set of questions on the table, questions that can't be answered definitively. These also have to do with Powers, his ritual failures, and the demands of his critics but attempt to get closer to Powers's understandings of "ought" and "must be." Was Powers the soldier, the ritual performer, confused about what he ought to do and why? Was there some justice in the superficially odious editorial penned by Holmes Alexander? To begin, Powers's task in war and captivity was not simple; he was required to reconcile ritual expectations derived from the general, national realm of civil religious "ought" with expectations from the more specialized military ritual realm in which he trained and prepared for his flights. He had to use his body to reconcile these expectations, and he had to do it in the unstable, disorienting, and unexpected ritual realm of war. The national realm expected embodied devotion, resistance, and sacrifice. The military realm provided Powers with ambiguous guidance: orders that were explicit and contradictory—talk of cooperation with captors, talk of resistance to captors—and orders that were more subtle—a needle tipped with poison. In the midst of a historic fall in a disintegrating aircraft, Powers chose to abide by one set of orders from the military realm; he chose to live and to avoid confrontation. Voices in the government said publicly that he had done as he had been ordered. Indeed, everyone with firsthand knowledge of Operation Overflight said that Powers was never given a direct order to kill himself. The congressional record contains his official orders in case of capture. They say nothing of suicide.

Whether this means that suicide was not expected depends on how one understands the preflight world in which those official orders were promulgated. Take this world to be already the world of the hunt, where words and actions represent what is actually done, and a spirit of polite openness was indeed the order of the day; the pin and the gun were truly only options, things to use if self-destruction seemed the sensible thing to do. On this reading of the ritual realms, Powers truly did do his best. One could argue, though, that the military ritual realm, in this case the preflight world, is not quite "the hunt," that it is, rather, a transitional zone with close and clear connections to the broader ritual culture of the military, the military ethic, and the mythology of the G.I. Messiah but indirect and unstable connections to combat. In that intermediate ritual world the military creates civil religious adepts through ritual acts, the literal meanings of which are often beside the point. Thus it would be naive to expect that the real expectations of Powers be spelled out in official orders or, as Sevareid suggested to Allen Dulles, in a contract. We are better off seeking those expectations in the silence that long hung over the question of what to do if one's U-2 went down over Russia and in the terse words of Powers's intelligence officer, "You may as well tell them everything, because they're going to get it out of you anyway." *Here, take this coin along if you want, there's a pin inside.* Troubling as one might find it, is it so improbable that the nation Powers served understood these implied orders to be operative in combat? The mechanism was in place for explaining and rendering meaningful a U-2 incident in which the pilot had died from a lack of oxygen. *The plane was unarmed. It was a research craft. The pilot's oxygen supply gave him trouble* (curare, the poison on Powers's needle, is an asphyxiant).[54] *We are sorry.* This explanation, which might have sailed for decades through the treacherous waters of the Cold War, ran aground on the living body of Francis Gary Powers.

If American observers of the U-2 incident suffered from a hyperextension of the ritual realm described in film, unfairly expecting soldiers to act according to that mythology, Powers, we might say, suffered from a hyperextension of the preflight ritual sensibility, proceeding in his public performances with little sense that expectations of him might be informed by other sources, little sense of the mythological significance of his words and deeds, little sense of the possibility that others would read his actions as cosmically significant. Powers repeated this ritual failure by treating the trial in Moscow as primarily *his* trial. By cooperating and confessing and apologizing, per his official preflight orders, rather than resisting with and sacrificing his body, per the mythology he embodied, Powers more closely resembled the hunter who addresses a bear face-to-face before attempting to kill it than the savvy hunter who kills as he must. But Powers did not kill his bear after addressing it, and what he said to it gave little evidence of a desire ever to kill or even to confront a bear. His performance not only threw the ritual system out of balance—a problem for which remedial rituals exist—it troubled the whole soldierly mythology and called into question, before a global public, American efforts to adapt that mythology to Cold War complexities.[55] Siberian communities might also find it troubling

if a hunter appeared to embrace the rituals of the bear hunt and then re-
jected the hunter/bear distinction on which their cosmos, not to mention
their survival, depended.

Coda

Francis Gary Powers died on August 1, 1977, when a television sta-
tion helicopter he was piloting fell to earth. He was returning from covering brush fires in Santa Barbara for Los Angeles's KNBC when he ran out
of fuel, lost control of the aircraft, and crashed near the Sepulveda Dam
Recreational Area in Encino, California. He left behind his second wife,
Sue, and two children, Dee and Francis Gary Powers II. KNBC broke the
news of the deaths of Powers and his cameraman George Spears. It was an
understandably difficult story for anchorman Jess Marlow, Powers's friend,
to handle, but he worked his way nobly through an impromptu eulogy. In
the course of the report he noted that some thought of Powers as a hero and
that others did not, giving space to the ritual failure that defined Francis
Gary Powers's life as a soldier.[56]

Powers is remembered for the day on which the expected unexpected
of combat reached 68,000 feet into the air, pulled his body earthward and
confronted him with the ritual expectation that he kill himself for the good
of the nation. Forgotten, though never really known in the first place, is
that prior to that fateful May 1, 1960, Powers had logged 500 hours of flying time and twenty-seven missions in the U-2. Each of those missions required him to breathe pure oxygen for ninety minutes before takeoff and
for the duration of the flight. Each required him to wear a pressure suit that
all but immobilized him. He could not eat, drink, or urinate in flight. He
wore his long underwear inside out because the seams would chafe him to
bleeding. Powers gave his body to the precarious task of flying a U-2. The
headaches and exhaustion, the welts and cramps wracked his body regularly
and still, faced with his failed sacrifice, his refusal of self-annihilation, Senator John Stennis needed to establish his citizenship for the record, "You are
an American[?]"[57]

Senator Stennis's question and much of the commentary surrounding
the U-2 incident reflected deep anxieties about the relationship between
the men preparing to fight the next war, wherever it would be, and the nation they were sworn to protect. The war in Korea raised questions about
the depths of civil religious devotion among men who were supposed to

give flesh to the word of the nation, questions that Powers forced once again into the public conversation. The war in Vietnam, in its infancy when Powers returned home, would press these questions even more forcefully, bringing politicians, commentators, soldiers, and students into debates and protests about what soldiering for America and, by extension, America itself meant.

CHAPTER 5

The Vietnam War as a Christological Crisis

Irony consists of apparently fortuitous incongruities in life which are discovered, upon closer examination, to be not merely fortuitous. Incongruity as such is merely comic. It elicits laughter. This element of comedy is never completely eliminated from irony. But irony is something more than comedy. A comic situation is proved to be an ironic one if a hidden relation is discovered in the incongruity. If virtue becomes vice through some hidden defect in virtue; if strength becomes weakness because of the vanity to which strength may prompt the mighty man or nation; if security is transmuted into insecurity because too much reliance is placed upon it, if wisdom becomes folly because it does not know its own limits.

—REINHOLD NIEBUHR, *The Irony of American History*, 1952

The American experience of the Vietnam War was deeply ironic. The virtue of using American blood and treasure to resist a cynical, dehumanizing, and oppressive ideology became the vice of squandering American blood and treasure in support of a cynical, de-humanizing, oppressive, and inept regime. The strength of a sophisticated military-industrial complex placing powerful weaponry in the hands of well-trained soldiers became the weakness of believing that a sophisticated military-industrial complex, powerful weapons, and well-trained soldiers could easily defeat an enemy thought to have none of these things in abundance. The security of a war waged with optimism and a managed presentation of results was transmuted into the insecurity of a war being waged by a government too optimistic and ultimately unable to reconcile its presentation of results with the results themselves. American wisdom became American folly because American wisdom not only did not know its limits, but failed to account either for varieties of wisdom in the American camp or for wisdom in the adversary's strategies and tactics. Perhaps the deepest irony of them all is that military and diplomatic victory in 1945 became wrenching military defeat in 1975 because, faced with a choice between supporting an already crisis-stricken French colonial regime and a Vietnamese nationalist leader with a Communist past, the United States chose the course deemed by many to be safest.[1]

For American soldiers fighting in Vietnam these ironies had life-altering, sometimes life-ending consequences. Strength became weakness became mutilation and death. Security became insecurity became powerlessness and frustration. Virtue became vice became volcanic viciousness. Wisdom became folly became complete disorientation, the inability to discern meaning or purpose in a one-year combat tour, not to mention a twenty-year campaign to build and protect a free Vietnam. Irony became suffering became tragedy, as it flowed into and around the bodies of soldiers. Many American soldiers felt the destructive pull of the ironies of Vietnam. Few felt them more deeply and more tragically than did Dwight Johnson.

On November 19, 1968, Sergeant Dwight H. Johnson stood before a president whose last name he shared to receive the Congressional Medal of Honor. Four other men were also there to receive the same award. Together they listened as President Johnson spoke. "Our hearts and our hopes are turned to peace as we assemble here in the East Room this morning. . . . All our efforts are being bent in its pursuit. But in this company we hear again in our minds, the sounds of distant battles." Sergeant Johnson heard those sounds as loudly as anybody in the room. He may even have smelled the smells, tasted the tastes, and seen the scenes. For him, the battles were distant in geography only. In later conversations about her son, Johnson's mother recalled that he stood in the receiving line "tears streaming down his face."[2] She remembered being confused. Wasn't he happy to have made it back?

The citation read and presented to Sergeant Johnson that day told a story that equaled the most heroic depictions of soldiering. The tall, crying man was one hell of a fighter. Evidence of this exploded into the consciousness of his fellow soldiers on January 15, 1968, near the village of Dak To. Johnson, then a specialist fifth class and a tank driver, was part of a rapid reaction force attempting to aid members of his platoon who were "in heavy contact with a battalion size North Vietnamese force." Johnson's tank lost a track and could not move. The Medal of Honor citation continues:

> Realizing that he could do no more as a driver, he climbed out of the vehicle armed only with a .45 caliber pistol. Despite intense hostile fire, Sp5c Johnson killed several enemy soldiers before he had expended his ammunition. Returning to the tank . . . he obtained a submachine gun. . . . Armed with this weapon [he] again braved deadly enemy fire to return to the center of the ambush site where he courageously eliminated more of the determined foe. Engaged in extremely close combat when the last of his ammunition was expended, he killed an enemy soldier with the stock of his submachine gun.

The first chapter of Dwight Johnson's morning of war ended with the deadly intimacy of hand-to-hand combat and the crushed skull of a North Vietnamese soldier. But as was so often the case in Vietnam, in spite of the strain, the gore, and the body count, the fighting was not yet over. The ambush continued, and so did Dwight Johnson. With bullets filling the air around him, Johnson made his way to the lead tank, "extricated a wounded crewmember," and carried him to relative safety. "He then returned to the same tank and assisted in firing the main gun until it jammed. In a magnificent display of courage, Sp5c Johnson exited the tank and again armed only with a .45 caliber pistol, engaged several North Vietnamese troops in close proximity to the vehicle. Fighting his way through devastating fire and remounting his own immobilized tank, he remained fully exposed to the enemy as he bravely and skillfully engaged them with the tank's externally mounted .50 caliber machine gun." Few citations for the Medal of Honor are as long as Dwight Johnson's, but few recipients of the award did as much fighting and killing and defending and saving as he. Johnson seems to have not stopped acting from the moment his unit was ambushed until, as his citation reads, "the situation was brought under control."[3]

Given the nature of this source—an official citation for combat heroism in the extreme—we should not be surprised to find that the narrative emphasizes classic martial virtues: bravery, selflessness, resourcefulness, controlled violence, the besting of a "determined foe," the forging of order out of chaos. Nevertheless, we have much to learn by studying the presentation of these attributes and by asking about the meaning of their embodiment in Dwight H. Johnson. For though these virtues are presented here,

5:1: Dwight Johnson receives the Congressional Medal of Honor from President Lyndon B. Johnson, November 19, 1968. (LBJ Library, photo by Yoichi Okamoto, White House Photo Office)

subtly, artfully, as timeless, they emerged out of a context and were narrated to a moment shot through with concern about a war that was going badly, a war that was withholding the cooling balm of victory from the burn of acid irony. President Johnson, whose vision for the nation and whose very presidency had been ruined by the war, whose party had lost the White House two weeks before Sergeant Johnson's Medal of Honor ceremony, may well have found comfort in the words and the ideas of the citation. Show courage in the face of danger. Fight the enemy with everything you have. Bring the situation under control. Sergeant Johnson provided an embodied argument that the war could still be won, that our soldiers could still save us.

Dwight Johnson grew up in poverty in Detroit, Michigan. He was raised by his mother in a crime-riddled neighborhood but was not dragged down by his environment. Johnson was "one of the few among thousands of poor black youngsters in Detroit who had struggled against the grinding life of the ghetto and broken free."[4] He had been a "good boy . . . an altar boy, and Explorer Scout." In his nineteenth year he was drafted, trained, and sent to Vietnam. The nation called, Johnson responded, and in the most extreme duress imaginable, he showed the enemy and his fellow soldiers the best of America. He gave flesh to the word of the nation. Johnson was on his way to aid friends in distress. His equipment failed him. He grabbed a pistol. It was one man with one gun against an entire battalion of Vietnamese Communists. Johnson shot with deadly accuracy. Having emptied one gun he grabbed another and fought off enemy soldiers who were advancing so aggressively that he had to kill one with the butt end of his gun. He then ran to save a friend, grabbed another pistol, and killed some more. Back on his tank at last, he grabbed the most deadly weapon in his arsenal, a .50 caliber machine gun, and fought on. The young man drafted from the ghettoes of Detroit rose to the heights of soldierly civil religious practice. He was brave, unselfish, and violent in defense of others. Dwight Johnson made visible in his very body the Johnson administration's hopes for society.[5] He also embodied the principles of American progressive warcraft. Fight to defend friends and allies. Fight to bring freedom and flourishing to the world. In his potentially self-sacrificing violence, Dwight Johnson became the G.I. Messiah.

Just off the page and yet thousands of miles away from the White House ceremony were two details of the fight that complicate this reading of Johnson's heroism. The first detail, recounted to *New York Times* reporter John Nordheimer by Stan Enders, the gunner in Johnson's tank, establishes a more complicated motivational frame for Johnson's actions. Enders and Johnson were together in the second tank of a four-tank convoy. The lead tank was manned by the crew Dwight Johnson had served with since arriving in Vietnam "eleven months and twenty-two days" before that violent morning. On any other day Johnson would have been in that tank. On January 15, 1968, he wasn't. Instead he watched as the lead tank, his usual tank, bore the brunt of a ferocious ambush. Johnson saw rockets slam into the vehicle carrying his friends. It caught fire immediately. Enders noted, "He was really close to those guys in that tank. . . . He just couldn't sit still and watch it burn with them inside." So Johnson rushed to help and was able to pull one injured man from the flaming wreck before fire ignited the tank's munitions. Enders continued, "When the tank blew up Dwight saw the bodies all burned and black, well, he just sort of cracked up."[6] Was it frustration, anger, a deep sense of injustice that drove him to fight as he did? Did Johnson embody American martial virtue, or was he gripped by an overwhelming desire to spill the blood and shatter the bodies of those who had killed his friends?

In the official narrative of the battle, Johnson's fellow soldiers recede. He appears to be the only man fighting. In Stan Enders's account, Johnson's fellow soldiers reemerge less as fighters and more as witnesses to Johnson's fighting and the after effects. "No one who was there could ever forget the sight of this guy taking on a whole battalion of North Vietnamese soldiers." Enders then added a second crucial detail omitted from the Medal of Honor citation, which concluded with "the situation . . . under control." The attack eventually ceased, he noted, but Johnson kept fighting. The situation may have been under control, but Dwight Johnson was not. Not at all. "He was raving," Enders said. "He tried to kill the prisoners we had rounded up." Unable to calm Johnson down after the fighting stopped, three men had to restrain him and administer three shots of morphine. A medical team placed the soldier from Detroit in a straitjacket and evacuated him to the U.S. Army hospital at Pleiku. Johnson was back with his unit the next day, but his days of fighting in the field were over. He collected his things and began the journey back to Detroit.[7]

The young man (he was still just twenty) arrived home in February 1968 but spoke not a word of the incident at Dak To. Then, in October, with campus tensions over the war running high and the nation reeling from a tumultuous, murderous spring and summer, the army forced Johnson's hand. Two military policemen arrived at the family's apartment to conduct a quick interview. Not long after they left, the telephone rang. A colonel was calling from Washington, D.C., to tell Johnson that he was going to receive the nation's highest military honor. Could he come to the White House? The president wanted to present the medal himself.[8]

Dwight Johnson's story appeared in the *New York Times* in May 1971, three years after he was awarded the Medal of Honor. The *Times* explored Johnson's bravery and heroism, his background, his personality, and his battlefield breakdown. The story was not, however, a standard profile in courage; it was not a celebration of soldiering for America. The *Times* reported on the Medal of Honor recipient from America's urban ghettos because Charles Landeghem, a store manager in Detroit, had done with one gun and five bullets what an entire battalion of Viet Cong had been unable to do. He had killed Dwight Johnson. Johnson entered his store late on the night of April 30, 1971, pulled a revolver, and "demanded money from the cash register." Landeghem produced his own gun and emptied it into the war hero. Johnson stood for a moment, told Landeghem that he was going to kill him, and then collapsed to the floor.[9]

The years following Johnson's return from the war had involved many moments of celebration and celebrity. He had gotten married, had a child, and been feted in his neighborhood and in the city. High schools invited him to talk to their students. People he met "would pump his hand and slap his back and say, 'Johnson, if you ever think about getting out of the Army, come look me up.'" The years had also involved a constant battle to stay employed, to control his emotions, to make sense of the day when he became a hero. The people so eager to promise him jobs and help rarely followed words with actions. His appearances at high schools often attracted militants who called him "a robot the Army was using to recruit blacks for a war in Asia." Johnson told an army psychiatrist that he was haunted by "winning a high honor for the one time in his life when he lost complete control of himself."[10] He spent roughly six months in the psychiatric ward of an army hospital near Valley Forge, Pennsylvania. "His personal life was becoming chaotic," *Baltimore Sun* reporter Henry Scarupa wrote in September 1971. "Bills had been piling up. He was subject to depression, wracked by bad dreams, full of doubts and guilt over what happened that eventful morning in Vietnam and afraid . . . he would lose control over himself as he had during the enemy attack a few years back."[11] After Johnson was laid to rest in Arlington National Cemetery, his mother wondered aloud if the robbery, so out of character for her son, had been a form of suicide. Perhaps, she said, he was "tired of this life and needed someone else to pull the trigger."[12] The man so celebrated for his ability to fight and kill had been stumped by the question of how to live and, in the end, how to die.

The decade in which American involvement in Vietnam grew from a barely noticeable Cold War sideshow to the central issue of American public discourse also brought extended engagement with American civil religion from many corners of society. As Dwight Johnson's actions and their sculpted presentation to the nation remind us, the government and the military forcefully asserted mythologies of American martial efficacy and masculine heroism in the face of more complex realities. They and, to be fair, a majority of Americans held a deep faith in America's ability to reshape the world in its image.[13] Other public voices—politicians, artists, clergy, activists—filled the 1960s with reflections on the many changes and challenges facing the United States and what Americans' actions and reactions said about the moral health of the nation.

No Vietnam-era figure shaped the scholarly discussion of civil religion quite as enduringly as Robert Bellah[14] Bellah's 1967 essay "Civil Religion in America" described American civil religion as a tradition of "beliefs, symbols, and rituals," a tradition with "its own seriousness and integrity." Bellah argued that this civil religion could be traced from the founding moments of the republic down to the mid-1960s, and that it expressed "common elements of religious orientation that the great majority of Americans share." Writing in and to the Vietnam moment, he noted that America's canonical wars had shaped civil religion in important, even constructive ways, but that civil religion in America was susceptible to jingoistic, militaristic "distortion." Bellah described with remarkable precision the manipulation of civil religious concepts in support of Cold War military action. "Those nations that are for the moment 'on our side' become 'the free world.' A repressive and unstable military dictatorship in South Vietnam becomes 'the free people of South Vietnam and their government.' It is then part of the role of America as the New Jerusalem and 'the last best hope on earth' to defend such governments with treasure and eventually with blood."[15] What Bellah saw less clearly, as uniformed Americans departed for and returned from Vietnam, as one year of war became another, was the intensely embodied nature of the civil religious crisis that the Vietnam War spawned. The question of the meaning of America, addressed eloquently and forcefully in words spoken and written by Bellah and many others, was also worked out in and through the bodies of American soldiers.

Like all wars and all experiences of soldiering, Vietnam provided men and women in the moment, and provides scholars now, with multiple interpretive options. As Americans managing, waging, and observing the war attempted to make sense of it, they drew on many aspects of American civil religion and differed, sometimes very sharply, as to how to apply them. This chapter argues that Americans interpreting the nation's actions in the war found themselves confronting a crisis over the meaning of soldiering for America, in the terms of this book, a Christological crisis for American civil religion. The crisis involved vivid characterizations of soldiering in Vietnam, rancorous disagreements about the morality of the conflict and of soldierly involvement in it, struggles over how the returned soldier should and should not position himself in public, and, not far below the surface, starkly different ideas as to the precise relationship between the soldier and the nation.[16] Were soldiers primarily the product of voluntary acts, men who worked to embody the noble ideals of the nation? Or were they better understood as products of compulsion and coercion, otherwise peaceful men whose minds and wills were displaced or reshaped by the nation and the military. The ancient Christological controversy to which I compare this modern soldiering crisis took centuries to resolve because the scriptural materials that early Christian leaders took most seriously were ambivalent, and because simple descriptions of the relationship between God and Christ were philosophically untenable, theologically troubling, or both.[17] The Christological crisis occasioned by the Vietnam War was rooted in ambivalence as well—the ambivalence of war experiences—and it took the shape that it did because civil religious faithful urgently needed to make sense of this ambivalence and of the actions of the American soldiers who were forced to live both in its midst and with its aftermath.

A Rumor of Religion, *A Rumor of War*

In his justly celebrated memoir, *A Rumor of War*, Philip Caputo wrestles with the deeply ambivalent experience of serving as a marine in the early stages of the Vietnam War. The memoir is shot through with religious imagery and the language of the study of religion—ritual, myth, symbol, sacred—not to mention insights connected to Caputo's own mid-century American Catholicism. The book also makes a case for the religiousness of soldiering as such, the catechesis of basic training, the binding together of men into communities of purpose, the revelatory power of combat. Caputo's work is, in short, a study in the durability of a religious reading of soldiering and war, even in Vietnam.[18] With a rhythm, the strength and persistence of which some might find surprising, Caputo writes of his affection for the war and his respect for and love of the men he came to know through it. By way of introduction to his story, he notes: "Anyone who fought in Vietnam, if he is honest about himself, will have to admit he enjoyed the compelling attractiveness of combat. It was a peculiar enjoyment because it was mixed with a commensurate pain. Under fire, a man's powers of life heightened in proportion to the proximity of death, so that he felt an elation as extreme as his dread. His senses quickened, he attained an acuity of consciousness at once pleasurable and excruciating." When he returned from the war to a society that talked endlessly about it but knew Vietnam very differently than he did, Caputo felt marginal. He joined the antiwar movement but was unable to share fully in the passions of fellow protestors. Issues that were blessedly clear to his friends were murky to him. "I would never be able to hate the war with the undiluted passion of my friends in the movement," he wrote. "Because I had fought in it, it was not an abstract issue, but a deeply emotional experience, the most significant thing that had happened to me."[19]

Caputo decided to join the Marine Corps based in large part on American mythos and his own belief in war as a civil religious ritual. "I joined

the Marines in 1960 partly because I got swept up in the patriotic tide of
the Kennedy era but mostly because I was sick of the safe suburban existence I had known most of my life." The ringing words of JFK, "that
most articulate and elegant mythmaker," combined with Caputo's desire
to "live heroically" to awaken him to his soldierly destiny. "I had one of
those rare flashes of insight: the heroic experience I sought was war; war,
the ultimate adventure; war, the ordinary man's most convenient means of
escaping the ordinary. The country was at peace then, but the early sixties
were years of almost constant tension and crisis; if a conflict did break out,
the Marines would be certain to fight in it and I could be there with them.
Actually there."[20] The combat, the actuality, the there-ness of the Marine
Corps spoke to Caputo's need to prove himself and to separate himself from
the banality in which he lived.[21] And though basic training, deployment
to Okinawa, and his eventual service in Vietnam would offer much by way
of disenchantment, they would not slake his thirst for action. Caputo first
longed for and then embraced the mission and the culture of the Marine
Corps.

He was in no way alone in his desire to embody the spirit of Camelot
through military service. The draft was in place during the Kennedy years,
generating roughly 20 percent of all uniformed service personnel, but the
rest of America's soldiery consisted of those who joined voluntarily.[22] To be
sure, not all volunteers enlisted because of romantic visions of military service or out of progressive desires to remake the world in Kennedy's image.
For some, it was simply the best job available. Still, the process of indoctrination and training went a long way toward converting a diverse cohort
of young men to belief in the transformative power of service, war, and
combat. Looking back, Caputo saw the religiousness of his own attraction
to service and of the process by which that attraction became, in him and in
others, the embodied reality of soldiering. "We were novitiates," he writes,
"and the rigorous training, administered by the high priests called drill in-
structors, was to be our ordeal of initiation." The initiation involved end-
less verbal abuse, close-order drill, marches to nowhere and back again, and
intense catechesis in the "mythology" of the Marine Corps.

Though imperfect, this initiation worked. Stepping outside of himself to ask why, Caputo wrote, "'Gung ho! Gung ho! Pray for war!' Like
the slogans of revolutionaries, these look ludicrous in print, but when re-
cited in unison by a hundred voices they have a weird, hypnotic effect on
a man. . . . In time he begins to believe that he really does love the Marine
Corps, that it is invincible, and that there is nothing improper in praying

for war." Moreover, Caputo came to love what he was doing and who he was becoming. Writing of the end of an exceptionally difficult and painful training march, Caputo described a moment when, having snaked through the Virginia landscape for thirty miles with his fellow marines, their destination came into view. The men began to sing. "The song was like a cry of defiance. . . . Nothing could subdue them. Hearing that full-throated *Woa-oh-oh-oh Little Liza, Little Liza Jane* roaring through the woods, I felt proud of that spirited company and happy that I was one of them." These men had learned to embody the word of the nation by suffering, serving, and subordinating their wills, eventually their lives, to the greater good.[23]

In reflecting on his service in Vietnam, Philip Caputo often turns to religious imagery to describe the men, the war, and the terrain. At moments of import and to ends both earnest and sarcastic, religion frames his interactions with the realities of war. The evening artillery is "vespers." The rounds he must make to have the orders that will return him to combat approved are "the Stations of the Cross." After leading his company through their first experience of sustained combat, Caputo describes the transformation as a completed and efficacious ritual. "Having received the primary sacrament of war, baptism of fire, their boyhoods were behind them. Neither they nor I thought of it in those terms at the time. We didn't say to ourselves, We've been under fire, we've shed blood, now we're men. We were simply aware, in a way we could not express, that something significant had happened to us." Caputo does not deploy the language of *imitatio Christi* as frequently as some in past wars did, but neither does he turn from it entirely. In relating the story of his company "tramping down a dirt road past a Catholic church built long ago by French missionaries," Caputo describes the intense heat, the punishing sun, and the sufferings of the entire company. But the machine gunner in front of Caputo evoked a particular image: "Head bowed, [he] is walking with his weapon braced across the back of his shoulders, one hand hanging over the muzzle and the other over the butt, so that his shadow resembles the Christ figure on the cross atop the gate of the church."[24]

Stepping back from Caputo's memoir—itself a step back from Caputo's experience—we can see the seeds of a civil religious Christological crisis and note the integrity and latent ferocity of different views of the soldier. On the one hand, Caputo longed for the kinds of experience that the marines gave him, at least insofar as he could imagine them. He chose the Marine Corps; he chose service; he saw boot camp for what it was; he knew the escape hatches. But he stayed in and was, on his own account, proud of having done so. He felt bound to his fellow soldiers and was happy to stick with them through the strains of training and into the strain of war. Caputo was in Vietnam because he wanted to be in Vietnam, wanted to fight, wanted to win. Even as things in his corner of the war went badly, he still embraced combat, still hoped to fight.[25]

On the other hand, Caputo clearly was drawn into the military by Hollywood and by cultural mythologies of martial heroism.[26] He was taken into a system designed to transform civilians in all their diversity into soldiers who work, fight, kill, and die together; a system designed to "destroy each man's sense of self-worth, to make him feel worthless until he proved himself equal to the Corps' exacting standards." He was trained to want what marines wanted, to value what marines valued, to talk and think like marines talked and thought. By the end of the process he and the other men had "acquired the military virtues of courage, loyalty and *esprit de corps*, though at the price of a diminished capacity for compassion."[27] The nation, through the Marine Corps, bent the wills of men, perhaps even emptied men of individual willing, and sent them out to save the world. The cultural, ideological, and natural environments into which the government inserted these men shaped them still more, as Caputo's recollection of a "summary execution" carried out by a private in his company shows. The private came across a badly wounded Viet Cong soldier, drew his pistol, and shot him in the face. Almost immediately he "looked at the pistol as if it had gone off by itself and said, 'Now what did I do that for?'" Caputo answers the question by pointing both to the natural setting, "in that dangerous swamp it seemed a perfectly natural thing to do," and to the marines' mission in Vietnam. "You men are here to kill VC," General Greene, commandant of the Marine Corps, had told the troops. "Well," Caputo writes, "that is what [Private] Marsden had done; he had killed Viet Cong, wiped out one small part of the Communist forces. He had accomplished his mission."[28] Private Marsden enacted policies developed by the nation. The nation, not Marsden, bore responsibility. For Caputo, a morally problematic experience of war began with hybrid experiences of soldiering: soldiering as an act of will was mixed with soldiering as coerced behavior.

In two telling moments separated by only five pages in the memoir, Caputo gives further expression to the ambivalent nature of the Vietnam War as a soldiering experience: the "both-and" of willing and coercion. As he is being driven to a new command which will allow him back into combat,

Caputo notices some marines heading out into the field. "They walked slowly and in single file, heads down, long hooded ponchos billowing in the wind. The stocks of their rifles, slung muzzle-down against the rain, bulged under the backs of the ponchos; hooded and bowed, the marines resembled a column of hunchbacked, penitent monks." The marines resembled men who had taken vows of what? Poverty? Service? Separation? Violence? The metaphor describes men who had chosen to be what and where they were even if the "what" and the "where" were miserable. The very next morning, after a night of rainy, confused combat, with his men moving through a snake-infested rice paddy, Caputo turned to a different metaphor. "One fire team, marooned on an island of high ground, had to borrow sampans from the villagers to get back to the road. Like prisoners in a labor gang, the marines marched toward camp joylessly and without expectation that the new day would bring anything different or better."[29] These marines, perhaps the same men described as "penitent monks" above, looked like men who had been forced, coerced, trapped. They looked like convicts, but what was their crime? Poverty? Altruism? Naiveté?

Caputo's sympathetic voice and staggering literary gift express well the deeply mixed experiences of soldiering in Vietnam. A willing volunteer in the war's early stages, Caputo moves further toward a feeling of being trapped and shaped against his will by policy and by the increasingly toxic environment of Vietnam. Caputo's own ambivalence on this point of soldiering helps clarify the problem with so much civil religious positioning of the American soldier in the Vietnam era. There were few ways to present or describe a soldier—few ways that were common at least—that did not do significant violence to the travails of this G.I. Messiah. To describe the soldier in ways that foregrounded his agency ("a valiant hero," "a feckless coward") was to deny the role of U.S. policy and the particularities of the Vietnam War in shaping his actions and attitudes. To describe the soldier as only an agent of the government ("a robot," "an automaton") was to reduce him to an instrument, a tool, and thus not only to obscure his own willing, doing, loving, and hating, but to cast as deviant and/or mindless those American soldiers who continued to support the war and to believe in its aims even as the narrative turned and the popularity of the war plummeted.

There is something enduring about Caputo's characterizations of men and combat. Soldiers of the Great War wrote in similar terms. Soldiers of America's most recent wars do too. One can find in and after America's wars soldiers moving away from larger, corporate frameworks of meaning, describing the pall of doubt that hangs over the conflict and involvement in its ritual processes and sanctified embodiments. To what end was the suffering? Doubts about the efficacy of soldierly sacrifice and the redemption wrought by American soldiers in Vietnam and on the home front were a small part of the Vietnam experience from very early in the war. These doubts did not invalidate civil religious orthodoxies wholesale. They did not immediately undermine soldiers' own commitments to the war, the cause, or the nation.[30] But they did build on a creeping ambivalence that grew steadily more public and that soldiers and commentators and politicians were forced to engage as they worked out the meaning of the Vietnam War. The Christological crisis developed as experiences of soldiering, some common, some specific to Vietnam, met a newly intimate public knowledge of war and were projected onto an already divided, conflict-ridden nation. Who was the soldier? What did he reflect? How should we make sense of his victories? How should we make sense of his failures? What kind of salvation did the *true* soldier offer the nation?

Christologies Performed and Contested

The ambivalence of soldiering expressed so clearly in Caputo's memoir is also evident in the sharply divergent portrayals of soldiers and soldiering developed and presented by Vietnam veterans on the home front. Divisions over the meaning of soldiering for America deepened and became more obvious in the early 1970s, when support for the war effort, once so high among Americans of all political affiliations, collapsed and a group of antiwar Vietnam veterans gained significant national attention. Vietnam Veterans Against the War (VVAW) presented the American people with bodies and voices not usually associated with civil religious devotion. As an organization, Vietnam Veterans Against the War was committed to "bringing the war home" to the American people. What members meant by this was forcing Americans to see, unmediated by the television set, what government policies, military tactics, and a dauntingly complex war were forcing soldiers to do in Vietnam, "what search and destroy missions in Indochina were really about."[31] To the end of awakening and saving a nation they viewed as overly complacent, VVAW used guerilla theater performances—pop-up, public enactments of common war scenarios—unofficial hearings and trials, and more traditional acts of group protest to foreground the brutality in which American soldiers engaged and to argue that this brutality was the natural outcome of American policies in Vietnam.[32] The hope was that, through performative political actions on the home front, returned soldiers could save the soldiers still deployed in Vietnam and could save the nation from itself.

Three VVAW events in 1970–71 used public civil religious performances and testimony to emphasize the coercive aspects of soldiering in Vietnam.[33] Operation RAW was an eighty-mile march with repeated guerilla theater performances along the way. It was followed by the Winter Soldier Investigations, two days of testimony regarding American war crimes and atrocities held in Detroit in February 1971. Operation Dewey Canyon III, which lasted from April 18 to 23, 1971, focused the efforts of VVAW members on Washington, D.C., and involved a rally on the National Mall, a march to Arlington National Cemetery, the return of service medals, and testimony before Congress. The controversial gospel preached at and by these events told of a government that coerced young men into service and turned them into murderers. It argued that looking with clear eyes at what American soldiers were doing in Vietnam revealed that the war and the government were morally corrupt and murderous. VVAW members used their bodies—some whole, some broken—and their voices to make these points repeatedly.[34]

VVAW members claimed, in spite of their countercultural appearances, to be the truest devotees of American civil religion. They laid claim at every opportunity to the sacred spaces, narratives, symbols, figures, and ideals of America. Not surprisingly, acts of protest and public testimony by VVAW brought rejoinders from other war veterans and commentators who supported the war effort and a more orthodox presentation of the soldier. These voices proclaimed that the men with the long hair and the plastic rifles gathering on the Mall, taking over the Statue of Liberty, and calling themselves war criminals were not true soldiers. They were, at best, a radicalized minority, at worst traitors to the nation, to their fellow fighting men, and to those who had died in Vietnam. In short, their gospel was misleading.

In the waning days of the summer of 1970, veterans dressed mostly in combat fatigues, carrying plastic machine guns, and looking rather unkempt for soldiers parading on the home front, marched from Morristown, New Jersey, to Valley Forge, Pennsylvania in an action that VVAW called Operation RAW.[35] Along the way, VVAW members and professional actors staged simulated search-and-destroy missions, violent interrogations, and home invasions. This march across a countryside draped in the mythos of the American Revolution was an embodied argument against the Vietnam War. *This is what soldiers are doing in your name to save the world. We have come back to show you the truth. America, not Vietnam, needs saving.* World War II veteran Ernest Cummings encountered members of VVAW participating in Operation RAW and aired his opinion of them. "You men are a disgrace to your uniforms. You're a disgrace to everything we stand for. You ought to go back to Hanoi."[36] Cummings grasped that this performance was more than a long walk across historic terrain, more than a critique of foreign policy. It was a challenge lodged by fellow veterans for the heart of American civil religion, a heart to which Cummings also had claim. The extended parade was a civil religious statement that delegitimized Cummings's own understanding of the tradition and challenged the meaning of his embodiment of it. As a practitioner and a symbol of American civil religion, he was compelled to protest. *These men only appear to be angels of light. Their gospel emanates from America's adversary.*

Six months after its first large-scale civil religious performance, VVAW convened the Winter Soldier Investigations, two days of preaching and prophecy on the question of American soldiers and criminality. Roughly 150 veterans came to a Howard Johnson's Motor Lodge in Detroit to detail the horrors of their Vietnam experiences. Revelations about the massacre at My Lai had forced upon the nation the question of how American soldiers could commit murder on such an appalling scale.[37] The answer from VVAW was that William Calley and his men were the embodiment of America in Vietnam, their actions, though horrible, were the logical outgrowth of American policies. VVAW members could state this with authority because they had been to Vietnam, seen the disordered violence, and according to their own testimony, had done similar things. The Winter Soldier Investigations generated a stunning archive of soldierly brutality in Vietnam. Each participant's story was highly particular, but the words of Sergeant Jim Weber and of Specialist Fourth Class Samuel Schorr capture the recurring themes and explanations. Weber served in Vietnam from November 1967 to November 1968; Schorr was a soldier in the Eighty-Sixth Combat Engineers from September 1966 to September 1967. Weber saw the process by which he became a soldier as one of coercion. His will was warped, if not replaced, by forces outside of him. Weber was drafted, sent to South Carolina for "murder training" and Louisiana for "advanced genocide training" and through these processes was taught "to hate, hate anything that wasn't like me. Anything that wasn't a fighting machine." According to Weber, a crucial aspect of this process was the destruction of "my complete moral worth" and a total resocialization "which they were very effective at doing."[38]

Samuel Schorr testified about the incidents of disordered violence authorized and encouraged by the resocialization that Sergeant Weber described. These included "recon by fire" and "random fire on civilians." "Recon by fire," he testified, "is when you go into an area and you're not exactly sure what is in the area. You want to find out, so you just fire into the jungle or into the surrounding vegetation in the hopes you hit the enemy or something." In directing lethal force at the unknown (which, to be sure, was a formidable adversary in Vietnam) Schorr ignored the requirement that soldiers discriminate between combatants and noncombatants, but it was accepted practice.[39] Random fire on civilians, as Schorr described it, was something altogether more malicious.

> "Random Fire" on civilians happened quite often, especially on bunker guard. You sit on bunker guard for a week, twenty-four hours a day, and you get pretty bored. So we'd play little games. The Vietnamese would be working in their rice paddies with South Vietnamese flags stuck in the paddies so you would know they were there. And we would try to knock the flags down. I had a machine gun, my friend a grenade launcher, we would shoot all over the area and the Vietnamese would just take off for the hills. They thought we were friendly and they put the flag up to let us know they were there and we fired at it anyway. This was out of sheer boredom and also because we just didn't give a damn.[40]

In these bits of testimony and the dozens of others that accompanied them, veterans recounted their wantonly, viciously destructive behavior—murder, rape, sexual mutilation. Their goal was to "tell Americans what *their country* was really doing in Vietnam." They were also "purg[ing] the guilt which grew out of an inability to find any moral reason for the brutality, the waste, the destruction, which they had seen."[41] The truly brutal, wasteful, destructive actors in this drama, however, were not the soldiers themselves, but the United States government and the military leadership whose will the soldiers were enacting.

The rhetoric of the VVAW during the high-water mark of their public influence emphasized coercion in soldiering to the point of absolving individual soldiers of moral culpability for their actions in war. Soldiers spoke of being "brainwashed" and "programmed" to make sport of hurting and killing children, to not think twice about raping and killing women. "When you become an automaton," Major John Bjornson argued, "you begin to follow orders—the idea of killing and sticking bayonets into the model soldiers, the whole business of gooks, the Vietnamese are inferior, which is constantly drummed into your heads [*sic*]. It's a kind of programming."[42] If the primary goal of VVAW actions was to bring to light the disordered violence in which American soldiers were involved, a barely secondary goal was to indict the U.S. government and the military for creating the conditions that—so the logic went—encouraged, even necessitated, war crimes. Veterans tried to turn themselves in as war criminals, spoke openly of the atrocities in which they had engaged, and presented war crimes as the battlefield norm in Vietnam. They did all of this not because they expected to be arrested and held responsible as individuals, but because they wanted to highlight the sinfulness of the government in drafting and training soldiers and then asking them to wage an excruciating, impossible, brutalizing war. As John Kerry, high-profile spokesman for the organization summarized the situation in 1971, "We did not send ourselves to Vietnam. We did not make the orders. We did not give commands. We did not write the policy."[43]

Those who presented this view of soldiering as coercion were still, however, very much dependent upon civil religious devotion to the G.I. Messiah. Their gospel drew its force from the fact that those preaching it were themselves former soldiers. Accounts from observers, from politicians, even from policemen charged with dispersing or arresting VVAW protesters underscored the legitimacy that accrued to these men by virtue of their service and their suffering. According to the *Washington Post,* "Jerry V. Wilson, metropolitan police chief, ordered the release of one demonstrator, William Wyman of Boston, who has no legs." Chief Wilson commented, "I just won't do it. I just won't arrest him." Wilson was not alone in feeling reverence. George Ashworth of the *Christian Science Monitor* wrote that in spite of "unkempt" appearances that diverged from the stereotype of "clean-cut young men willing to serve their country," these men spoke with authority. Clearly, "they had fought hard, many of them, for their country." He then delved more deeply into the question of authority. "The authentic veterans in the group that assembled in Washington did enjoy one tremendous advantage over others who have protested—their credibility as sources of criticism of at least some validity. It is far easier for doubters to suspect the motives of protesters against the war than it is to doubt those who have done what their country asked and returned to say, 'Foul.'"[44]

Protesting veterans themselves were keenly aware of their authority. Mike Milligan, a twenty-two-year-old marine from Philadelphia, wounded in July 1970, commented, "People have never seen protesters like us. . . . We didn't dodge the draft. Our guerilla theater is effective because we were the guerillas. Nobody is going to doubt the sincerity of a guy who got both his legs blown off in the Nam. We're finally bringing the war home." Another veteran continued, "A million college kids don't count as much as a thousand of us."[45] The uniforms, the wounds, and the discharge papers clashed with the hair, the testimony, and the politics, but it was all reconciled within a logic of salvation worked out for the nation by the G.I. Messiah. Stated concisely by John Kerry in his testimony before Congress, these former soldiers were working "so when thirty years from now our brothers go down the street without a leg, without an arm, or a face, and small boys ask why, we will be able to say 'Vietnam' and not mean a desert, not a filthy obscene memory, but mean instead the place where America finally turned and where soldiers like us helped in the turning."[46]

If we take VVAW members at their word, and I see no reason to do otherwise, the acts in which they engaged—especially the Winter Soldier Investigation and Operation Dewey Canyon III—were emotionally difficult, fraught with feelings of confusion and betrayal, but driven by a civil religious urgency. America could fight wars. America could send sons and daughters to die. But the nation had to operate from a position of restraint, had to wage war only in response to real threats to America's well-being. The Vietnam War, they said, was a betrayal of these principles and of the men and women being asked to kill and to die. It was, in John Kerry's words, "the biggest nothing in history."[47] Because Vietnam was a betrayal, it was the duty of American soldiers to alert America, to invert civil religious performance, to short-circuit a superficial civil religious sacred with heavy doses of "true" civil religious orthodoxy.

The VVAW members did not take their civil religious duty lightly. In the wake of Operation Dewey Canyon III—five days in April 1971 when one thousand members of VVAW camped on the Mall in Washington, D.C.—former marine captain Rusty Sachs told two reporters for the *Wash-*

ington Post that returning his Silver Star and Purple Heart was "the final act of contempt for the way the executive branch is forcing us to wage war." Throwing his medals over a fence erected near the Capitol left Sachs awash in a sea of emotion. "It was like two hours before I could stop crying. . . . I was just standing there crying." Explaining his own tears, John Kerry expressed the sense, quietly but surely, that returning his Bronze Star and three Purple Hearts was a betrayal of other civil religious adepts. "I just cried for ten minutes afterward," he told Joe Pilati of the *Boston Globe*, "because I've lost friends whose mothers only had the medals I gave back."[48]

Criticism of VVAW and of less organized attempts to portray soldiering as coercion was vociferous. One of the most strident public critiques came from John O'Neill, spokesman for Vietnam Veterans for a Just Peace. O'Neill appeared opposite John Kerry on the *Dick Cavett Show* in May 1971. A navy veteran like Kerry, he sought to undermine both Kerry and the VVAW and to defend the millions of individual soldiers whom he believed had been betrayed by VVAW's civil religious heresies. When the two men sat opposite each other on national television, the depth of their civil religious difference and of the soldiering crisis generated by Vietnam became glaringly apparent. O'Neill saw soldiering as so completely an act of willing that he could not entertain the notion that soldiers' actions were anything but their own or that critiques of the war were anything but personal. O'Neill spoke first that evening. "[John Kerry] is the same little man who on nationwide television in April spoke of, quote, 'crimes committed on a day-to-day basis with the full awareness of officers at all levels of command,' who was quoted in a prominent news magazine in May as saying, quote, 'war crimes in Vietnam are the rule and not the exception,' unquote." O'Neill went further, "This man has attempted the murder of the reputations of two and a half million of us, including the 55,000 dead in Vietnam, and he will never be brought to justice. We can only seek justice and equity from the American people." John O'Neill was, of course, aware of the ugliness of war. He knew about William Calley and the My Lai massacre. But he saw Calley and the entire incident as isolated and anomalous, a tragic failure authored by individuals and best addressed individually: "The law," he noted, "will operate in his case."[49] To argue that the problem was more systemic, that the nation had chosen an unjust war, that military commanders and circumstance required that it be waged unjustly, was to murder reputations.

Attempting to discredit Kerry by either calling his bluff or implicating him in the alleged criminality, O'Neill asked him whether he had committed any war crimes himself. Kerry responded, "I did take part in free fire zones and I did take part in harassment interdiction fire. I did take part in search-and-destroy missions in which the houses of noncombatants were burned to the ground. And all of these, I find out later on, these acts are contrary to the Hague and Geneva Conventions and to the laws of warfare." Kerry then clarified the VVAW position on American soldiers as war criminals: "But we're not trying to find war criminals. That's not our purpose. It never has been. . . . What we're looking for is an examination of our policy by people in this country, particularly by the leaders before they take young men who are the objects of that policy and try them rather than examine the policy at the highest level where it was in fact promulgated." This reasoning made little sense to O'Neill, who saw soldiers as willing individuals and could not, or would not, divorce assertions of war criminality from accusations of individual culpability. Hence O'Neill's relentless characterization of Kerry and the VVAW as cowards, traitors, and liars and his summary of the consequences of their civil religious performances. "Never in the course of human events," he proclaimed, "have so many been libeled by so few."[50]

Not every critic provided the kind of civil religious challenge that met VVAW marchers en route to Valley Forge or John Kerry on the *Dick Cavett Show*. Not every voice in the silent majority branded the protesting veterans as hippies and rabble-rousers, militants and conspirators, traitors and cowards, the mentally depraved.[51] What some argued was that individual experiences of war differed and that the VVAW and individual radicalized soldiers did not represent either the Vietnam veteran or the American soldier more generally. This was the official reaction of the American Legion and the Veterans of Foreign Wars, whose national commanders issued statements in the wake of Dewey Canyon III questioning "the value of this type of publicity" and expressing regret that "any veteran [feels] it necessary to return medals to the government." Both organizations pointed out further that their membership numbers were growing and that returning Vietnam veterans showed no unusual reluctance to affiliate with them. And though VVAW garnered significant media attention beginning in 1970, its numbers were indeed small in absolute terms, barely significant as a percentage of those who served in Vietnam. It may have been the case, as one Dewey Canyon III participant stated, that one thousand VVAW veterans counted for more than one million college students. How, though, does one measure VVAW veterans against non-VVAW veterans? VVAW's most widely publicized protest—Operation Dewey Canyon III—brought 1,000 members to the Mall in Washington. At its peak in 1972, VVAW counted 20,000 members on its rolls. According to *Los Angeles Times* reporter Nick Thimmesch, by April 1971, when John Kerry testified and VVAW protesters gathered, lobbied, and camped, 700,000 Vietnam veterans had joined either the VFW or the American Legion.[52] This left roughly 1.8 million veterans undeclared in their affiliation. If one were to divide that pool between the two parties according to the ratio (35:1) they present, 1.75 million would lean toward the Legion and the VFW, 50,000 would lean toward the VVAW. This is hardly a detailed survey of soldiers' attitudes toward the nation, the military, and the war, but it should cast doubt upon simple narratives of post-Vietnam disillusionment and the notion that VVAW spoke for "the American soldier."

In the aftermath of Operation Dewey Canyon III, the *Los Angeles Times*'s Thimmesch raised the question of the VVAW's soldierly authenticity by focusing on what he believed to be the apolitical majority among Vietnam veterans. "The overwhelming majority are buying new clothes, looking for girls, trying out new cars and life-styles, some booze, maybe, and a little pot. Some found jobs and many didn't." They will not protest en masse he argued. They don't care for or have time to give to radical organizations. "The Vietnam veterans pretty much reflect their generation, with the added dimension being they have been through an unpopular, perplexing war." The veteran could certainly use a little more appreciation for what he has been through, Thimmesch wrote, perhaps an invitation to lunch and a sympathetic ear. But "the Vietnam veteran . . . will likely end up much more of a 'middle American'" than the "elitist" politicians who had "fawned over" the protesters.[53] These men had, like men before them, gone to war, fought well, and come back eager to reintegrate into society. Those for whom the script was different were simply that: different; products of their own inability or unwillingness to get through war and get on with life.

A Voluntarist Christology and an All-Volunteer Military

The Vietnam War did not begin as a crisis, Christological or other. A mix of volunteer and draftee soldiers waged the war from 1965 to 1967 with the strong support of the American public and with little public concern over the course of the conflict. Crises emerged as U.S. involvement escalated, as the draft took certain Americans in large numbers and other Americans only rarely, and as men and women on the home front learned more about the war and about the actions some Americans were taking to win it.[54] There was nothing new in drafting young men into service. American soldiers in other wars had committed acts of disordered violence. The United States had certainly been responsible before for targeting and killing civilians. Soldiers had previously turned from war to advocate for peace, lodged harsh criticisms against the government, and struggled mightily to reorient their lives and their bodies in postwar society. But the Vietnam War brought these old sins of soldiering and war out into view, and the clearer it became that the righteousness of victory would not cover them, the more urgently observers posed the questions. Who is the American soldier? Why does he act as he does? What do his actions say about America?

To interpret the Vietnam War as a Christological crisis is to notice in the civil religious positioning and practices of American soldiers a deep concern for the meaning of the soldier as a symbol and a desire for answers, once easier to come by, as to what in America he represented. The experiences of Vietnam blurred the meaning of service, suffering, sacrifice, and salvation and forced a reevaluation of the G.I. Messiah.[55] Treating the period as one of Christological crisis also keeps in the foreground the fact that those engaged in protesting the war were not, in most cases, rejecting the soldier as a central civil religious symbol. The crisis over soldiering in Vietnam, like the ancient Christological controversy, arose among those deeply committed to the Christ figure, certain of his importance, and convinced of the reality of his saving work. Yet, as historians of the ancient Christian churches will attest, to agree on the importance of a figure or to say "the Word became flesh" is to settle not a single argument as to why, how, or to what extent, much less to work through the theological and soteriological implications of various answers. Questions of Christology that vexed the ancient world vexed America as they pertained to the soldier. Why would God / the nation send a son / sons to suffer? What did the son's / sons' words and actions say about God / the nation? Did God / the nation suffer along with the son / sons? If so, to what end? If not, what kind of God / nation was this?

Two soldierly Christologies—I will call them voluntarist and adoptionist—can be discerned in the civil religious rhetoric and performances of the Vietnam War era. These Christologies correlate closely to competing understandings of soldiering as a willing expression of devotion and soldiering as compelled or coerced behavior. The voluntarist Christology features a belief in the essential strength and virtue of the state and imagines military service as a willing act of devotion on the part of the citizen. The perfect soldierly incarnation involves a citizen bending his or her will to the will of the nation, submitting to the demands of service, and then serving energetically. By this soldierly Christology the union of word and flesh is a process the success of which depends on the strength of the flesh. Moments of remarkable courage and heroism are evidence of the soldier's strength. Moments of cowardice or disordered violence demonstrate the soldier's weakness. The adoptionist Christology also emphasizes the strength and the virtue of the individual, but it imagines the process of incarnation as an act of state power, as the process by which the will of the state replaces the will of the soldier. By this Christology the union of word and flesh is more complete and, therefore, more revelatory of the true nature of the word. A soldier's actions in war are not his own as much as they are expressions of the nation's will, the inevitable outgrowth of military training. Moral problems, weaknesses, even a tendency to evil emerge not from the soldierly flesh per se, but from the word within it. Soldiers who are involved in acts of war that shock the civil religious devout are more victims than perpetrators, suffering servants who, without the word in them, would not have tossed that grenade, stabbed that child, pulled that trigger, lost control.

Voluntarists and adoptionists described soldiering in terms they found meaningful, embraced the returning soldiers who hewed most closely to those terms, and imagined the majority of Vietnam veterans in their image. By virtue of their access to mass media, Philip Caputo, Vietnam Veterans Against the War, John Kerry, John O'Neill, and editorialists writing both for and against the war were able to articulate their soldierly Christologies and to make the moral implications of their positions clear. Caputo's presentation blends the two Christological models but tends toward adoptionism in the end. VVAW and John Kerry are clear adoptionists. John O'Neill is clearly a voluntarist. Dwight Johnson did not leave an archive of his thoughts on military service for us to interpret, but his experiences of an ambivalent war yield equally well to adoptionist and voluntarist readings. Neither reading can capture every nuance of Johnson's time as a soldier. What the readings can capture is the civil religious importance of establishing the voluntarist Christology as right doctrine and right practice in the face of America's experience of Vietnam.

An adoptionist reading of Dwight Johnson's experience near Dak To would likely emphasize that he was a draftee and that, unlike young men of middle- and upper-class backgrounds, he had no legal means to avoid the call. It would emphasize too the training and transformation of a quiet young man into a person ready to unleash awesome lethality. Equally important would be the moments of war that pushed him to do what he did, that led him to "crack up" on the battlefield: the horror, the helplessness of watching friends die, the unpredictability of the war, the palpable, frustrating futility of it all. The training, the loss, the violence, and the breakdown are, in the adoptionist reading, all of a piece and were forced on Johnson by the United States. The adoptionist Johnson stands in as an American everyman, chosen, made, used up, restrained, and then sent home. Dwight Johnson's actions in and after the war reveal an unjust America to America. In considering Johnson's race, the adoptionist would take a systemic view, emphasizing the particular vulnerability of the impoverished to the economic incentives of military service in general and to the coercive force of the draft. One might then read Johnson's violence and rage as reactions to, or against, the injustices and the poverty of inner-city America, even an expression of the cultures of violence that surrounded him in his childhood. A nation capable of inflicting such suffering and authoring such injustice in and through its soldier sons could hardly offer redemption to its own people, much less the world. Rather, as the adoptionist Messiah testified, the nation offered violence, corruption, and power for power's sake. Salvation could come through these adoptionist messiahs, but only in so far as their postwar words and actions revealed the true nature of the national divine and brought about, in John Kerry's words, "a turning."

The voluntarist interpretation, set forward most clearly in Johnson's Medal of Honor citation, places an American fighting man in a situation fraught with danger, a chaotic "fatal environment."[56] In the jungle to fight Communism and defend the South Vietnamese, Johnson empties himself completely into the battle. He stands his ground. He kills justly and effectively. The danger to his comrades spurs him to action, of course, but danger and death are important mainly insofar as they are part of the war effort, a reminder to Johnson of the stakes and the importance of his dedication to the fight. His willingness to face danger, his ability to kill, his drive to save his comrades are all expressions of his devotion to cause, comrades, and country. Johnson's need for morphine and a straitjacket, not mentioned in his Medal of Honor citation, makes sense in the voluntarist Christology because different men handle war differently; always have, always will. The voluntarist might also look at Johnson, an African-American war hero, and see in his uniformed body proof of racial progress if not race equity, and of shared capacities for the heights of military masculinity. At the same time, some might consider his "crack up" as a manifestation of a racial tendency toward uncontrolled violence, tainting the voluntarist messiah with common prejudices against African Americans. On the voluntarist reading, the heights of civil religious devotion evident in Dwight Johnson's war experiences reflect his strength as an American and the enduring power of war to reveal the hero. The problems he encountered in his more personal battles, though, belong to him and him alone.

The Christological crisis of the Vietnam War was a discursive problem and an intensely embodied one as well. These different presentations of the soldier informed protests and counterprotests, undergirded assertions of civil religious orthodoxy, and drove charges of heresy and betrayal. They seem also to have shaped soldiers' memories and interpretations of war. In navigating the moral complexities of their own experiences and the actions and inactions of their comrades, soldiers followed logics similar to those I have described: presenting themselves and their close comrades in voluntarist or adoptionist terms, sometimes both, and imagining the salvation they might bring to the nation in terms of either exposing the coercion and revealing the truth or encouraging more men of firm will to join the fight. When John Kerry spoke of the "new soldier" helping America in "turning," he meant a turning from the unjust, disordered violence that he saw as endemic to the American effort in Vietnam, and the physical, psychological, and civil religious damage such violence did to soldiers like Dwight Johnson. O'Neill hoped for a turn toward deeper devotion to America's struggle against Communism, the kind of effective and fierce devotion given bodily expression by Dwight Johnson.

The Vietnam War involved much turning. In the case of the G.I. Messiah, it involved a resolution as well. The irony of this resolution was not lost on Robert L. Turner of the *Boston Globe*, who wrote in early 1973, "It may be considered one of the anomalies of the age that a war as unpopular as Vietnam could be followed by establishment of an all-volunteer military."[57] Turner was not wrong to note the anomaly. In the first years of the 1970s, the most public faces and bodies in American civil religion had been those who emphasized, first, the coercive aspects of military service; second, the atrocities into which service had forced them; third, the corruption of the government and the military they had served; and fourth, the limited vision (to put it charitably) of those who disagreed with them.

Through repeated and brilliantly choreographed embodied acts of civil religious devotion, VVAW and its sympathizers had laid claim to the mythology, the symbology, even the sacred spaces of American civil religion and reminded Americans of aspects of that religion that, VVAW argued, had been occluded during America's involvement in Vietnam. Turner was not wrong about the irony of a turn to voluntarism. Yet he also was not as right as he could have been. On the one hand, although VVAW and related organizations garnered significant media coverage, they did not represent that vast majority of Vietnam veterans regardless of class, race, or gender. On the other hand, though working with a conflicting vision of soldierly Christology, veterans who protested the war or became radicalized in other ways often built their protests on assumptions central to the valorization of the G.I. Messiah, assumptions that they shared with non-protesting, non-radicalized, voluntarist veterans.

Conversations about the feasibility of an all-volunteer military began well before the Vietnam War. The idea had been bouncing around the Pentagon since the late 1940s. The first congressional hearings to address the issue convened in the final days of the Kennedy administration. In 1964, when Vietnam was still one problem among many, President Johnson convened a working group to look into the feasibility of transitioning from a mostly volunteer force to an all-volunteer force. But by 1968, when candidate Richard M. Nixon pledged to end the draft, and by 1973 when he finally did, conscription, coercion, racial and economic inequality, and unjust violence had all become attached to the draft, to soldiering, and by adoptionist logic, to the United States as well.[58] The problem faced by the architects of an all-volunteer military was, in short, how to make voluntarism attractive enough that adoptionist practices and their pressing practical and civil religious problems could end. Much of the discussion about how to achieve this goal focused on economics. What were the social and fiscal costs of the draft? What would be the commensurate costs of an all-volunteer force? What level of pay, what financial incentives would attract sufficient numbers of men and women to the profession of soldiering? How much would it cost to keep them in the service for an entire career?[59]

Discussions also touched on race and how ending the draft might change the color of the G.I. Messiah. In general, those who supported the draft argued that without it the military would become at once too lower class and too black. One scholar commented: "In point of fact, an all-volunteer army would liberate the middle class from the legal necessity of serving but commit others to compulsory service by economic circumstance. Is this not, in effect, forcing the poor and the less fortunate into the armed forces? Is this truly democratic?"[60] There was no question that the Dwight Johnsons of America would continue to enlist and serve. They had no better place to turn for work, or so the logic went. But what of the John Kerrys, the Philip Caputos, and the John O'Neills? Adoptionism was the only way, draft advocates argued, to keep the military looking like America. Those who supported ending the draft argued that government compulsion was almost never the best answer to a question of domestic policy and that it was far better to rely on a mix of rational economic choice and civil religious devotion to fill the ranks.

Smuggled into this conversation—sometimes quite poorly—was the concern that African Americans were not only not fully American but would threaten American society in direct proportion to their representation within the military. It was, of course, desirable to have some African-American men in uniform. It was also necessary to have white men serving with them. Unconsciously echoing the concerns that fed vicious race riots during America's mobilization for the Great War, military sociologist Morris Janowitz opined that ending the draft would create "a predominately or even all Negro enlisted force in the Army, an 'internal foreign legion' which would be disastrous for American political democracy." Some who favored voluntarism were alert to the overtly racist assumptions of draft proponents. Milton Friedman observed: "It is a good thing not a bad thing to offer better alternatives to the currently disadvantaged. The argument to the contrary rests on a political judgment: that a high rate of Negroes in the armed service would exacerbate racial tensions at home and provide in the form of ex-soldiers a militarily trained group to foment violence."[61] America's sons, given the proper incentives, would choose devout service and would not turn violence back in on the nation.

Already in 1967 Martin Anderson, a Columbia University business professor and adviser to Richard Nixon, was thinking about how best to frame the discussion of ending compulsory service. Anderson felt that conscription imposed a duty of service that ran counter to the best libertarian traditions. He also found it troubling because it burdened a mostly professional military with unnecessary costs and inefficiencies. Drafting men into the service guaranteed a high level of turnover and chronic morale problems. It allowed the government to compel those who were drafted to pay an unfair tax in the form of income lost for the time of their service.

Anderson noted further that the government had gotten lazy in valuing service, paying soldiers nowhere near "reasonably fair wages."[62] In response to these conditions, he articulated a vision of soldiering that wove modern economic logic and the need for a robust military together with key themes of American civil religion. Anderson concluded a paper written for Nixon in July 1967, "Therefore, because it is moral and fair, because it increases our national security, and because it is economically feasible, we should establish a volunteer armed force that will offer the young people of our country the opportunity to participate in her defense with dignity, with honor, and as free men." The warrior image Anderson constructed drew on contemporary realities—dignified, honorable, free American men and women entering the armed forces of their own will—but envisioned them purified of less salutary realities and reconnected convincingly, completely to a voluntarist Christology.[63]

Nixon found Anderson's reasoning both convincing and politically expedient, and by November 1967 he was arguing publicly that "the nation must move toward a volunteer army by compensating those who go into the military on a basis compatible with their civilian careers."[64] In October of 1968, candidate Nixon presented this sentiment in language more resonant with civil religious mythology. "I feel this way: a system of compulsory service that arbitrarily selects some and not others simply cannot be squared with our whole concept of liberty, justice, and equality under the law. Its only justification is compelling necessity. . . . Some say we should tinker with the present system, patching up an inequality here and there. I favor this too, but only for the short term. But in the long run, the only way to stop the inequities is to stop using the system." As with so many campaign promises, the promise to end compulsory military service took years to realize. In the meantime, the war ground on and widened. Protests against it grew louder. More soldiers killed and suffered and died. Reenlistment rates decreased, and the number of draftees as a percentage of the armed forces serving in Vietnam reached its height for the war. Reports of a crisis of morale and of high rates of drug use and soldier-on-soldier violence filled home-front media.[65] And more men returned, some articulating clearly and forcefully an adoptionist rationale for the atrocities of which they accused themselves and for the psychological and social struggles they faced in the aftermath of their war experiences.

One month after Nixon's statement, Dwight Johnson traveled to the White House to receive the Medal of Honor. Just over a year later he was admitted to the military hospital outside Valley Forge for psychiatric evaluation and treatment; he went AWOL. Johnson returned to Detroit in April 1971, where, in his last act, he attempted to rob a small grocery store. Dwight Johnson was returned to the nation's capital in May 1971 for burial in Arlington National Cemetery. As Johnson's life unraveled, the VVAW slowly but steadily developed a public voice and an embodied civil religious argument against the system that made Dwight Johnson a hero—though not against the heroes themselves. In an oddly synchronized, unintentional dance with Dwight Johnson, VVAW members also marched to Valley Forge. Perhaps Johnson heard their protest. The VVAW held war crimes hearings in Detroit while Johnson, back in his old neighborhood, struggled to hold himself together. He may well have seen local coverage of the Winter Soldier Investigation. In the final days of Johnson's life, VVAW members performed their vision of soldiering by returning medals won in a war they called criminal. Two weeks before Johnson was laid to rest, VVAW members and a few Gold Star Mothers marched to Arlington National Cemetery and were barred from entering. When they returned the next day and confronted the cemetery superintendent, they were allowed access to this epicenter of the civil religious sacred.[66]

When a resolution to the Christological crisis finally came, it came as a silence. In March 1973, the Nixon administration decided, in the words of Secretary of Defense Elliot Richardson, "that it will not be necessary to extend the draft induction authority beyond its expiration date of July 1, 1973."[67] This "final act in implementing the all-volunteer force" put an end to the adoptionist Christology of soldiering for America. Questions of coercion and indoctrination did not end, to be sure. Close-order drill remains close-order drill. Military mythology remains central to the forging of soldierly identity. But forced service and its taint on soldierly suffering vanished, and it became harder to draw straight lines from the sins and indiscretions of the sons to the actions or the will of the Father. From now until the reinstitution of the draft (an event as unlikely as it would be unwise), the men and women suffering, fighting, killing, and dying "over there" are there as a matter of choice; complex choice, but choice nonetheless. Their sufferings are not coerced. The meaning of their service is legible in terms consonant with the America's civil religious mythos. "Thank you for your service," however sweet or saccharine the sound, makes sense again for the very first time.

CHAPTER 6

Safety, Soldier, Scapegoat, Savior

Everyone (hawks, doves, patriots, subversives) can find something to celebrate in Pat Tillman.
—*Sports Illustrated*

The dawn of a new millennium was, for many Americans, an occasion to reflect on the changes the United States had undergone in the space of the last century. One hundred years of near-constant global conflict and the rise and fall of a half dozen empires left America an uncontested, though not an unblemished, superpower. The faces and faiths of Americans had changed considerably as well. A surge in immigration dating to the mid-1960s altered the racial, ethnic, and religious fabric of the nation. Religions retained much of their vibrancy and had added layers of diversity unimagined by previous generations of Protestants, Catholics, and Jews. Significant gains in the struggle against race- and gender-based discrimination had moved the United States closer to realizing its promise of liberty and justice for all.

The American military and its soldiery had changed as well. The all-volunteer force had become a reality. Proving naysayers wrong, the military had developed into a smoothly functioning, fully professionalized, widely revered institution composed of men and women who chose service freely and who, in theory at least, worked each day to embody the will of the nation in tasks ranging from payroll management to physical fitness training, aircraft maintenance to intelligence gathering. One result of this transition to a voluntarist model was that even as the military came to reflect more accurately the demographics of the United States, an emotional, geographical, and political space reopened between the military and the broader American community.[1] Images of the warrior hero and fantasy echoes of wars past, crafted to exorcise the "ghosts of Vietnam," filled the space between soldiers and most civilians, giving an overwhelming majority of Americans strongly positive feelings about soldiering but little, if any, direct knowledge of military life. When young people worried about the draft in 2001, their thoughts were of the professional prospects of 224 elite college football players, not the military fates of physically qualified men between the ages of eighteen and thirty. Military budgets, driven upward during the Reagan era and cut only slightly under George H. W. Bush and Bill Clinton, were astronomical in both absolute and relative terms. Mid-century fears about a rising military-industrial complex, famously articulated by President Dwight Eisenhower, had been fully realized. Very few Americans seemed bothered. In the last decade of the twentieth century the military had ample opportunity to impress the nation and the world. Interventions in Iraq and the Balkans showed a military that packed a punch and made reasonable efforts to be precise and justified when throwing it.[2] The country could not agree on the most desirable successor to President Bill Clinton, but it could agree that soldiering for America was a virtuous enterprise.

When airplanes hijacked by Al Qaeda operatives slammed into the World Trade Center towers, the Pentagon, and a field near Shanksville, Pennsylvania, the United States experienced a civil religious revival. The sight of such horrific destruction—falling bodies, falling buildings—prompted Americans to gather in acts of mourning, solace seeking, and remembrance. The attacks also led Americans to give themselves over to the nation as soldiers in numbers that exceeded expectations.[3] The motives of this large and diverse body were surely complex, but they were certainly informed by myths of warfare and by devotion to the G.I. Messiah. With America under continuing threat and with militant Islamists the self-declared enemy, many citizens looked once again for national salvation to come through the soldierly body.

No single American was gripped by this sense of devotion and by the mythology of warfare and soldiering as famously as was Pat Tillman. In the early stages of a startlingly successful career as a safety for the Arizona Cardinals of the National Football League, Tillman traded his rising star on the biggest stage in American sport for the experience of soldiering. He walked away from a contract that would have made him a millionaire to enlist in the army and, if all went well, to become a Ranger. He realized this goal with his brother at his side and completed one tour in Iraq before he was killed by friendly fire in Afghanistan on April 22, 2004. Tillman's life, service, death, and the battle for his memory are an appropriate subject for the final chapter of this book for at least two reasons. First, Tillman's story demonstrates the enduring power of the G.I. Messiah in American civil religion and the equally enduring burdens of embodying that ideal. Many aspects of the Tillman saga are presaged in earlier chapters of this book and in previous episodes of American war-craft. Second, the way that the story of Pat Tillman unfolded and then unraveled may indicate a significant loosening of the nation's hold on the memory of its war dead and on the devotional power it derives from them. Although the precise expressions that demonstrate this change should give us pause, the loosening itself may well lead to a fuller accounting of the meanings of soldiering for America in the twenty-first century.

This chapter proceeds in two parts. I will begin by discussing the influence of the G.I. Messiah ideal on Pat Tillman and will situate him and his military service on the post-9/11 civil religious landscape. The second half of the chapter considers invocations of Pat Tillman after his death and the parallels between these pronouncements and the Levitical scapegoat ritual. As different as were the agendas behind public discussions of the fallen Tillman, as apparently secular as most pundits' pronouncements were, they were remarkably similar in their structure and their purpose. Twenty-first-century commentators spoke of Tillman as if he were a ritual sacrifice and imagined his death as atonement for national sins. The Tillman episode demonstrates that even in the midst of a diverse America characterized by eclectic religiosity and multidirectional cultural influences, presentations and interpretations of the soldier still draw on recognizably scriptural patterns and echo biblical understandings of sacrificial death.

Pat Tillman, the American Soldier, and the Power of the Ordinary

There have been two biographies—one a *New York Times* bestseller—and a widely acclaimed documentary film. There have been articles, editorials, and blog posts, eulogies, commentaries, and encomia from all corners of American society. The narrative arc of his life has the familiar cadence of a beloved American hymn. *He overcame a lack of size with heart and grit. He proved all doubters wrong and made himself an elite athlete. From the promised land of professional football he heard the call of his country and the call of history. He gave up wealth, career, and finally life for the cause of freedom.* The words used to describe Pat Tillman the athlete, the soldier, the person are equally familiar: brave, smart, tough, daring, heroic, relentless, uncommon. The most widely discussed soldier and the most carefully studied death of the wars in Afghanistan and Iraq have generated so much copy that most attempts to discuss them become exercises in creative repetition. With official documents redacted and evidence relating to his death destroyed, with direct revelation cut off, what remains to be said about Pat Tillman by those who are not his family?

What remains to be said about Pat Tillman, if we are to fathom fully the religious dynamics of his life and death, is that he was not extraordinary. Moreover, the most important lesson, the most fundamental fact of the entire Tillman saga from enlistment to service to combat to death to memorialization is just how ordinary it all was. Drawn to service by myths of military heroism, held there by his commitment to the soldierly ideal and by affection for his corner of the military community, Tillman waged a morally complicated war that many Americans thought of in simpler terms. He disliked some military procedures and policies; he criticized his leaders. Like many soldiers, he struggled with the forms of obedience that the military forced him to accept. His death was the result of confusion that, while avoidable, is common in combat. Those around him crafted a narrative of his death that was fully compatible with American martial mythology and the figure of the G.I. Messiah. The purpose of this official telling of Tillman's death was to shore up the mythology, defend the symbol, and to derive some political power both from these enduring features of American civil religion and from Tillman's embodiment of them. Similarly occluding yet revealing narratives have been told innumerable times in the midst of past conflicts and have comforted mourning families by rendering heartbreaking losses meaningful. None of this is extraordinary.

To describe Pat Tillman as ordinary or common is to contradict nearly every word written about him to date. But it is also to create a necessary tension among Pat Tillman the soldier, the claims so frequently rehearsed about him, and the scholarly task of making sense of both. To designate someone as uncommon, extraordinary, or exotic is to risk losing track of meaningful connections between that subject and the society in which he or she exists.[4] It is also to risk letting awe or reverence on the one hand, disgust or bewilderment on the other, short-circuit efforts to explain and to understand. This linguistic and conceptual move is of enhanced importance in the study of soldiering because vocabularies of the exceptional are so central to the civil religious construction of the American soldier. Americans watch, read, and otherwise consume stories of soldiers' extraordinary experiences. The very act of donning a uniform renders young men and women exotic in their communities. Soldiers' ribbons, medals, and sometimes their very bodies are evidence of a willingness to do exceptional things. One can feel almost heretical using the label "common." But this move matters not only for our understanding of the Tillman case but for the cases of thousands of soldiers who were *not* Pat Tillman. For it is my contention that the sacrificial dynamics so clearly in evidence in interpretations of Tillman's death have a much broader reach within and beyond the soldiery, undergirding myriad public reflections on the G.I. Messiah.

There are two additional reasons to begin a discussion of the life, death, and afterlife of Pat Tillman by emphasizing his ordinariness. First, he seems to have wanted to be perceived and treated this way.[5] He somewhat naively resisted all media and government attempts to hold him up as exceptional, expressing in word and deed his desire to be treated as common. Second, exceptionalist accounts of his life and death both commit and reinscribe violence. Portrayals of Pat Tillman as superhuman, flawless, mythic rely on accounts of his life and actions that are at best partial and at worst deliberately distorting. These accounts do violence to a memory and to those who would preserve it. Further, by telling stories of Tillman's exceptional sacrifice, exceptional sense of duty, and exceptional valor, authors and commentators, often unwittingly, give added vitality to a mythology that elevates and venerates ideal types of those who wage war rather than the flawed women and men who actually do. These narratives of exception extract, sacralize, and encourage imitation of the aspects of Tillman's life that commentators imagine as good, useful, essentially American while sequestering and ignoring qualities that are questionable or inconvenient. *Pat Tillman saw his duty clearly. This is how pure heroism looked when he walked among us. Imitate him if you can.* Always keeping in mind that Tillman was, as Senator John McCain noted by way of eulogy, "a good son, brother, and husband, a loyal friend, an excellent student, an overachieving athlete, a decent, considerate person, a solid citizen in every respect," and that he was loved and mourned intensely, we do well to think of Pat Tillman as, first and foremost, ordinary.

This is, admittedly, a challenge. Pat Tillman was already a nationally known professional athlete when he enlisted. Unlike sports celebrities who served in previous wars, Tillman's image was built and disseminated through weekly national broadcasts of his football games and, between the Internet and cable television, a near-constant public presence. One of two starting safeties for the Arizona Cardinals, his departure for military service was immediately noticeable in ways that the enlistment of a high school graduate from upstate New York or a twenty-something waitress from Texas was not. Fittingly, journalists covering war and sport made much of the fact that Pat Tillman gave up a tremendous amount—money and fame primarily—to serve his country. This, they said, made him remarkable. There are, of course, very few people in the world who at Tillman's age earn an annual salary of $1.2 million. Fewer still make such money as athletes. Pat Tillman was indeed a statistical anomaly when he entered the army; few models of rational choice would have predicted his behavior. But in joining the military, becoming a soldier, he fled from the athletically remarkable, the financially uncommon, the professionally noteworthy to pursue a more commonly available "uncommon," an uncommon that he believed to be more real, more authentic, more genuinely heroic, and, perhaps, redemptive. That which is common in Pat Tillman is both what he became, a soldier, and his ideas about what becoming a soldier meant and what service in wartime would entail.

When Pat Tillman entered the army in April 2002, he did so in the same way millions of young men and women have entered the military since the transition to an all-volunteer force. He consulted with a recruiter, signed the appropriate paperwork, and reported for induction and basic training.[6] He was one of thousands of Americans shaken by the attacks of September 11, 2001, motivated by a mix of outrage and vulnerability, to rethink the patterns of their lives and to imagine themselves as soldiers. Many voices, public and private, connected 9/11 backward to December 7, 1941, and the last large-scale attack on American territory. In an interview that he gave the day after the attacks, Tillman conveyed this common sentiment, "My great-grandfather was at Pearl Harbor and a lot of my family has . . . gone and fought in wars and I really haven't done a damn thing as far as laying myself on the line like that and so I have a great deal of respect for those that have and what the flag stands for."[7] Tillman did more than just respect those

6:1: Specialist Pat Tillman marches with Captain Christopher Deale during graduation from boot camp, October 25, 2002. (*Columbus Ledger-Enquirer*/McClatchy-Tribune)

who had laid themselves on the line; he sought to emulate them through embodied service. For the Pat Tillman of 2001–2, no more noble expression of love of country was possible than to don the uniform and go to war. The supreme embodiment of national devotion, that for which "the flag" stood, was, in his eyes, the battle-tested soldier. Whatever other complexities and heterodoxies were part of Pat Tillman's persona, on this point of American civil religion he was a perfect catechumen.

Tillman's devotion to the ideal soldier brought him into temporary conflict with members of his family who were deeply concerned about his safety and struggled to understand the timing of his decision—shortly after his wedding, in a pivotal year of his football career.[8] Frustrated and bewildered by his conversion from football player to soldier, they tried to convince him to reconsider, to count the costs, to think of the danger. But Tillman refused to be swayed. The thoughts he recorded on April 8, 2002, are evidence of this commitment and take us still deeper into the ordinary Tillman. "For much of my life I've tried to follow a path I believed important," he wrote. "However, these last few years, and especially after recent events, I've come to appreciate just how shallow and insignificant my role is. I'm no longer satisfied with the path I've been following . . . it's no longer important." The antidote to unimportance, he believed, was soldiering. "I'm not sure where this new direction will take my life though I'm positive it will include its share of sacrifice and difficulty, most of which falling squarely on Marie's shoulders. Despite this . . . I am equally positive that this new direction will, in the end, make our lives fuller, richer, more meaningful. My voice is calling me in a different direction."[9] Tillman called this "voice" his own, and it certainly expressed itself in a Tillman idiom. But his voice paraphrased an American ur-text that equates ease and comfort with stagnation, "sacrifice and difficulty" with growth and meaning. This same text valorizes individualism and mastery of self and presents violence and conquest of the wilderness as redemptive. The muscular faith it expresses is so ordinary that we struggle to see it as faith.[10] *Prove yourself soldiering for the United States,* the text reads, *and you have proven yourself for good.* The fact that Tillman chose to embody this faith by soldiering for the United States makes him a man of firm but common civil religious devotion.

Tillman's religion, understood as his lived relationship to the divine, was also quite common. Tillman did not believe in a god, did not attend church, and, according to his brother Kevin, did not want a chaplain involved in his memorial service. He was, however, respectful of others' religious views and was interested enough in them to read scriptures. If Pat Tillman had responded to the American Religious Identification Survey (ARIS) in 2008, he would have been among the "Nones," a group that includes atheists, agnostics, humanists, and those who claim no religious affiliation. This group includes 34 million Americans or roughly 15 percent of the adult population.[11] If responses are classified based on stated beliefs only and not on explicit group identification, Tillman's cohort of atheists, agnostics, and the unaffiliated grows to 24 percent of the adult population, 54 million Americans, or slightly fewer than those who identify as Catholic. If we place him in the significantly smaller group comprising only other professed atheists and agnostics, he is still no more or less exotic than an Episcopalian or a Jew.

Having heard the mythic call and chosen, as did 110,923 others in 2002, to join the military, Tillman entered boot camp, the military's common rite of initiation.[12] This extended ritual, and the many rituals within the ritual, break down old bonds, disorder stable relationships, undermine individual identities all to the end of rebuilding them to fit the distinctive *communitas* of the American military. The ritual of boot camp is disorienting by design. It was doubly disorienting for Tillman because he found so many of his fellow recruits to be so objectionable. "They're resentful, ungrateful, lazy, weak, and unvirtuous, as often as not. They bicker, complain, lie, tell tall tales, mope, and grumble incessantly." But, as commonly happens, he also found some like-minded fellow travelers.[13] Like many who went before him and many who will follow, Tillman did not enjoy boot camp, but he endured. He found parts of his training to be ridiculous, but he completed them. One reason for his perseverance was his belief in the goal toward which this ritual was leading him. Pat Tillman wanted to be a Ranger, which meant going to jump school, which meant going to boot camp. It is a well-worn path. The conclusion of basic training found Tillman challenged by a common final training exercise but ready to move on. "Get me the fuck out," he wrote.[14] A communal graduation ritual marked the end of this rite of passage.

Upon arrival at his Ranger battalion Tillman was again subjected to "merciless rituals" designed to reinforce the "pecking order," but now he was less bothered. "He regarded being a Ranger as one of the most serious challenges he'd ever undertaken."[15] According to Tillman's mother, to Tillman himself, and to biographer Jon Krakauer, the closer he got to his goal of "laying myself on the line," the greater affinity he felt with those around him and the greater fidelity he felt to his inner voice. But to fulfill this martial desire completely, to reach his goal of a richer more meaningful life, Tillman had to encounter combat, the most intensely transformative stage in the rite of passage that is war. The potential for harm to come, the risk of sacrifice, the proximity of death and violent chaos were to him the horrifying, fascinating, invigorating, and truly transformative aspects of the soldiering experience. Tillman's reaction to being denied the opportunity to fight in Iraq demonstrates vividly his firm commitment to this common belief.

When Tillman's Ranger unit deployed to Iraq he was still a junior soldier with no combat experience. As commonly happens, Tillman was "left in the tent" when his unit went forward on patrol. Following this perceived snub he wrote that he felt like "the last kid picked," and then gave vent to his frustration. "I did not throw my life to shit in order to fill sandbags and guard Hummers. This is a fucking insult that boils my blood. All I want to do is rip out the throat of one of these loudmouth fucks who's going as opposed to me. . . . Here, nothing is based on merit. . . . I want someone to . . . [r]ealize we are not normal privates, break the fucking rules, and put us in a position to add value." The rite of passage is incomplete without a "baptism by fire." And though he wasn't "left in the tent" for the entirety of his tour in Iraq, Tillman left the country without seeing combat. "We did not fight, or find ourselves in any life-altering situations," he wrote. "Perhaps in time this whole experience will seem larger than it does and more exciting. I admit that it was not what I expected of 'going to war.'"[16] This is a common non-experience. There is nothing extraordinary in the disappointments of war.

The chaos that resulted in Pat Tillman's death was also common. Confusion, chaos, paralysis, firing on one's own troops, and equipment failures are all ordinary aspects of combat and all of them can bring about unnecessary or accidental death. The American military has devoted a great deal of training and technology to the elimination of "fratricide," and still American bullets and bombs cause between 10 and 24 percent of U.S. combat deaths.[17] Far more American soldiers are killed by enemy fire, to be sure, but deaths by so-called friendly fire are no statistical rarity. A soldier at war cannot know whether or not a bullet will bring his life to an end, but he can know that in combat straight lines will bend, black and white will become gray, and that failure will be as much a part of the longed-for combat experience as success.

In Tillman's case the deadly confusion began with a decision by senior officers—resisted vehemently by his unit's commanding officer—to split his Ranger company into two groups or "serials" in order to tow a disabled vehicle out of a narrow canyon. Pat was in the lead serial—Serial One— when the second serial—Serial Two—which was supposed to travel by a different route, came under mortar fire. Tillman's serial turned around to provide help. He and his fellow soldiers left their vehicles and headed up the canyon walls hoping to suppress the mortars or simply to provide covering fire. Fleeing the ambush at high speed, Serial Two came upon Serial One members positioned above them in the canyon and, thinking they were Taliban fighters, unleashed a hailstorm of bullets. Their stunned comrades did not have enough cover to protect themselves from the men they were trying to protect and, try as they might, could not convince Serial Two to cease fire. Two members of Serial One were injured. Two, including Pat Tillman, were killed.[18]

The single most disturbing aspect of the Tillman case, the way the army concealed the truth about the circumstances of his death, is also undeniably common. According to extensive coverage, the army had been busy from the moments after Tillman was killed hiding and destroying evidence, suborning falsehoods, concealing as much as they possibly could about the "true" circumstances of his death, rushing to bury the dead.[19] From Tillman's immediate superiors to those close to the president it was judged best, however craven, however illegal, to make his death mythic. The army initially described the events of April 22, 2004, as a recapitulation of the sacrificial death of the G.I. Messiah. Tillman's unit, they lied, had been caught in an ambush. Without so much as flinching Tillman recognized the danger of the situation and, not thinking of himself, charged up a hill into enemy fire, sacrificing himself so that his fellow soldiers could live on.[20] To give material expression to Tillman's imagined heroics the army awarded him a Silver Star for valor. To add narrative expression and combat-verified credibility, Steve White, a Navy SEAL whom Tillman had come to know during his tour in Iraq, spoke at his funeral. Paraphrasing the award citation, White said, "He made the call; he dismounted his troops, taking the fight to the enemy. This gave his brothers in the downed vehicle time to move off that target. He directly saved their lives with that move. Pat sacrificed himself so that his brothers could live."[21]

The extent to which the re-narration of Tillman's death is commonplace becomes apparent as we break it down into two parts: myth and motive. From the standpoint of myth, specifically the myth of the sacrificial soldier, the story told about Tillman's last moments is thoroughly ordinary, not to mention deeply orthodox. One would be hard pressed to count the number of similar stories told about soldiers, both fallen and not. *There was combat. There was fear. One remained calm. One did what was needed to save his comrades. One died (or would have) so that others might have life.* The narrative pattern is familiar and in this case employs common though antique vocabulary—"dismount"—and common though substantial euphemisms—"brothers"—to generalize and mythologize war experiences and war deaths across time and space.[22] American military cemeteries around the world do this same work in a nontextual medium, placing gleaming white crosses, uniform symbols of suffering, sacrifice, Christ-likeness, over the bodies of men whose deaths may have shared certain characteristics but were anything but uniform. The stories told by their gravestones, like the story initially told about Pat Tillman, make no distinction between one type of death and another. All are heroic; all are salvific. *Greater love hath no man than this.* Official accounts of Tillman's death were, then, fictional in the sense that they did not describe the circumstances accurately, but they were also truer than true, expressing the mythic essence of the G.I. Messiah.

This constancy of mythmaking is matched if not surpassed by the constancy of motive. Why did the army assert heroism and then destroy evidence to the contrary? Why did the army tell a story that was truer than true to a family that just wanted facts? Why the white crosses at Normandy American Cemetery? Why the Eternal Flame at the Tomb of the Unknowns? The tendency in film, biography, and blog has been to emphasize the personal aspects of the army officers' motives in the Tillman deception, particularly as they intersect with public perception. High-ranking men were worried, these accounts go, about the implications of having killed Pat Tillman.[23] This analysis certainly has merit, but there are good reasons to resist such an exotic framing. Pat Tillman was not the first soldier whose death was narrated according to mythology rather than fact. His was not the first funeral for a hero whose actions in war were not extraordinary. Tillman's funeral and award citation are connected to hundreds of thousands of other memorial acts by the nation's desire to imagine its soldiers as embodiments of the G.I. Messiah and to derive power from rhetorics and performances that encourage and express devotion to the soldier-savior. In other words, presenting the Tillman family with a false account of their son's death was a secondary or, perhaps, tertiary action subordinate to the common ritual processes by which fallen soldiers officially come to embody G.I. Messiah. To the extent that they were thinking of the Tillman family at all, army officers were likely thinking of them first as citizens of the United States who had given their son in service and who would be comforted, as hundreds of thousands of families have been, by myths of soldierly sacrifice. And in this effort the nation, led by one of the more divisive presidents in American history, was at first quite unified.

The Soldier as Scapegoat

So much was common in the service and death of Pat Tillman that we must be open to the possibility that the patterns evident in his memorial treatment, uncommonly voluminous as it clearly was, are also common. Put another way, the fact that Americans wrote, talked, and thought more about Pat Tillman than any other fallen soldier of the wars in Afghanistan and Iraq does not mean that the ways in which they talked were extraordinary. Articles, editorials, eulogies, and blog posts described Tillman as uncommon, exceptional, exotic—an exemplary devotee of American civil religion. But they did more than this. In describing his virtues and looking for meaning in his death, authors frequently framed his death as a ritual sacrifice. By this I mean that discussions of the fallen Pat Tillman bear striking structural and rhetorical similarities to the ancient scapegoat ritual described in the book of Leviticus. In this ritual, two goats are brought before the tabernacle to atone for "the uncleanness of the children of Israel." Leviticus 16:5–22 instructs the priests to cast lots upon the goats, to sacrifice one as a sin offering, and to confess over the other "the iniquities of the children of Israel, and all their transgressions in all their sins" before letting this scapegoat go to "bear their iniquities unto a land not inhabited."[24] The innocent goat, a ritually pure creature, absorbs both the sins of Israel and the punishment Israel deserves.

Why turn to an ancient Israelite goat to help interpret an American soldier? What can the biblical guidelines for an ancient sacrifice ritual possibly reveal about a twenty-first-century war death? To begin, the understanding of sacrifice articulated in Leviticus not only shaped Israelite understandings of communal responsibility and the purpose of ritual violence, it also influenced Christian theories of the meaning of the Crucifixion. The notion that an innocent being could bear the sins of a people and be sacrificed as atonement for those sins is not as historically or culturally distant as it might at first seem. American understandings of soldierly suffering and death are themselves freighted with this ritual and theological baggage. Moreover, the Levitical sacrifice is far from culturally unique. Similar scapegoating rituals—rituals that attempt to resolve social tension or heal social division by directing violence at a third party—have been part of numerous societies, both contemporary and premodern.[25] In our current era of religious diversity and complexity, regular, public invocations of explicitly Christian myth and symbol are less common than in past eras of American history. This does not mean, however, that Americans no longer theologize sacrifice. Society, instead, builds its memorial rituals on equally religious but less noticeable substructures. These rituals often feature proclamations of the ritual purity of the fallen, an enumeration of the "iniquities" of society, and an argument that in a soldier's death America has an opportunity for renewal. There is, in short, more going on in soldierly eulogies than meets the eye.

In using the language of ritual sacrifice, I do not mean to lend support to theories that Tillman's death was intentional.[26] Rather, my goal is to chart the relationship that a wide range of thinkers and writers forged with the dead Pat Tillman, to present religious dimensions of that relationship, and to demonstrate the highly ritualized ways in which Americans approach dead soldiers. Attention to commentaries on Tillman's life and death reveals a consistent ritual form with two distinguishable, if not always distinct, parts: (1) a proclamation of his ritual purity as a sacrificial victim and (2) a clear articulation of the societal sins for which his death atoned. The proclamation of purity is better understood as an assessment of ideological affinity, having far less to do with moral practices per se and a great deal to do with a commentator's ability to imagine Tillman in her/his image. The pronouncement of societal sins, a feature of the scapegoat ritual at least since its description in Leviticus, serves both to enhance the perceived purity of the sacrifice (he was *that* pure, we are *this* degraded) and to channel the power derived from the sacrifice toward a particular vision of social redemption. Ritual pronouncements on Tillman unfolded in predictably political ways. Some adopted a jeremiadic tone—lamenting the loss of courage, honor, virtue, love of country, and sacrificial spirit—and called Americans to a Tillman-like embodiment of these qualities. Others focused on corruption and abuses within the military and the federal government—highlighting the impoverished, ossified views of the nation/deity held by those who celebrated Tillman first—and called Americans to an embrace of Tillman-like truth-seeking and critique.

This phase of the Tillman story is both tragic and accusing. For if there is one additional commonality among those who took part in memorial rituals and authored memorial proclamations, it is that veneration of Tillman was often about using his memory as a weapon against political opponents with little regard for the complex man or for his family's desire to be precise in their memories of him. While these commentators were asserting that Tillman was uncommon, they were making a case for public ownership of his legacy as they understood it, arguing that he should be our new norm, our new common, and reminding those who listened that he had absorbed violence for us and washed America in his blood. The exotic Pat Tillman became a ritually pure sacrifice for the sins of twenty-first-century America. He was imagined this way for the legitimacy that his sacrifice could lend to accounts of America as it was and, more important, America as it should be.[27]

On April 21, 2004, Pat Tillman's story did not matter much beyond the locker rooms of the Arizona State Sun Devils and the Arizona Cardinals, and of course the Tillman family's homes. But when news came back on April 22 that Pat Tillman was dead on a hillside in Afghanistan, people all over the nation began to tell his story. And that story was a very shiny object. It was part Horatio Alger: Tillman was selected by the Arizona Cardinals in the seventh and final round of the NFL draft.[28] Seventh-round draft picks are not supposed to make the team, let alone succeed in the NFL, but Tillman did both and in his second full season set the team record for tackles. His story was also part rebuke to the greedy: he turned down a five-year, $9 million contract offer from the Saint Louis Rams for a three-year, $3.6 million contract with the Cardinals.[29] His story was, above all, a story of embodied civil religious devotion, for after playing out the first year of his new contract, the 2001 season, he walked away from the $1.2 million annual salary for the roughly $18,000 annual paycheck of a private in the U.S. Army. Serving the United States as an Army Ranger was worth a fortune to him. The AP article announcing his death reported, "The news of Tillman's death stunned those who knew him, and those who cheered him on," which is surely a true statement, but in the short arc of his adult life sacrifice had already been a theme (money, fame, comfort), and I suspect that many who knew him found meaning in the symmetry.[30]

Encomia to Pat Tillman came immediately from many corners. Bob Ferguson, the man who selected Tillman in the NFL draft, reacted by saying, "Pat represents all that is good with this country, our society and ultimately the human condition in general. . . . In today's world of instant gratification and selfishness, here is a man that [sic] was defined by words like loyalty, honor, passion, courage, strength, and nobility. He is a modern day hero." Arizona Cardinals president Michael Bidwill, the man who signed Tillman's last NFL paycheck, agreed: "He is a hero. . . . He was a brave man. There are very few people who have the courage to do what he did, the courage to walk away from a professional sports career and make the ultimate sacrifice."[31] Ann Coulter, writing for the conservative FrontPageMagazine .com, juxtaposed Tillman, "an American original—virtuous, pure, and masculine like only an American male can be," and former VVAW leader and recently defeated presidential candidate Senator John Kerry, whom she described as an "America-bashing trophy husband." Pat Tillman and Kerry were alike, she wrote, in that both were awarded a Silver Star. But Tillman, unlike Kerry, "did not write his own recommendation or live to throw his medals over the White House fence in an anti-war rally." She continued, "The stunningly handsome athlete . . . died bringing freedom to 28 million

Afghans. . . . There is not another country in the world . . . that could have produced a Pat Tillman."[32] Those professionally close to Tillman and those who had never met him saw in his death the loss of someone of exemplary civil religious purity.

There is, however, much more to notice about the structure and content of these memorial statements. Their authors were quite specific as to the contours of Tillman's purity and the sins for which his death atoned. Bob Ferguson described his purity in terms of masculine virtues and called him a representative of "all that is good" in humanity. According to Ferguson, Tillman bore America's sins of self-centeredness and instant gratification into the wilderness, showing the nation a deeper, truer way of living. For Michael Bidwill, bravery, a sacrificial spirit, and perhaps even his status as a professional athlete constituted Tillman's purity and made him fit to bear the national sin of insufficient courage. According to Ann Coulter, Pat Tillman could stand in for less virtuous Americans not only because he was the quintessentially American American man—bringing freedom to the oppressed and looking good doing it—but also because he so perfectly embodied civil religious orthodoxy as Coulter understood it. His heroism was a true, pure heroism, the kind verified by others, the fatal kind. Even if he had lived, Coulter implied, Tillman would never have lodged a critique against the war he had volunteered to wage. His embodiment of national virtue was too complete for such effeminate drivel. The meaning of Tillman's death was thus completely contained within familiar meaning-making devices and the timeless, almost ontological quality of the categories into which he was placed: purity, virtue, courage, loyalty, honor, strength, nobility, bravery, passion.[33]

On May 3, 2004, Arizona senator John McCain traveled to San Jose, California, for a nationally televised memorial service and delivered a brief eulogy that reiterated and expanded on the praises uttered by Bidwill, Ferguson, and Coulter. McCain noted that he was "poorer" for not having met Tillman and, as quoted above, listed Tillman's many virtues as a family member and a citizen. But as in the eulogies of Bidwill, Ferguson, and Coulter, McCain framed Tillman's virtue with ritual statements of societal vice. McCain spoke of "his uncommon choice of duty to his country over the profession he loved and the riches and comforts of celebrity." Sounding somewhat the Jeremiah, he noted, "We're not as familiar with courage as we once were. . . . Pat's best service to his country was to remind us all what courage really looks like." Finally, McCain averred that "Pat Tillman

6:2: Senator John McCain speaks at the memorial service for Pat Tillman, May 3, 2004. (AP Photo/Gene Lower, Pool)

understood his obligations . . . better than many of his contemporaries" and proclaimed, "We have to love our freedom, not just for the ease or material benefits it provides . . . but for the goodness it makes possible."[34] In death Tillman provided Americans with a "welcome lesson in courage and honor," a lesson that McCain hoped could strengthen the nation by increasing ritual devotion to it. McCain understood the suffering that Tillman's sacrifice caused and, in closing, attempted to provide solace with a generally Protestant portrayal of the afterlife. "And you will see him again, when a loving God reunites us all with the loved ones who preceded us in death." The sacrifice of Pat Tillman was more like a long-term loan that God would repay with interest.

But that which was once fully contained and interpreted according to civil religious orthodoxy soon burst its interpretive shell in three important ways. The first signs of rupture emerged at the memorial service. After McCain described the meaning of the soldierly sacrifice, Tillman's brother Rich offered a counterinterpretation that upended, among other things, the narrative of heavenly reunion. "Pat isn't with God. He's fucking dead. He wasn't religious. So thank you for your thoughts, but he's fucking dead."[35] This was an early indication of the Tillman family's discomfort with the rituals and doctrines of American civil religion and the relationship being forged between their son and the nation. Indeed, Lieutenant Colonel Ralph Kauzlarich, one of Tillman's commanders in Afghanistan and an important shaper of the official narrative of his heroism, came to see the Tillman family's lack of Christian faith and lack of faith in the nation as different sides of the same coin. Speaking about the Tillman case and the family's relentless questioning, Kauzlarich said that if one rejects the notion of a "better life" to follow this one, "what is there to go to? Nothing. You are worm dirt." He continued, "[In the Tillman family] there is not a lot of trust in the system or faith in the system."[36] Second, it soon came to the surface that Tillman harbored deep concerns about the war in Iraq, allegedly telling a fellow soldier it was "fucking illegal." These words posed problems for those who expected Tillman's voluntary military service to be an act of full-hearted devotion, and who had embraced him on this basis. Coulter's assertions to the contrary, Pat Tillman may have had quite a bit in common with John Kerry when it came to assessing the war he had waged. Finally, as discussed above, contrary to official reports that Tillman had died what Drew Gilpin Faust has termed a "good death," the army soon admitted that Tillman had been killed by American bullets.[37] This revelation raised an urgent question. Was the death once seen by some as a deeply meaningful, willing sacrifice indicative of the sins and virtues of the American people, actually meaningless? If a death is a mistake, can it also be a sacrifice?

Meaninglessness and soldierly death are uncomfortable bedfellows. We should not be surprised, then, that those who arrayed themselves against the early and orthodox portrayals of Tillman's life and death were equally eager to provide interpretations. Their pronouncements also framed Tillman as a ritual sacrifice, declaring his purity and naming the sins for which he died. In the eyes of this second group of interpreters, Tillman's ritual purity was verified by his apparent opposition to the war in Iraq, his affinity for left-leaning writers, and his lack of interest in Christianity. In an editorial titled "Pat Tillman, Our Hero," published eighteen months after Tillman was killed, the *Nation*'s Dave Zirin eulogized a very different Pat Tillman than the one lifted up initially. Zirin described a man who was critical of the war in Iraq, strongly anti-Bush, and "an avid reader whose interests ranged from history books . . . to the works of Noam Chomsky." This Tillman was "a critically thinking human being."[38] In Zirin's eyes these qualities—as much as his ability to make Ann Coulter "seethe"—marked Tillman as ritually pure. His sacrifice was an opportunity to enumerate national sins related to the war in Iraq and to highlight the Bush administration's dishonesty, which was painfully evident in its handling of Tillman's death. Politicians had told the Tillman family lies and treated them as "props" at a "charade" memorial service; "Pentagon spinmeisters and their media stenographers" had conspired to make Tillman a GI Joe and engaged in "callous manipulation" by committing themselves too much to the narrative of white football hero turned soldier. Zirin also saw Tillman's death as occasion to call attention to President Bush's sinfully false masculinity. Bush, he wrote, led an administration of emasculated "chicken hawks" whose spirit he embodied, "[He] loves the affectations of machismo but runs from protesting military moms."[39] Zirin did not call Bush a "trophy husband," but he worked just as hard as Ann Coulter had to feminize the ritually impure. Real men, like Pat Tillman, backed up words with actions. For our society's lies, failures to seek truth, and tolerance of a half-man as president, deadly violence fell on the head of "the real Pat Tillman."

A second set of left-leaning commentaries focused not on Tillman's masculinity, courage, and honor, but rather, as Lieutenant Colonel Kauzlarich had, on Tillman's religion. According to these commentaries, Tillman's sacrifice was closely related to the sin of "Christian Supremacism" in the military and the society the military purports to defend. On April 26, 2007, blogger Austin Cline, writing on atheism for About.com, took up the topic of "Pat Tillman, Christian Supremacism in the Military, and Atheists as Worm Food."[40] Cline used his essay to point out the dangers that a converted military posed to "not just secular, civil government, but also a religiously pluralistic society in America." He also noted several instances of intolerance of religions other than "conservative, evangelical Christianity," in which he saw a pattern of "anti-atheist, religious bigotry" in the military. In the eyes of Cline, Tillman's sacrifice offered an opportunity to describe and address this bigotry. But like Coulter on the one side and Zirin on the other, Cline needed a ritually pure Tillman for this sacrifice to be efficacious. His intratextual fashioning of Pat Tillman's religiosity is evidence of his deep desire for an atheist, and therefore pure, Tillman. Cline did not know the details of Tillman's religiosity at the time that he wrote. He acknowledged this early in his piece—"It should be noted that the Tillman family hasn't said whether they are atheists or not. They may be or they may not be"—and wrote later, with reference to Christian "supremacist" perceptions, "Ultimately . . . it doesn't really matter if Pat Tillman was an atheist or not. . . . The fact that [the Tillman's] are not Christians . . .

was sufficient for them to be treated as inferior to Christians." Nationalist Christians had fashioned a confirmed atheist and substituted him for a possible atheist. Perhaps, but then Cline pulled a similar switch. "What's really got to be sticking in the craw of these people is the contradiction between the real Pat Tillman and the mythological Pat Tillman they tried to create. The real Pat Tillman was an atheist who, after getting to the Middle East, perceived the truth and described the invasion of Iraq as 'so fucking illegal.' The real Pat Tillman was inconvenient."[41] Yes, he was. And few were willing to be inconvenienced by their G.I. Messiah.

Of Purity and Glory

Jon Krakauer's *Where Men Win Glory: The Odyssey of Pat Tillman* is a thorough account of Tillman's life, service, and the scandal that followed his death. It is an impressive work of biography, augmented with discussions of wars gone wrong in Iraq and Afghanistan. Jon Krakauer uses his considerable skills as a researcher and writer to craft an exceptionalist narrative par excellence, seeing Pat Tillman as a rugged idealist betrayed twice, even three times over, by the nation he sought to serve. Krakauer is an eloquent chronicler of the human condition as it is expressed in and against unforgiving landscapes. As a longtime, up-close observer of outdoor life, he has looked for, studied, and often judged those who share his love for the wilderness, for risk taking, for adventure. Coursing through Krakauer's writings is a belief, inherited from Fredrick Jackson Turner, G. Stanley Hall, Theodore Roosevelt, and more generally, the Muscular Christianity movement of the early twentieth century that such environments reveal and refine character and that those who have encountered and conquered these environments deserve a special place in American culture.[42]

Moreover, Krakauer is aware of and engaged with the ritual rhetorical structures present in the pronouncements of Coulter, McCain, Zirin, Cline, and others. Most renderings of Pat Tillman, Krakauer writes, have been constructed in support of political agendas using partial understandings of the man. "Unencumbered by biographical insight, people felt emboldened to invent all manner of personae for Tillman after his passing. Most of these renderings were based on little more than rumor and fantasy. The right-wing harridan Ann Coulter claimed him as an exemplar of Republican political values. The left-wing editorial cartoonist Ted Rall denigrated him in a four-panel comic strip as an 'idiot' who joined the army to 'kill Arabs.'

Neither Coulter nor Rall had any idea what motivated Pat Tillman."[43] This last statement aside, Krakauer's description is spot on. Men and women from all corners of the political world invented a Pat Tillman who was, in one way or another, incomplete. These inventions were not, as Krakauer asserts, unrelated to the whole Pat Tillman, but the particulars they emphasized were largely determined by a priori conceptions of American sin and American virtue.

Yet, as Krakauer sets out to address the problem of a distorted Tillman fashioned from selectively emphasized facts, he often engages in a more subtle version of the process he critiques. To be clear, there is no comparison between Krakauer and Zirin or Coulter on the deeply relevant questions of genre and biographic detail. One author, Krakauer, cared about the details of Pat Tillman's life. The others cared about a much smaller subset of details. But this difference in genre and in degree of attention does not render the presence of the Levitical scapegoating dynamic any less relevant. Instead it forces questions of the depth of the influence of the G.I. Messiah and our own enmeshment in the ritual structures and social dynamics of ritual sacrifice in spite of our best intentions. As much as any commentator on Tillman, Krakauer needs a ritually pure soldier to bear the sins of the nation.

The Pat Tillman who died for Jon Krakauer's America was smart, fit, capable, confident, idealistic, and fearless. He was a perfect balance of the civilized and the savage. According to Krakauer's account, Tillman displayed this balance almost out of the womb and maintained and perfected it throughout his youth and adolescence.[44] As early twentieth-century theorists would have claimed and as Krakauer echoes, Tillman's regular ventures into the canyons around his home and, eventually, his exploits on the football field provided the physical challenges and controlled violence that allowed him to grow into the civilized, masculine man he became.[45] The Tillman family exercised their intellects in "clamorous discussions" where Pat learned not to be afraid to "buck the herd." Outdoors, on the field, and in occasional fights they exercised their bodies. And there was virtue in the fighting. "Despite Pat's quickness to resort to fists, he was in many ways the antithesis of the bully . . . he fought only kids who were bigger than he was, and on several occasions he intervened to rescue nerdy classmates who were being hassled by older, larger tormentors. But when Pat fought, he fought to win and never capitulated."[46] This balanced, truth-seeking, noble Tillman—an embodiment of the proper use of American power—is the ritually pure Tillman, the perfect sacrifice for an unquestioning, sedentary, bully nation.

In writing Tillman's story, though, Krakauer had to account for moments of imbalance and potential impurity. His treatment of two incidents in particular evidences a struggle to explain flaws in the scapegoat hero without troubling or polluting the sacrifice. The first of these incidents occurred in 1993 when Tillman was seventeen. While out with a group on a November night, Tillman severely beat a nineteen-year-old man, Darin Rosas, whom he mistakenly believed to be roughing up a friend. A witness recounts, "Darin was on the ground and Pat was kicking him, so I jumped in between them to try to stop it. . . . Darin was sort of curled on his side in a fetal position . . . and Pat kept kicking him in the face and chest and stomach. He was enraged, absolutely enraged."[47] Tillman was charged with felony assault and was eventually convicted of a reduced charge. In the hands of Krakauer, this incident becomes a case of virtue improperly regulated.

> Much of Pat's brilliance on the football field derived from his uncanny ability to anticipate the moves of opposing players, react without hesitation, and tackle the ball carrier with a tooth-rattling hit. But Pat had just turned seventeen, and like those of other kids that age, his dorsal lateral prefrontal cortex—the region of the brain that weighs consequences—was far from fully developed. In this instance, his dubious adolescent judgment was further distorted by both alcohol and his conviction that one of his duties in life was to be the protector of the vulnerable, the guardian of his friends and family. The upshot was that Pat flattened the wrong guy.[48]

According to Krakauer and those he interviewed, Tillman was immediately sorry and learned from the short time he spent in jail. Nothing about the incident as Krakauer describes and accounts for it reflects anything significant about Tillman. Blame it on an underdeveloped dorsal lateral prefrontal cortex, a bit of booze, and misdirected chivalry.

Krakauer describes a second impurity in less detail, though it reflects just as clearly his desire to find in Tillman the perfect balance of spirit and flesh. This incident took place roughly six years later when Tillman, now a professional football player, was hiking with his brother Kevin. The two came upon a pine tree growing up from the canyon floor to the height of the canyon rim where they were walking. Tillman decided to jump from the rim to the tree. (Jumping from high places was a regular activity for Tillman, though he generally jumped into water.) This was a risky undertaking for anyone; doubly risky for someone whose career was so tightly connected to physical health. Krakauer narrates, "After several long minutes, he approached the edge yet again and then launched himself into the void with all the power he could generate." But Tillman had "jumped harder than necessary, causing him to slam into the tree with excessive force. He held on, but it wasn't pretty." Explaining the why of this harder-than-necessary jump, Krakauer writes not of misjudged distances or misjudged strength, but rather cites the fact that "so much adrenaline was surging through his bloodstream."[49]

Krakauer clearly loves the rugged individual and sees Tillman as a prime example thereof. Yet he turns to lay neurology when faced with the violent Pat Tillman, the man who made a living in a violent game, the man who moved from that violent game into the violent profession of the military seeking involvement in violence. Krakauer loves the deep-thinking Pat Tillman, the man whose thirst for knowledge seemed unquenchable. Yet he turns to lay endocrinology when looking upon a man who made bad judgments and sometimes lost sight of his limits. In Krakauer's skillful authorial hands these qualities become accidents, not essentials, the result of physiological tics rather than expressions of imbalance, however temporary.

It is not my point that Jon Krakauer invented his Pat Tillman from whole cloth. He didn't. Rather, he described a Pat Tillman who could properly, purely, bear the sins of the Bush administration and Bush-led America. These sins can be stated as the opposites of Tillman's virtues, but they revolve most tightly around judgment, truth, and faith. Tillman sought truth tenaciously; the Bush administration fled from and manufactured it. Tillman economized belief, withholding it from things (most things) remote; the Bush administration lavished belief on the unseen and asked America and the world to do the same. Tillman exercised sound judgment based on sound mind and sound body; the Bush administration miscalculated, took unnecessary risks, and failed. And an America torn between timidity and bellicosity, indulgence and prudishness, credulity and cynicism went along with Bush, sacrificed Tillman, and realized too late the mistake it had made.

From Scapegoat to Savior

The traditions of ritual sacrifice, René Girard has observed, have long been bound up with purity, sin, substitution, and at a deeper level, with efforts to relieve social tension.[50] Violence done to a third party, a scapegoat, allows two conflicting parties to articulate their grievances, obtain some measure of satisfaction for them, shed some blood, and to live on in relative peace. The death and postmortem cooptation of Pat Tillman present these themes within an American civil religious context, making uncommonly clear just how persistent they are. The safety became a soldier, the soldier became a scapegoat whose sacrifice provided an opportunity for various priesthoods to describe American virtue, rail against American sin, and call America back to some vision of collective glory. The conversation could end here but for one matter. Pat Tillman was not a goat. He did not bleat as he died. According to one Ranger, he shouted repeatedly, "'I'm Pat fucking Tillman, damn it!'" The witness continued, "He said this over and over again until he stopped."[51]

Public treatments of Pat Tillman as a ritual sacrifice, an American scapegoat, obscure the fact that Tillman was a complex individual who made choices and, like all of us, had many sides. A *New York Times* story written at the beginning of Tillman's military career made this point more clearly than any of the postmortem material considered here. The author, Mike Freeman, described Tillman as "a strange, at times contradictory blend of machismo and humility, of ego and selflessness." Freeman continued, "By joining the Army, Tillman has a lot of people—both in and out of the sports world—calling him a hero while simultaneously questioning his sanity."[52] Death did one thing to Pat Tillman beyond destroying his body: it flattened his voice. According to his brother Kevin, Tillman was aware that "fighting as a soldier would leave us without a voice," and we cannot ignore the extent to which Tillman was complicit in his own muting—refusing interviews, asking family members not to speak, and so on[53]—and, therefore, in the process by which he became a symbol.

The lingering question—a question of significant civil religious urgency—is whether Tillman's voice or the voice of any fallen soldier can be fully recovered, somehow disentangled from the interpretive webs of American civil religion. I suspect that the answer in Tillman's case is no and that the prognosis for other, less famous modern soldiers isn't much better. But we can, I hope, see modern civil religious scapegoat rituals for what they are, critique them, and look again at the life and death of a soldier. I have tried to do this with Pat Tillman, and I have arrived at a few tentative observations about the man and the soldier. In life, Pat Tillman was unpredictable. He chose a very big salary over an even bigger salary. He then chose a very small salary over the very big salary. He chose the deadly violence of an army at war over the merely injurious violence of the NFL. He chose silence over clarification. He chose change over stasis. He chose obedience to military authorities over active dissent. But he did not choose blind devotion. What more can we say? Perhaps we can hazard that in life and in death Pat Tillman testified to the importance of serving a higher good and wrestling with that higher good when its goodness seemed suspect. To carry the analysis one step further, he seems to have seen the service and the wrestling as of a piece, challenging both those who would serve without wrestling and those who would wrestle without serving.

Pat Tillman's story also challenges the families of soldiers, living and fallen. The Tillmans grieved their son, brother, husband. They mourned him publicly. But they resisted efforts to narrate his death according to civil religious orthodoxy. When the nation claimed his body, they dug in their heels, making counterclaim after counterclaim. This is an immense burden for families to bear in the face of world-altering losses, but it is its own form of devotion to nation and to soldier, and it may, in the end, bring its own form of redemption. The Tillmans' struggle did not end in a public triumph. There was no permanent, public shaming of Pat Tillman's chain of command. But their efforts brought to the surface things usually buried and reminded those paying attention of the full humanity of Pat Tillman and of his irrevocable connectedness to a family, not a nation, to stories, not myths.

In the twenty-first century the tools for making such civil religious counterclaims are more abundant than ever. The voices woven into this chapter made use of the Internet, of mass media, and of legal processes to apply pressure to those content with the common narratives of civil religious orthodoxy. As troubling and as firmly rooted in scapegoating rituals as were the uses of Tillman, the avenues by which commentators disseminated their interpretations encourage, or at least allow, an unprecedented degree of engagement with the lives and deaths of soldiers and a high degree of civil religious pluralism.

And still the G.I. Messiah rises. After the release of Amir Bar-Lev's documentary *The Pat Tillman Story*, Tillman's younger brother Richard (he of the profanity-laced counter-eulogy) appeared on the *Bill Maher Show* to discuss his brother and the making of the film. The self-proclaimed atheist did not have a beer in hand as he did at Pat's funeral, but he was as ready as he had been six years earlier to jar the audience. Sharing his feelings about his brother, Richard announced, "I think he's fucking Jesus . . . and I don't even think there's a Jesus. He was the real Jesus." To a cheering throng of a studio audience, Tillman the Younger preached Tillman the G.I. Messiah. National sacrifice? Clearly. Personal savior? Yes, that too.

Of Flesh, Words, and Wars

While traveling home from Washington, D.C., in early August 2014, I found myself in an exceptionally crowded corner of Washington National Airport. The skies were clear and it wasn't a holiday weekend, so I was confused and a bit dismayed that the area around my gate was so full of other travelers. The reason for the crowding became clearer to me as I noticed a large number of men —perhaps one hundred of them— wearing red T-shirts and the navy blue, mesh-back baseball hats that are common in the military. The crowd consisted of veterans, Vietnam veterans mostly, whom a national airline was treating to an "honor flight." The veterans and their spouses had been flown from Oshkosh, Wisconsin, to the nation's capital and given a tour of the "powerful memorials dedicated in their honor."[1] They were now preparing to fly home from the same gate as my not-honor flight, which explained the red, white, and blue bunting around the door to the jet bridge.

The veterans' shirts announced their participation in the honor flight program and proclaimed, by way of civil religious reminder, "It's never too late to say thank you." The mood of the group was jovial. I heard no stories of war or its tragedies. I saw no signs of trauma or of old animosities bubbling to the surface. It was just a group of men and their wives, milling about, enjoying the camaraderie, checking their cell phones, waiting to fly.

Conspicuous in the crowd was one man wearing sunglasses, an olive-drab baseball cap, and a T-shirt that did not match the uniform of those around him. The back of his shirt showed the outline of a soldier in combat gear carrying what looked to be an M-16. The figure was superimposed over a cross. Above the scene were words from the Gospel of John, "Greater love hath no man than this: that a man lay down his life for his friends." I studied it for minutes, transfixed.

I know little of the life stories of the men and women from Wisconsin who populated the terminal that Friday afternoon, beyond the fact that soldiering and war figured in their lives. I know little more of the man with the soldier-cross T-shirt, though I assume he is a Christian. Still, this unexpected crowd of people confronted me not only with a fascinating embodied expression of American civil religion—I have never been happier to stand in the middle of an airport crowd—but also with the methodological conundrum and the argument of this book.

Draped on the body of one man was a presentation of soldiering as thick with Christian theology as one could hope to see in an airport terminal. There, on a T-shirt, standing before a cross, was a battle-ready American soldier. Lest one mistakenly assume that the soldier just happened upon a cross while out on patrol, the scriptural quotation explained, using words attributed to Jesus, that a man (a soldier) shows the world its greatest love when he "lays down his life" (dies in combat). The coming together of the soldier, the cross, and the Gospel words accomplishes an impressive amount. At the intersection of symbol and scripture, death in war is sanitized. It is made an act of willing. The soldier does not have life torn, blown, cut, or crushed from him. He is not burned to death or atomized by an enemy shell. Rather, he lays life down. At this same intersection, soldiering for America is sanctified. The shirt presented the soldier as living and ready to fight, but death was an implied possibility for him. He had not yet demonstrated that greater love, but the image encourages us to devotion nonetheless. It is not only dying that demonstrates love. It is the willingness to die, telegraphed by the accouterments of soldiering for America. What is a citizen to do when confronted with such an intensely embodied, but implied, love? Emulate it? Admire it? Express gratitude for it? More numerous in the terminal by far—and more noticeable because of their large numbers—were the red T-shirts, shirts that unified a group and set them apart from fellow travelers, shirts that described the appropriate civil religious attitude—gratitude toward the soldier—and served simultaneously as material evidence that someone, somewhere had lived out that ethic. These red T-shirts rendered men who had been to war visible and mapped a simple route to civil religious redemption. "It's never too late," the shirts counseled, "to say thank you."

I have argued throughout this book that we must see the overtly Christian civil religious moments woven throughout the twentieth century, and cultural objects like the soldier-cross T-shirt, not as relics or cottony coincidences but as indications of the theological threads out of which the relationship between America and the American soldier is woven. These threads run through the past century. They are part of the fabric of America's memorials and commemorative rituals. They connect spoken, written, and symbolic discourse. They give American civil religion much of its binding power and emotional force. The two T-shirts are distinct, but their messages and the civil religious tendencies they present demonstrate that they contain the same thread. American attention to the soldier and the meaning of his actions builds upon notions of redemptive suffering and sacrifice that are recognizably Christian, but this attention is often expressed in an idiom of civic ecumenism. Our understandings of what soldiers have done or might do, and of the proper response to those actions—an absolutely central civil religious practice—parallels a generally Christian stance toward the figure of Jesus. As symbols of American civil religion, soldiers must participate in this dynamic of sacrifice and gratitude. As practitioners they must configure their actions and attitudes in relationship to complex and diverse experiences of war and to the demands of soldiering.

Soldiering and the Present Past

This group and their T-shirts also confronted me with the reality that the history described in this book is a history that reaches persistently into the present even as it is reshaped and reimagined by a waxing and waning American empire. The nation, its citizens, politicians, and major corporations work to settle old accounts with former soldiers, to provide meaningful rituals of reintegration—an honor flight, for instance—and belated expressions of gratitude—bunting, a party, a T-shirt. As mythic warriors age and new warriors seek treatment for their wounds, the nation must reckon with other unsettled accounts. When reports of neglect in a Phoenix-area VA hospital surfaced in early 2014, crisis followed close behind. The problems were systemic, not local, and commentators wondered how the nation could be so neglectful of those who have given so much. The soldier remains a revered and, in some respects, a privileged figure in society, one whose work is consecrated to the nation; one whose injuries are tended by the nation; one whose willingness to serve and, potentially, "lay down his life," citizens, politicians, and soldiers themselves recognize, admire, and venerate. When the health care system expands to cover salesmen and part-time teachers, the nation is being hijacked. When the health care system in place for veterans contracts or falters, the nation is betraying its heroes.

The release of Sergeant Bowe Bergdahl was front-page news of a different sort. Held five years by the Taliban after disappearing under questionable circumstances, Bergdahl was freed on May 31, 2014, in exchange for five detainees held at Guantanamo Bay. *Time* magazine used its cover to ask, "Was he worth it?" Veterans of the war in Afghanistan angrily blamed the deaths of friends on Bergdahl, claiming that efforts to find him had led them into dangers they would otherwise have avoided.[2] Congress spoke again of executive overreach. Letters to the editors of major and minor newspapers went back and forth on the exchange. Some saw it as unproblematic, the kind of thing that a nation ought to do to "bring the boys home." In the eyes of others, the terms of Bergdahl's redemption were a clear sign that the terrorists had won. More than five decades after Francis Gary Powers fell from the sky and then from American grace, Bowe Bergdahl's capture and release prompted similar questions and concerns. Had civil religious infidelity led him into captivity? Did he stand firm when tempted in the wilderness? Or had he become a traitor, a G.I. Judas? Could he be redeemed and reintegrated? Should he be? As the focus of veneration and as sites for expressing the values and anxieties of the nation, soldiers matter immensely in American civil religion. And every indication is that stories of the American soldier will remain prominent fixtures of our news cycle.

The foreign policy issues that confront the United States in the second decade of the twenty-first century are complex and dangerous. It is as if the world is marking the centenary of the Great War by creating the conditions for another Great War or two. Fighting in Ukraine, Syria, and Israel has re-primed old pumps of hatred and ill will; amidst civil chaos in Syria a grotesque caricature of an Islamist movement has gained power, land, and a perverse legitimacy. A deadly virus is on the rampage in West Africa, bringing agonizing death and fear to communities already plagued by poverty. In spite of the gloom, one can look at these situations and conclude that the world has come a long way since 1914. The conflicts are, for the most part, local. Mechanisms of deterrence (diplomatic, economic, and military) are in place and have been effective. Ebola is not yet threatening to become a global pandemic on the order of the Spanish flu. The most powerful nations in the world are not lined up against each other on the battlefield.

Yet one can also look at these same situations and wonder what one hundred years of soldierly suffering and sacrifice has accomplished. Are we on the doorstep of a thousand-year reign of peace? Is this what salvation looks like? Because military achievements are and will continue to be this-worldly, theologically inflected questions about them often seem jarring. But such questions are fully in line with expectations set by American civil religion and directed through the American soldier over the past century. Through him the nation hoped to build and defend a better world, a world of progress, a world with less evil in it. Through him the nation has tried to bring salvation, if not to eternal souls, at least to oppressed bodies and benighted minds,. As of this writing, American soldiers are preparing new iterations of old saving works on battlefields that are too familiar. American military personnel are planning coalition operations to degrade and destroy the Islamic State in Iraq and Syria (ISIS). President Barack Obama recently told a gathering of NATO nations that overt incursions from Russia into Ukraine and the Baltic states would trigger a military response. "An attack on one is an attack on all," he said, "and so if, in such a moment, you ever ask again, 'Who'll come to help?' you'll know the answer: the NATO alliance, including the armed forces of the United States of America."[3] American soldiers continue to wage war in Afghanistan, thirteen years after the initial invasion. In addition to all of this, American soldiers have traveled to West Africa to build Ebola treatment centers.

The foreign policy problems facing the United States are enormous. But the men and women whose bodies are needed to resolve these problems are not. They are as limited, as finite, as flawed as other Americans. The American soldier is and has been nothing more and nothing less than a person who can fight and kill, damage and repair, love and hate, suffer and die. The cases presented in this book make this point abundantly clear. They also make clear that Americans working out what it means to be good Americans often struggle to see this full humanity. I have argued that these soldiers and their observers practice American civil religion as they imagine and enact soldiering, and that the space between the imagined and the enacted, though it continues to fill with myths, symbols, and echoes, is a deep and dangerous place. The stories of Charles Whittlesey and Pat Tillman demonstrate as clearly as any from this long American century the power of civil religious orthodoxy and its martial mythology to draw someone toward war, the strength of a person to bear up under war's strains, and the thrill Americans derive from witnessing embodied civil religious devotion. At the same time, these stories show clearly the precariousness of it all: rituals go wrong; adulation depresses the living and devours the dead; individual soldiers are victimized by symbolizing processes that have no interest in tensions or complexities within the symbolized. These dynamics reach into the present as well. The narratives they feed have an eerie familiarity.

Salvatore Giunta received the Congressional Medal of Honor in November 2010. He was the first living recipient of the honor since the Vietnam War. What he did on October 25, 2007, is recounted in his award citation. While on patrol in Afghanistan's Korengal Valley, Giunta and his squad were ambushed "by a well-armed and well-coordinated insurgent force." After an initial engagement with the enemy, Giunta "exposed himself to withering enemy fire" in order to protect and treat his injured squad leader. He then rejoined the fight. In the midst of continued heavy fighting, Giunta and his squad advanced to treat other wounded soldiers, but realized that one of their own was missing. At this point, Giunta broke from the squad and rushed forward. "As he crested the top of a hill," the citation reads, "he observed two insurgents carrying away an American soldier. He immediately engaged the enemy, killing one and wounding the other. Upon reaching the wounded soldier, he began to provide medical aid, as his squad caught up and provided security." Three years after that day of deadly combat, Giunta stood before President Obama who presented the medal and confessed, "I really like this guy."[4]

An Associated Press article from January 2011 described Salvatore Giunta's life since news of the award began to break. People suddenly wanted to be near him: President Obama, David Letterman, Stephen Colbert; they wanted to tell and to hear and to marvel at his story. When he wasn't appearing on national television and receiving praise from the famous and the powerful, he was attending receptions in Times Square and at the Iowa State House; he even appeared on the field as part of the Super Bowl XLV halftime show. Giunta went to these events because this is what civil religion demands of the G.I. Messiah. But he spoke too of the burdens of heroism, the darker side of incarnation. "I've never seen anyone else asked what was the worst day in your life and let's break it down piece by piece and please go into detail. . . . For some reason they continually ask me every single day and multiple times a day." Giunta continued, "I lost two friends that day. They mean absolutely everything and people brush by their names. And they keep saying 'Giunta. Staff Sgt. Giunta.' That doesn't feel right." At the end of his enlistment, Giunta separated from the army and decided to return to college.[5]

Public venerations of the G.I. Messiah are complicated, multivalent matters. It is too easy to think of them as ritual moments that "honor," "remember," even "worship" the truest of Americans. Though these moments clearly celebrate, they can also bewilder and exhaust the person or people at whom they are directed, raising questions about the purpose of the ritual and how much of the soldier the nation truly celebrates. To what extent is the ritual concerned with "the flesh," the embodied practitioner of American civil religion? To what extent does the ritual serve only to celebrate the enduring righteousness of the word, made mighty by uniformed flesh? To what extent did Americans want to see and be near Salvatore Giunta not because of who he is but because in doing what he did and surviving he gave life to and validated their faith?

The story of another staff sergeant made the front page of the *New York Times* the same day that the profile of Giunta appeared on the AP wire. Staff Sergeant David Senft, two years Giunta's senior and the product of a tumultuous California childhood, joined the army following the September 11 attacks. He eventually deployed as a Blackhawk helicopter crewman, once to Iraq and twice to Afghanistan. It is reasonable to believe that he encountered the familiar recruitment pitches—to be an army of one, live the adventure, aim high—and that he found those pitches not incompatible with his desire to grow, mature, accomplish, even escape. Yet friends and family could tell that wartime service was not changing him for the better. They saw that his life-altering experiences of combat, his baptisms of fire, were layering trauma upon trauma. Fellow soldiers also noticed that he was struggling. Senft was a sensitive person and was deeply troubled by some of the gruesome scenes he encountered in Iraq. He spoke of suicide and attempted it twice; he missed a deployment to Iraq because of his mental health and spent time in a treatment center. Senft deployed to Afghanistan in 2010, came home on leave, married, and then returned to complete his tour. On November 15, 2010, he was found dead in an SUV on Khandahar Air Base, a single bullet hole in his head. His suicide note, the article explains, was a text message.[6]

Much has been written and reported about the increased suicide rate in the military since the wars in Afghanistan and Iraq began over a decade ago.[7] One theme that emerges in the reporting was expressed by General Peter

Chiarelli, then army vice chief of staff, "Each suicide is as unique as the individuals themselves."[8] While it is hard to disagree with that statement—a close look at suicide notes written in ink or on phones would surely support Chiarelli and the individualist interpretation—it is also important to note the ways that it subtly shores up the mythology of the G.I. Messiah. Self-sacrificial heroes such as Salvatore Giunta capture and express a national and communal ideal. Through the acts they author with their bodies, we see the best of America. Suicides, those who literally self-sacrifice, represent nothing beyond their own struggles. They are "unique." They are "individuals." They are separated from or anomalies in the midst of the heroic enterprise of waging war, the fruit of a ritual gone wrong, a rite of passage interrupted.

Incarnation and Excarnation

From a historical vantage point much different than our own, Reverend Aaron Allen Heist described soldiering for America in intensely Christological terms. In "Present Day Incarnation," his sermon for Christmas Day 1919, he spoke of the ideals of the nation becoming flesh in the doughboy: "It was when the Word became flesh," he preached, "that the Word became mighty." What Giunta, Senft, the other soldiers considered in this book, and, I submit, hundreds of thousands more help us to see is another side of the civil religious incarnational theology toward which Reverend Heist gestured in 1919, something more aptly described as *excarnation*. By excarnation I mean the extraction from the soldierly body of that which the nation, the military included, understands to be its spirit and the re-presentation of that spirit to devoted publics within and beyond the military. Excarnation is necessarily selective, necessarily careless of human particularities. It is the edge of American civil religion that cuts the soldier as it attempts to heal him. But excarnation does not describe a sacrificial system. It does not point to an a priori national need for blood or for broken bodies, a need that is satisfied when soldiers die in combat. Rather, the national need for these elements is synchronous with and defined by the bleeding and the breaking, and it grows larger and more complete the more complete the bleeding and the breaking are. Moreover, the power and efficacy of excarnation depends as much on the narration of the sacrificial act as on the act itself. Spilled blood and broken bodies are never sufficient in themselves as elements of American civil religion. They must be made intelligible by blood preserved and bodies kept whole, by the witness who transforms blood into ink, the survivor whose uniformed body stands in for the fallen.

I am aware of and concerned about the possibility that this book participates in something like the incarnational/excarnational dynamic it describes: perpetuating myths, giving added strength to symbols, investing in bodies meanings that are not their own; doing civil religious hagiography in a less orthodox register. I have told a history and built an argument based on stories of lives and descriptions of embodied action, not the lives and the bodies themselves. There is no way around the need to present something less than the whole of these things, and in doing so losing something, obscuring some relevant detail. But I have tried to tell these stories with attention to human particularity and agency, balancing discussion of the symbols and discussion of the people. When Robert Bellah wrote that American civil religion "requires the same care in understanding that any other religion does," he likely did not envision a turn to practice, the soldier, and war.[9] If my reading of the tradition is decidedly different than his, I hope at least to have lived up to his call for "care in understanding."

Where I have indeed fallen short and must ask forgiveness of readers (and several former shipmates) is in describing and theorizing the effect of women in uniform on the G.I. Messiah and on American civil religion more generally. The story of Felicita Hecht, presented at the beginning of chapter 3, reminds us that the actors in American wars are not all male and that the stakes for women waging war for America have been very high and also, most often, distinct. But with combat roles officially open to women since 2013, the usual and pervasive gendering of soldiering as male encounters a rather significant challenge.[10] I am not one to underestimate the power of myth and symbol to adapt to new realities, and it remains to be seen if the reclassification of combat roles (something of a relic of old frontal models of waging war) will affect the number of women who are involved in combat.[11] If women become much more prominent in America's combat efforts, how will American civil religion respond? Will narratives of female suffering in war follow well-worn domestic tropes where women's roles, wherever they are lived out, are primarily supportive, their wounds primarily emotional? Will we see further elaborations on New World captivity narratives, stories of kidnapping and life among "savages," as was the case in the capture and rescue of Private Jessica Lynch?[12] Or will American martial mythology expand to encompass a new norm in which women kill, suffer, and die heroically as they wage war for the nation? Will the nation embrace a woman soldier who fights and saves like Daniel Edwards, Dwight Johnson, or Salvatore Giunta? How will female practitioners of American civil religion engage and contest the tradition with their bodies and their words?

America's ongoing commitments in the world all but guarantee future opportunities to observe the evolution of soldiers as symbols and as practitioners of American civil religion and to describe and discuss the often destructive tension between these two modes. If there is a reliable way to reconfigure the dynamics of soldiering for America, to alter excarnational practices and rhetorics in American civil religion, I have not yet encountered it. Will better theology change the contours of citizens' devotion to the United States and to those who wear its uniform? Will awareness of ritual language make recruits alert to the commitments they make and represent with their bodies? Will pointing to the connections between scapegoating rituals and eulogies for the notable fallen halt the rush to claim a dead soldier for this platform or that cause? The problem in these cases is not just that theology is always culturally situated, that ritual and rhetorical patterns have deep roots and powerful, world-ordering effects. The problem, if we want to call it a problem, is that the symbolized soldier, the soldier practitioner, and American civil religion more broadly do not work only for ill, do not call forth only, or even mainly, national and personal demons. The soldier also presents qualities that Americans of diverse cultural backgrounds and political inclinations admire: communalism, devotion to a cause, altruism. In this less militant register—evident in earthquake and tsunami relief in Indonesia, the developing Ebola intervention in West Africa—the soldier can inspire a public to benevolent action, remind a public of the importance of people and realities larger than themselves, and relieve a public concerned that such virtues have been routed from American life by rampant, selfish individualism. Symbols and the people they generalize are mixtures of truth and falsehood, virtue and vice: they can express rancor and sow division; they can also foster understanding and encourage reconciliation.

For now perhaps it is enough to have recognized a phenomenon, shown its deep rooting in American Christianities and its centrality to American civil religion, and prompted some critical reflection to go along with the quite appropriate pride and respect the circulates around, among, and within soldiers. My hope is that future engagements with American civil religion will turn to the complex humanity that continues beneath and beyond the uniform and will notice the fact that respect and gratitude can cut both ways, drawing the soldier just this close, holding the soldier just that far away. Knowing her well enough to name her death a tragedy, but not knowing her well enough to recognize when mourning becomes using. Knowing him well enough to ask that he bear our sins, but not knowing him well enough to see, or to care, that he has plenty of his own to carry.

Notes

Introduction

1. A WorldCat search during the second week of January 2014 yielded 3,530 books published since 2003 that have "America" and "war" as part of their designated subject. During the same period 4,734 books were published with "America" and "military" in the subject listing. These numbers include some duplicates. A separate WorldCat search during the same week yielded 1,431 books published since 2003 that have "America" and "religion" as part of their designated subject. It proved impossible to answer with perfect precision the number of titles on religion in the United States and the number of titles on war or the military and America, but a ratio of roughly 1:3 seems to hold with reasonably limited search criteria.

2. For excellent resources on the development and deployment of images of the warrior in American history, see Jason K. Dempsey, *Our Army: Soldiers, Politics, and American Civil-Military Relations* (Princeton: Princeton University Press, 2012); Andrew J. Huebner, *The Warrior Image: Soldiers in American Culture from the Second World War to the Vietnam Era* (Chapel Hill: The University of North Carolina Press, 2008); Edward T. Linenthal, *Changing Images of the Warrior Hero in America: A History of Popular Symbolism* (New York: E. Mellen, 1982).

3. Dempsey, *Our Army*, xv; Linenthal, *Changing Images of the Warrior Hero in America*, 120.

4. Joan W. Scott, "Fantasy Echo: History and the Construction of Identity," *Critical Inquiry* 27, no. 2 (Winter 2001): 284–304; Samuel Stayman, "A Comparison of Judas Maccabeus and Geo. Washington," *Jewish Advocate*, July 25, 1918, 3; *Stars and Stripes*, August 2, 1918, August 9, 1918, February 28, 1919; Melinda Pash, *In the Shadow of the Greatest Generation: The Americans Who Fought the Korean War* (New York: New York University Press, 2012), 11, 12, 21.

5. John Bodnar, *The "Good War" in American Memory* (Baltimore: Johns Hopkins University Press, 2010).

6. Samuel P. Huntington, *The Soldier and the State: The Theory and Politics of Civil-Military Relations* (Cambridge: The Belknap Press of Harvard University Press, 1957), 222–69. Huntington's chapter, titled "The American Military Profession," describes well these developments and the resistance to them. "The ability of the professional officers and their impressive record in leading the forces and conducting the operations of the two world wars were acquired because of, not despite, their rejection at the end of the nineteenth century" (230).

7. Ibid. Huntington connects negative attitudes toward the military, ranging from dismissiveness to disdain, both to the attitudes of Thomas Jefferson and Andrew Jackson and to the rise and influence of big business which, out of self-interest, was eager to portray war and militaries as things of the past. This critique fits Huntington's overall juxtaposition of military communalism and clear-eyed responsibility with America's wide-ranging and persistent selfish individualism. He writes of the early twentieth century, "The arrogance, individualism, and commercialism of American society gave the military the outlook of an estranged minority" (268).

8. Ibid., 193–211. Here Huntington details Jeffersonian and Jacksonian concerns about a standing army and the alternatives they proposed. Huntington is also quite clear about the practical problems of these alternatives, to wit: an ill-prepared, ill-equipped army run by inept political appointees.

9. Ibid., 193–211, 222–30, 270–88.

10. Andrew Bacevich, *The New American Militarism: How Americans Are Seduced by War* (New York: Oxford University Press, 2006) is one example of an articulate critique of the structures and philosophies that have come to define both the twenty-first-century military and America's relationship to it.

11. Samuel Huntington occasionally used religiously inflected language in *The Soldier and the State* but did not develop his thinking along those lines. Edward Linenthal's *Changing Images of the Warrior Hero in America* is an excellent work from the mid-1980s and reflects quite strongly the Cold War moment out of which it emerged. For more recent treatments of religious aspects of civil-military relations, see Kelly Denton-Borhaug, *U.S. War-Culture, Sacrifice, and Salvation* (Sheffield, UK: Equinox, 2011), and Stanley Hauerwas, *War and American Difference: Theological Reflections on Violence and National Identity* (Grand Rapids, Mich.: Baker Academic, 2011).

12. http://www.cmohs.org/recipient-detail/2542/holderman-nelson-m.php.

13. http://www.cmohs.org/recipient-detail/2521/edwards-daniel-r.php.

14. For scholarly discussions of the sanctification of the United States in the late twentieth and early twenty-first centuries, see Bacevich, *New American Militarism;* Hauerwas, *War and American Difference;* and Denton-Borhaug, *U.S. War-Culture, Sacrifice, and Salvation.* Discussions of similar dynamics related both to the nation and to specific regions of the nation can be found in Jonathan H. Ebel, *Faith in the Fight: Religion and the American Soldier in the Great War* (Princeton:

Princeton University Press, 2010); Drew Gilpin Faust, *This Republic of Suffering: Death and the American Civil War* (New York: Alfred A. Knopf, 2008); Richard Gamble, *The War for Righteousness: Progressive Christianity, the Great War, and the Rise of the Messianic Nation* (Wilmington, Del.: ISI Books, 2003); Harry S. Stout, *Upon the Altar of the Nation: A Moral History of the American Civil War* (New York: Penguin Books, 2006); Charles Regan Wilson, *Baptized in Blood: The Religion of the Lost Cause, 1865–1920* (Athens: University of Georgia Press, 1980).

15. See Hauerwas, *War and the American Difference;* Carolyn Marvin and David Ingle, *Blood Sacrifice and the Nation: Totem Rituals and the American Flag* (Cambridge: Cambridge University Press, 1999); George Mosse, *Fallen Soldiers: Reshaping the Memory of the World Wars* (New York: Oxford University Press, 1990).

16. Stanley Hauerwas, Kelly Denton-Borhaug, and Harry S. Stout offer sharper theological and moral critiques in their books cited above. See also Jon Pahl, *Empire of Sacrifice: The Religious Origins of American Violence* (New York: New York University Press, 2010).

17. Bruce Lincoln, *Holy Terrors: Thinking about Religion after 9/11* (Chicago: University of Chicago Press, 2003). I am drawing here and elsewhere on Lincoln's four-part definition of religion (discourse, practice, community, institutions), which I have found especially helpful in imagining and presenting American civil religion as a religion.

18. Visitors' Center, Normandy American Cemetery; discussions of the religious imagery of ABMC cemeteries can be found in Thomas North, *General North's Manuscript,* unpub. manuscript, Files of the American Battle Monuments Commission, Garches, France; Ron Robin, *Enclaves of America: The Rhetoric of American Political Culture Abroad, 1900–1965* (Princeton: Princeton University Press, 1992); Kate LeMay, "Forgotten Memorials" (Ph.D. diss. in progress, University of Indiana).

19. For photos, descriptions, and a searchable database of soldiers buried in America's overseas military cemeteries, visit www.abmc.gov.

20. "Whole Again" is available in its entirety on YouTube. http://www.youtube.com/watch?v=FadwTBcvISo (accessed December 11, 2013).

21. Jonathan Z. Smith, *Imagining Religion: From Babylon to Jonestown* (Chicago: University of Chicago Press, 1982), 53–65; Smith, *Relating Religion: Essays in the Study of Religion* (Chicago: University of Chicago Press, 2004), 145–56.

22. Kathryn Lofton, *Oprah: Gospel of an Icon* (Berkeley: University of California Press, 2011). Lofton provides a thorough account of the regular religious dynamics of the *Oprah Winfrey Show* and of its star, as well as an account of the commercialism and therapeutic consumption performed by Oprah and her guests. It is not surprising, in light of Lofton's work, that Oprah would be the voice of this advertisement, which fuses American civil religion, consumption, and therapy.

23. Robert Bellah, *The Broken Covenant: American Civil Religion in Time of Trial* (Chicago: University of Chicago Press 1992 [1975]); see also Robert N. Bellah and Steven M. Tipton, eds., *The Robert Bellah Reader* (Durham, N.C.: Duke University Press, 2006). I have consulted the following essays by Bellah on civil

religion. "Civil Religion in America" (1967); "Religion and the Legitimation of the American Republic" (1978); "The New Religious Consciousness and the Crisis of Modernity" (1976); "The Kingdom of God in America: Language of Faith, Language of Nation" (1988); "Citizenship, Diversity, and the Search for the Common Good" (1991); "Is There a Common American Culture" (1997); "Flaws in the Protestant Code: Theological Roots of American Individualism" (2000); "The New American Empire" (2002); and "God and King" (2005). Other works on civil religion include: Catherine Albanese, *The Sons of the Fathers: The Civil Religion of the American Revolution* (Philadelphia: Temple University Press, 1976), and *America: Religions and Religion* (Belmont, Calif.: Wadsworth, 1992); Ray Haberski, *God and War: American Civil Religion since 1945* (New Brunswick, N.J.: Rutgers University Press, 2012); Russel E. Richey and Donald G. Jones, eds., *American Civil Religion* (New York: Harper Forum, 1974); See also the contributions to a roundtable on American civil religion at the 2009 annual meeting of the American Academy of Religion. The papers are available through *The Immanent Frame* and include Daniel Vaca, "Obama's Civil Religion," December 5, 2009; Philip Gorski, "A Neo-Weberian Theory of American Civil Religion," January 8, 2010; David Morgan, "The Social Body of Belief," January 15, 2010; Ebrahim Moosa, "Civil Religion and Beyond," January 22, 2010, and "Civil Religion of a Different Kind," January 29, 2010; David Kyuman Kim, "All Used Up," February 5, 2010; Catherine L. Albanese, "Echoes of American Civil Religion," February 12, 2010; and Pamela Klassen, "Fantasies of Sovereignty," February 19, 2010 (accessed February 21, 2010). David Morgan's "The Social Body of Belief" is a thoroughly compelling call to the kind of engagement with civil religion that I am interested in. He writes, "Expanding the register of analysis in order to avoid reducing civil religions to creedal assertions, to something that people say they believe, will require us to consider the relation between concept, symbol, and practice." And, further, "The work of a civil religion happens in the medium of feeling, so it is felt life that we must study."

24. Benedict Anderson, *Imagined Communities: Reflections on the Origins and Spread of Nationalism* (New York: Verso, 1983); Liah Greenfeld, *Nationalism: Five Roads to Modernity* (Cambridge: Harvard University Press, 1992); Daniel Van Kley, *The Religious Origins of the French Revolution: From Calvinism to the Civil Constitution, 1560–1791* (New Haven: Yale University Press, 1996). For one influential portrait of the role of religion and class in the rise of American "national" sentiment, see Rhys Isaac, *The Transformation of Virginia, 1740–1790* (New York: Norton, 1988). "Patriotism" and related terms ("patriot" and "patriotic") highlight well the affective dimensions of collective identity—love of country—but bear an attitudinal specificity that hinders the term's application to dissenting or disaffected groups within a collective. This problem is magnified on the American landscape, where patriotism's connection to the founding period and its subsequent usage in political discourse make it more a contested term within civil religion than civil religion's analytical equivalent. "Nationalism" and its related terms ("nationalistic," "nationalist") are perhaps less ideologically charged than patriotism vis-à-vis one's

relationship to the collective. Yet because the term emerged in conjunction with specific historical projects deeply invested in secular rather than religious identities, it tips the scale away from analysis of the religious dimensions of those identities. Attaching the adjective "religious" to "nationalism" further confuses analysis by invoking nation-building processes based primarily on religious identity and by foreclosing the possibility that the thing itself, nationalism, is either religious or a religion. Of equal concern is nationalism's tendency to forward a two-tiered conception of collectives, one in which ruling elites and cultural custodians imagine a community and convince those below them to embrace and, if necessary, fight and die for it. Benedict Anderson has shown beyond refutation the validity of this conception at key moments in the emergence of certain nations. Yet he would surely concede, as subsequent scholarship demonstrates, that the lives of national collectives have been and are considerably more complex and dynamic; Bellah, *Broken Covenant*, xiv.

25. Bellah, "Civil Religion in America," in Bellah and Tipton, *Robert Bellah Reader*, 229.

26. See Haberski, *God and War*. Haberski's book is an extremely valuable contribution to the blossoming, third wave of scholarship on American civil religion. Its source base, however, is intensely textual. This is not surprising given Haberski's training as an intellectual historian, but it does leave unaddressed questions of bodies and practices taken up here and in Denton-Borhaug's *U.S. War-Culture, Sacrifice, and Salvation*, and Michael Allen, *Until the Last Man Comes Home: POWs, MIAs, and the Unending Vietnam War* (Chapel Hill: University of North Carolina Press, 2009); For two examples of scholarship that engages civil religion creatively, see Grace Kao, "Of Tragedy and Its Aftermath: The Search for Religious Meaning in the Shootings at Virginia Tech," in John Carlson and Jonathan Ebel, eds., *From Jeremiad to Jihad* (Berkeley: University of California Press, 2012); and Jerome Copulsky and Grace Kao "The Pledge of Allegiance and the Meanings and Limits of Civil Religion," *Journal of the American Academy of Religion* 75, no.1 (March 2007): 121–49.

27. David Hall, ed., *Lived Religion in America: Toward a History of Practice* (Princeton: Princeton University Press, 1997); Laurie F. Maffly-Kipp, Leigh E. Schmidt, and Mark Valeri, eds., *Practicing Protestants: Histories of Christian Life in America, 1630–1965* (Baltimore: Johns Hopkins University Press, 2006); Albanese, *America: Religions and Religion*. Albanese provides an account of the emergence of the tradition and makes reference to practitioners but does not develop the discussion much beyond her account of waning interest in Memorial Day and the somewhat tepid celebration of the bicentennial.

28. Robert Orsi, *The Madonna of 115th Street: Faith and Community in Italian Harlem, 1880–1950* (New Haven: Yale University Press, 1985); Christine Heyrman, *Southern Cross: The Beginnings of the Bible Belt.* (New York: Alfred A. Knopf, 1997); Albert Raboteau, *Slave Religion: The Invisible Institution in the Antebellum South* (New York: Oxford University Press, 1980).

29. Albanese, *America: Religions and Religion*, 446.

30. For discussions of the religious textures of American secularisms in the twentieth and twenty-first centuries, see Tracy Fessenden, *Culture and Redemption* (Princeton: Princeton University Press, 2006); Winnifred Fallers Sullivan, *The Impossibility of Religious Freedom* (Princeton: Princeton University Press, 2005); Charles Taylor, *A Secular Age* (Cambridge: The Belknap Press of Harvard University Press, 2007); Chad Seales, *The Secular Spectacle: Performing Religion in a Southern Town* (New York: Oxford University Press, 2013); and Michael Warner et al., eds., *Varieties of Secularism in a Secular Age* (Cambridge: Harvard University Press, 2013).

31. For a recent scholarly engagement with civil religious diversity, see the recent multiauthor forum "Religion and American Public Life: Presidential Expressions of Christianity," in *Church History* 82, no. 3 (September 2013): 647–87. The forum features Cara L. Burnidge, "The Business of Church and State: Social Christianity in Woodrow Wilson's White House"; Sara Georgini, "John Quincy Adams at Prayer"; and Andrew Polk, "'Unnecessary and Artificial Divisions': Franklin Roosevelt's Quest for Religious and National Unity Leading up to the Second World War."

Chapter One. Incarnating American Civil Religion

1. For background on the IWW in the Pacific Northwest and a balanced account of the Centralia Massacre, see the web-published essays, "The Centralia Massacre" and "The I.W.W. in Washington," at https://content.lib.washington.edu/iwwweb/index.html. The event is also recounted in John L. McLelleand, Jr., *Wobbly War: The Centralia Story* (Tacoma, Wash.: Washington State Historical Society, 1987).

2. "Bullets Fell War Veterans; I.W.W. Hanged," *Chicago Tribune*, November 12, 1919, 1; "Centralia Misses a Hanging Holiday," *American Legion Weekly*, April 2, 1920, 10–11.

3. "Urges Revenge for Centralia: Head of Sons of American Revolution Demands Drastic Penalty for Anarchists," *Indianapolis Star*, February 26 1920, 8; "Parlor Bolshevism a Menace," *Indianapolis Star*, November 17, 1919, 6.

4. Timothy Egan, *The Good Rain: Across Time and Terrain in the Pacific Northwest* (New York: Vintage Books, 1991). Egan offers a typically gripping account of late twentieth-century efforts to navigate the Columbia River Bar.

5. Russell E. Clay, "Aaron Allen Heist," (obituary), Aaron Allen Heist Papers, box 1, Southern California Library for Social Studies Research (cited hereafter as Heist Papers, SCLSSR). The storm lasted from December 9 to 11 and dropped as much as sixty inches in some parts of the state. Totals were between fifteen and eighteen inches near Astoria. http://www.wrh.noaa.gov/pqr/paststorms/snow.php.

6. "Present Day Incarnation," Heist Papers, box 1, SCLSSR.

7. "Scene of Outrage," *Chicago Daily Tribune*, November 12, 1919, 2.

8. Ebel, *Faith in the Fight;* William Pencak *For God and Country: The American Legion, 1919–1941* (Boston: Northeastern University Press, 1989).

9. "Echoes," *Chicago Tribune*, November 14, 1919, 13.

10. Robert E. Speer, *The New Opportunity of the Church* (New York: Mac-Millan, 1919), 15.

11. Clay, "Aaron Allen Heist," Heist Papers, box 1, SCLSSR

12. For an account of post–Great War pacifism and liberal activism, see Joseph Kip Kosek, *Acts of Conscience: Christian Nonviolence and Modern American Democracy* (New York: Columbia University Press, 2009)

13. Lincoln, *Holy Terrors*, 3.

14. Reports of the incident were front-page news nationwide the next day. See "Reds Shoot Down Marching Veterans; Mob Lynches One," *New York Times*, November 12, 1919, 1; "Bullets Fell War Veterans; I.W.W. Hanged," *Chicago Tribune*, November 12, 1919, 1.

15. Mosse, *Fallen Soldiers;* Stout, *Upon the Altar of the Nation;* Denton-Borhaug, *U.S. War Culture, Sacrifice and Salvation.*

16. Orsi, *Madonna of 115th Street;* John Corrigan, "New Israel, New Amalek: Biblical Exhortations to Violence," in John D. Carlson and Jonathan H. Ebel, eds., *From Jeremiad to Jihad: Religion, Violence and America* (Berkeley: University of California Press, 2012); Eddie S. Glaude, Jr. *Exodus! Religion, Race, and Nation in Early Nineteenth-Century America* (Chicago: University of Chicago Press, 2000), 107–8.

17. *Stars and Stripes*, December 16, 1918, 4.

18. Mircea Eliade, *Myth of the Eternal Return* (Princeton: Princeton University Press, 1971). I use the term "axis mundi" in a way that is admittedly different than Eliade's usage, but that I hope bridges the gap between sacred figures and sacred landscapes and underscores the significance with which Heist, via scriptural allusion, invested the American soldier.

19. "The Centralia Awakening," *New York Times*, November 14, 1919, 12.

20. Committee on the War and the Religious Outlook (CWRO), *Religion among American Men: As Revealed by a Study of Conditions in the Army* (New York: Association Press, 1920), xv.

21. Ibid., 22, 25.

22. Philip Sheldrake, *Spaces for the Sacred: Place, Memory, and Identity* (Baltimore: Johns Hopkins University Press, 2001), 94. Emphasis added.

23. Dempsey, *Our Army*, entire.

24. Sheldrake, *Spaces for the Sacred*, 90. His fourth chapter, "The Practice of Place: Monasteries and Utopias," is especially helpful. He writes further, "Monasticism, too, is a counter-site, in some sense representing an idealization of critical elements of human community yet, at the same time, effectively contesting the contingent reality of existing social structures" (100).

25. Ibid., 97.

26. CWRO, *Religion among American Men*, 40.

27. Huntington, *Soldier and the State*, 465.

28. CWRO, *Religion among American Men*, 120.

29. Huntington, *Soldier and the State*, 7–18; 456–66. Huntington's first and final chapters enumerate these values in especially clear terms. His final chapter does so by contrasting them to the disordered liberalism of commercial, nonmilitary

America, a lifestyle similar to that which Bellah termed "utilitarian individualism." See Bellah and Tipton, *Robert Bellah Reader*, 322. Bellah used this term also in *Habits of the Heart*.

30. Andrew Strathern and Pamela Stewart, "Embodiment Theory in Performance and Performativity," *Journal of Ritual Studies* 22, no. 1 (2008). Strathern and Stewart argue that the "actual or perceived effects on the world" of a ritual act are determined by the "cosmos," which they describe in concrete terms as "the whole world as inhabited by people and apprehended by them, including the life-worlds of spirits and deities. The cosmos at any time also includes perceptions of history and its effects and the enduring significance of mythology."

31. Lt. Col. David Grossman, *On Killing: The Psychological Cost of Learning to Kill in War and Society* (New York: Back Bay Books, 1995). Grossman's fascinating and widely read work describes the difficulties (and several notable failures) in getting soldiers to shoot to kill.

32. Robert Bellah and Samuel Huntington, two very different thinkers, agree to a surprising extent in their mid-century writings on the importance of American communalism and the dangers of varieties of individualism.

33. Huntington, *Soldier and the State*, 11. Huntington attributes the phrase "management of violence" to Harold Lasswell; Philip Caputo, *A Rumor of War* (New York: Henry Holt, 1977). Caputo's is one of many accounts that make this point based on excruciating personal experience.

34. Strathern and Stewart, "Embodiment Theory in Performance and Performativity."

35. CWRO, *Religion among American Men*, 140.

36. Smith, *Relating Religion*, 145–56.

37. Albanese, *America: Religions and Religion*, 460. Albanese writes, "Civil religion could give Americans a creed, a code, and a cultus, but it could not—save in Exceptional wartime moments—transform them into one community."

38. Arthur van Gennep, *The Rites of Passage* (Chicago, University of Chicago Press, 1960); Victor Turner, *The Ritual Process: Structure and Anti-Structure* (Chicago: Aldine, 1970); Mathieu Deflem, "Ritual, Anti-Structure, and Religion: A Discussion of Victor Turner's Processual Symbolic Analysis," *Journal for the Scientific Study of Religion* 30, no. 1 (1991):1–25. See also Edward Linenthal, *Changing Images of the Warrior Hero in America*, xii–xv. Linenthal writes further, "Thus, war becomes a powerful initiatory ordeal from which the novice emerges transformed into a warrior. . . . Revered for the power of his acts and the mystery of the world he functioned in, the warrior often became a model, embodying the ideals of a society" (xv).

39. CWRO, *Religion among American Men*, 87.

40. Huntington, *Soldier and the State*, 270–88. Huntington describes this view as a product of neo-Hamiltonianism among the political and literary elites of the late nineteenth and early twentieth centuries. General Leonard Wood was, on Huntington's account, the most important representative of the neo-Hamiltonian position vis-à-vis the military.

41. CWRO, *Religion among American Men*, 88.

42. Everest served stateside; there was an organization of veterans that was closer in political inclination to Everest than to the Legion. They called themselves the Private Soldiers and Sailors Legion of the United States of America.

43. "Centralia Misses a Hanging Holiday," *American Legion Weekly*, April 2, 1920, 10–11.

Chapter Two. Symbols Known, Soldiers Unknown

1. Mary Frances Adams, *Arlington National Cemetery and the Burial of the Unknown Dead* (Washington, D.C.: W. F. Roberts, 1923), 49, microfilm index #89-14008, World War—Dead—Unknown Soldier—Arlington, 11-11-21, Archives of the American Legion, American Legion Headquarters, Indianapolis, Ind. (hereafter AL Archive); *Souvenir Booklet: America's Unknown Hero of the Great World War* (Washington, D.C., n.p.), microfilm index #89-4008, World War—Dead—Unknown Soldier—Arlington, 11-11-21, AL Archive.

2. *Souvenir Booklet;* Philip Bigler, *In Honored Glory: Arlington National Cemetery: The Final Post* (St. Petersburg, Fla.: Vandamere, 2005).

3. Adams, *Arlington National Cemetery*, 57; "Program of the Ceremonies Attending the Burial of An Unknown and Unidentified American Soldier Who Lost His Life During the Great War," 5, microfilm index #89-14008, World War—Dead—Unknown Soldier—Arlington, 11-11-21, AL Archive.

4. Adams, *Arlington National Cemetery; Souvenir Booklet;* Joseph K. Dixon to Charles H. Burke, Commissioner of Indian Affairs, November 4, 1921. Wanamaker Collection, Indiana University. I spell Chief Plenty Coos's name as it was spelled in the official program and in correspondence between Mr. Dickson and Mr. Burke.

5. The full epitaph for all unknown American soldiers of the Great War reads, "Here Rests in Honored Glory an American Soldier, Known but to God."

6. Robert J. Laplander, *Finding the Lost Battalion: Beyond the Rumors, Myths and Legends of America's Famous WWI Epic* (Waterford, Wisc.: Lulu Press, 2006), 42–43; See also Richard Slotkin, *Lost Battalions: The Great War and the Crisis of American Nationality* (New York: Henry Holt, 2005); Huntington, *Soldier and the State*, 280; Slotkin, *Lost Battalions*, 29–34. Both Huntington and Slotkin place General Leonard Wood at or near the center of the Preparedness movement and the establishment of the Plattsburgh Camp.

7. Laplander, *Finding the Lost Battalion*, 46, 545. The author writes of Whittlesey, "all-important 'orders' were things not to be trifled with, sometimes coming through for reasons not . . . readily clear at the time." He writes later, "But what one can say is that in following his orders so closely—even when others would not, and did not—that he paid a higher and more terrible price for upholding a value system that apparently knew no limitations." See also Slotkin, *Lost Battalions*, 366.

8. "Lost Battalion's Commander Home: Lieut Col Whittelsey Tells of Frightful Ordeal in Argonne," *Boston Daily Globe*, November 15, 1918; For more detailed accounts of the fighting see Laplander, *Finding the Lost Battalion*, 228–512;

Slotkin, *Lost Battalions,* 305–63; and Thomas M. Johnson and Fletcher Pratt, *The Lost Battalion* (Lincoln: University of Nebraska Press, 2000). Johnson's and Fletcher's book was first published in 1938 by Bobbs-Merrill.

9. Carl Peterson, *Lost Battalion* (Hayfield, Minn: n.p., 1939). See also Laplander, *Finding the Lost Battalion,* 352; Slotkin, *Lost Battalions,* 333; William E. Moore, "How the Lost Battalion Was Lost: The True Story of an Heroic Incident of the World War in the Light of a Tragedy of Peace," *American Legion Weekly,* December 23, 1921, AL Archive. Early legends of the Lost Battalion and of Whittlesey's heroics proclaimed that when handed a note of surrender Whittlesey shouted, "Hell no!" He denied ever having uttered such a thing. William Moore wrote in frustration about the persistence of this and other misconceptions about the war: "When we first came back some of us tried to correct these errors when we first heard them repeated, but it didn't take long to realize that our fellow citizens resented having the myths exploded. They wanted to believe the foolish and improbable things they did believe." See also Laplander, *Finding the Lost Battalion,* 531; Slotkin, *Lost Battalions,* 364–82.

10. Robert Alexander, *Memories of the World War, 1917–1918* (New York: Macmillan, 1931) 229–34. As one might expect of a general officer, Alexander weaves the incident into a broader strategic narrative of advance against the German forces and into a mythic narrative of American martial heroism. Alexander is generous in his praise of Whittlesey and his men. Laplander and Slotkin lean more heavily on the tension between Alexander and Whittlesey, with Slotkin arguing that Alexander's actions in the aftermath of the incident contributed considerably to Whittlesey's emotional distress. Slotkin, *Lost Battalions,* 364–67. The text of Whittlesey's citation can be found at http://www.cmohs.org/recipient-detail/2609/whittlesey-charles-w.php (accessed January 3, 2014).

11. Will Irwin, "Letters from Franco-America," *Saturday Evening Post,* December 7, 1918, 8, 38–48. Irwin writes in his entry for October 8, 1918, the day on which he and Runyon set out to interview survivors of the Lost Battalion episode, "To-day Runyon and I went hero hunting." Irwin did not, however, describe Whittlesey's rejection of the German surrender note using the mythic, "Hell no!" or "Go to hell!" He wrote, rather, quoting a survivor, "Whit just grinned and crumpled it up and put it in his pocket. It didn't need an answer." An account characteristic of Lost Battalion myth-making appeared in the *Pueblo Chieftain* on October 11, 1918, with the title, "Heroic Defiance Was Answer of Lost Battalion." See also Laplander, 530–31. Interestingly, in describing the aftermath of the incident and quite successfully getting "beyond the rumors myths and legends," Laplander writes himself into the civil religious orthodoxy of soldiering as a rite of passage. He writes, "Filthy men, ravaged by the situation and in terrible pain from rotting, infected wounds, still flashed broad smiles. . . . They were boys that [*sic*] had been thrown into a difficult and terrifying situation who had come out as men; perhaps bloodied and scarred but, at least for the time being, emotionally unaffected and still possessed of their youthful outlook." Laplander, *Finding the Lost Battalion,* 530.

12. *Stars and Stripes,* October 18, 1918.

13. Laplander, *Finding the Lost Battalion,* 556.

14. See Levi Smith, "Window or Mirror: The Vietnam Veterans Memorial and the Ambiguity of Remembrance," in Peter Homans, ed., *Symbolic Loss: The Ambiguity of Memory and Mourning at Century's End* (Charlottesville: University Press of Virginia, 2000), 105–21. The instability of symbols is a prominent feature of Homans's edited collection but is also implied in Clifford Geertz's definition of religion and Bruce Lincoln's response to it. See Clifford Geertz, "Religion as a Cultural System," in Geertz, *The Interpretation of Cultures* (New York: Basic Books, 1977); and Lincoln, *Holy Terrors,* 3–5.

15. An especially colorful example of this line of reasoning is the fundamentalist, militant, Christian rock drummer and evangelist Bradlee Dean, who, in addition to imagining himself as a soldier for God, regularly wraps his ministry in the American flag and speaks of the blood of American soldiers turning battlefields red. The website for his *Sons of Liberty* radio program features a picture of Dean crouching, with an American flag draped over his arms and the white marble crosses of American Battle Monuments Commission cemeteries imposed, receding, into the background. See http://sonsoflibertyradio.com (accessed January 3, 2014).

16. Bigler, *In Honored Glory.* To this day all but one of the unidentified dead are buried in overseas cemeteries beneath headstones that read, "Here rests in honored glory an American soldier known but to God."

17. Hamilton Fish to John Weeks, March 9, 1921, microfilm index #89-14008, World War Dead—Unknown Soldier—Arlington, 11-11-21, AL Archive.

18. *Souvenir Booklet,* 4. Accounts of the selection of the casket differ slightly in this detail. The official website of Arlington National Cemetery mentions a single white rose whereas an article in the *American Legion Weekly* describes a "wreath of roses." William Slavens McNutt, "The Soldier Comes Home," *American Legion Weekly,* November 11, 1921, 5–6.

19. Adams, *Arlington National Cemetery,* 47; *Souvenir Booklet;* See also the website of Arlington National Cemetery, www.arlingtoncemetery.mil (accessed January 3, 2014).

20. "America's Unknown Soldier," microfilm index #89-14008, World War—Dead—Unknown Soldier—Arlington, 11-11-21, AL Archive. This document is a draft of the text printed in the *Souvenir Booklet*

21. *Souvenir Booklet.* The compiler of the booklet explains that the poem first appeared in the *Providence Journal.*

22. The best treatment of the frontier myth in American history is the trilogy authored by Richard Slotkin. See *Regeneration through Violence: The Mythology of the American Frontier, 1600–1860* (Middletown, Conn.: Wesleyan University Press, 1973), *The Fatal Environment: The Myth of the Frontier in the Age of Industrialization, 1800–1890* (New York: Atheneum, 1985), and *Gunfighter Nation: The Myth of the Frontier in Twentieth-Century America* (New York: Atheneum, 1992).

23. "An American Lucknow," *Outlook,* December 25, 1918, 651.

24. "Thousands See Lieut. Col. Whittlesey Decorated with Congressional Medal on Boston Common." *Boston Daily Globe,* December 25, 1918, 12; "Present Whittlesey Medal Here Today" *Boston Daily Globe,* December 24, 1918, 5

25. N. K. Averill, "Memorial Address," in Lee Charles McCollum, *History and Rhymes of the Lost Battalion* (n.p., 1929), 6–8. Colonel Averill's eulogy describes Whittlesey's charitable actions in general terms, connecting them to his "gentle sympathetic nature" and the fact that he was "a ready friend." See also Slotkin, *Lost Battalions,* 466–80; and Laplander, *Finding the Lost Battalion,* 551–53. "Whittlesey Intercedes for Polish Stowaway," *New York Tribune,* September 7, 1920.

26. Laplander, *Finding the Lost Battalion,* 555–56.

27. Jonathan Ebel, "The Great War, Religious Authority, and the American Fighting Man," *Church History: Studies in Christianity and Culture* 78, no. 1 (March 2009): 99–133; See also Slotkin, *Regeneration through Violence; Fatal Environment,* and *Gunfighter Nation.*

28. Linenthal, *Changing Images of the Warrior Hero in America,* xiii–xv, 4.

29. "Program of the Ceremonies Attending the Burial of an Unknown and Unidentified American Soldier Who Lost His Life during the World War," 4, 8. See also, Adams, *Arlington National Cemetery;* and *Souvenir Booklet;* John S. Arkwright, *The Supreme Sacrifice and Other Poems in Time of War* (London, Skeffington and Sons, 1919), 17. http://www.oxforddnb.com/templates/article.jsp?articleid=98215&back (accessed January 3, 2014).

30. "Program of the Ceremonies Attending the Burial of an Unknown and Unidentified American Soldier Who Lost His Life during the World War," 4–6.

31. Laplander, *Finding the Lost Battalion,* 39. According to Laplander, the Whittlesey family attended First Presbyterian Church in Florence, Wisconsin.

32. Laplander, *Finding the Lost Battalion;* Slotkin, *Lost Battalions.*

33. Laplander, *Finding the Lost Battalion;* Slotkin, *Lost Battalions.*

34. McCollum, *History and Rhymes of the Lost Battalion,* 6–7. See also "1,000 Attend Memorial for Col. Whittlesey," *New York Tribune,* December 5, 1921. Whittlesey's mother spoke similarly of his suicide. "We feel . . . Charlie received his death blow in the Argonne. He gave his life to the great cause as did thousands of others and we are thankful he was spared to us for three years." "Liner's Captain Confirms Death of Whittlesey," *New York Tribune,* November 30, 1921.

35. Anderson, *Imagined Communities,* 9.

36. Adams, *Arlington National Cemetery,* 45. The opening pages of Mary Frances Adams's account of the interment ceremony are a prime example. She writes, "No event in our history stands out in its cameo-clearness as the solemn services attending the re-interment on Armistice Day, November 11, 1921, of one brave lad whose heart-blood stained the sod of France with drops as red as the poppies that grew on the fields of Flanders."

37. Frederick Palmer, "Known but to God," *American Legion Monthly,* April 1937.

38. http://www.findagrave.com/cgi-bin/fg.cgi?page=gr&GRid=6022334 (accessed September 3, 2012); Adams, *Arlington National Cemetery.*

39. James F. Barton, "Memo to Department Commanders and Department Adjutants: Department Pilgrimages to the Tomb of the Unknown Soldier in Arlington," January 6, 1930, microfilm index #89-14008, World War—Dead—Unknown Soldier—Arlington, 11-11-21, AL Archive.

40. Mary Frances Hall to Ralph T. O'Neill, National Commander, November 15, 1930, microfilm index #89–14008, World War—Dead—Unknown Soldier—Arlington, 11-11-21, AL Archive.

41. H. Edmund Bullis to James Barton, National Adjutant, September 15, 1930, microfilm index #89-14008, World War—Dead—Unknown Soldier—Arlington, 11-11-21, AL Archive; letter from Bullis to unnamed Legion personnel, February 9, 1930, microfilm index #89-14008, World War—Dead—Unknown Soldier—Arlington, 11-11-21, AL Archive.

42. Bullis to James F. Barton, September 15, 1930, microfilm index #89-14008, World War—Dead—Unknown Soldier—Arlington, 11-11-21, AL Archive

43. Levi Smith, "Window or Mirror."

44. Palmer, "Known but to God."

Chapter Three. In Honored Glory, Known but to God

1. "The Martyrdom of Saints Perpetua and Felicitas," in Herbert Musurillo, ed., *The Acts of the Christian Martyrs* (Oxford: Oxford University Press, 1972), 123, 129, 131.

2. Virginia War History Commission survey (VWHC), Felicita Wootlow Hecht. Hecht's survey (filled out postmortem, likely by Sister Olympia) and many others have been digitized and are available through the Library of Virginia. http://lva1.hosted.exlibrisgroup.com/F/?func=file&file_name=find-b-clas13&local_base=CLAS13 (accessed January 3, 2014).

3. Ibid. Hecht's unit identification is confirmed by the American Battle Monuments Commission database, www.abmc.gov.

4. Ibid. Page 3 of Hecht's VWHC survey consists of the letter, mistakenly dated January 3, 1918, from Maude Parson to Sister Olympia.

5. "Oise Aisne American Cemetery," American Battle Monuments Commission, www.abmc.gov.

6. Ibid.

7. A recent DVD about ABMC cemeteries, produced in cooperation with PBS, is titled *Hallowed Grounds.*

8. Numerous historians have demonstrated beyond reasonable argument that war memories are an important aspect of modern western cultures and that we have a great deal to learn from attention to the sites and the institutions by which and through which these memories are shaped and perpetuated. See Allen, *Until the Last Man Comes Home;* Bacevich, *New American Militarism;* Faust, *This Republic of Suffering;* Paul Fussel, *The Great War and Modern Memory* (Oxford: Oxford University Press, 1975); Ed Linenthal, *Sacred Ground: Americans and Their Battlefields* (Urbana: University of Illinois Press, 1993); Charles Regan Wilson, *Baptized*

in Blood: The Religion of the Lost Cause, 1865–1920 (Albany: University of Georgia Press, 1980); Olivier Wieviorka, *Divided Memory: French Recollections of World War II from the Liberation to the Present,* trans. George Holoch (Palo Alto: Stanford University Press, 2012); and Jay Winter, *Sites of Memory, Sites of Mourning: The Great War in European Cultural History* (Cambridge: Cambridge University Press, 1995). These scholars have also drawn attention to the contested nature of war memories and to the potentially contested nature of sites and landscapes associated with the war dead. Those working within the field of religious studies have long been concerned with two topics central to this chapter: constructions of the sacred and understandings of death. Numerous works have engaged with these topics alone but those who have worked at their intersection inform this chapter most directly. See Peter Brown, *The Cult of the Saints: Its Rise and Function in Latin Christianity* (Chicago: University of Chicago Press, 1982) and *Authority and the Sacred: Aspects of the Christianization of the Roman World* (Cambridge: Cambridge University Press, 1995); Homans, *Symbolic Loss;* Ed Linenthal and David Chidester, *American Sacred Space* (Bloomington: Indiana University Press, 1995); Gary Laderman, *Rest in Peace: A Cultural History of Death and the Funeral Home in Twentieth-Century America* (Oxford: Oxford University Press, 2005); Marvin and Ingle, *Blood Sacrifice and the Nation;* and Sheldrake, *Spaces for the Sacred.*

9. Scholars of the history of art and architecture, especially those who focus on the design of landscapes, have directed considerable interpretive energy toward the study of American cemeteries and the myriad ways that they have reflected and shaped Americans' relationships with their nation and their dead. See Elizabeth G. Grossman, "Architecture for a Public Client: The Monuments and Chapels of the American Battle Monuments Commission," *Journal of the Society of Architectural Historians* 43, no. 2 (May 1984): 119–43; Kenneth T. Jackson, and Camilio José Vergara, *Silent Cities: The Evolution of the American Cemetery* (Princeton: Princeton Architectural Press, 1989); Robin, *Enclaves of America;* Kirk Savage, *Monument Wars: Washington, D.C., the National Mall, and the Transformation of the Memorial Landscape* (Berkeley: University of California Press, 2009); David Charles Sloane, *The Last Great Necessity: Cemeteries in American History* (Baltimore: Johns Hopkins University Press, 1995); Joachim Wolschke-Bulmahn, ed., *Places of Commemoration: Search for Identity and Landscape Design* (Washington, D.C.: Dumbarton Oaks, 2001), see especially essays by Michael Stern and Patrick Hagopian. Their efforts allow us to situate ABMC cemeteries within a broader narrative of the aesthetics of memorialization in twentieth-century America and, as exegetes of the "texts," to be more attentive to their many levels of meaning.

10. Homans, *Symbolic Loss,* 1–38. Peter Brown's work on the "special dead" in ancient Roman/ancient Christian community life is exemplary.

11. I take the phrase "literary portraiture" from Sheldrake, *Spaces for the Sacred,* 41; See Brown, *Authority and the Sacred,* especially chapter 3, "Arbiters of the Holy," for a discussion of ancient hagiography and the broader meaning-making function of the genre.

12. Thomas North, *General North's Manuscript*, Files of the American Battle Monuments Commission, Garches, France, 1–8. Major General Thomas North served with the ABMC for nearly forty-six years and wrote an account of his service which has not been published. This document was provided to me by James Woolsey of the ABMC. According to General North, the practice of allowing epitaphs was discontinued almost immediately due to "light response" and to prevent "invidious distinctions" among the dead. For an early discussion of what and what not to place on the markers, see "Durable Markers in the Form of Crosses for Graves of American Soldiers in Europe," *Hearing Before the Committee on Military Affairs, House of Representatives*, 68th Cong., March 1924 (Washington, D.C.: Government Printing Office, 1924).

13. The ABMC cemeteries are not unique in this regard. They have counterparts established and maintained by England, France, and Germany. See especially Mosse, *Fallen Soldiers*, chapter 3.

14. Michel Foucault and Jay Miskowiec, "Of Other Spaces," *Diacritics* 16, no. 1 (Spring 1986): 22–27. Originally presented as a lecture in 1967, this version of "Des espace autres" was translated by Jay Miskowiec for the journal *Diacritics*. I am citing Foucault here because his notion of the heterotopia influenced me in my thinking about ABMC cemeteries; Huntington, *Soldier and the State*, 464–66.

15. Linenthal, *Sacred Ground*. Linenthal provides an excellent account of this contest of interpretation at America's battlefields.

16. North, *General North's Manuscript*, entire; Mosse describes similar developments in Weimar Germany in conjunction with what he describes as "the Myth of the War Experience" and the "Cult of the Fallen Soldier" and argues that these cultural forces and the war cemeteries they shaped were of great importance in the rise of National Socialism; North, 1–10. North also discusses the extent to which American memorial efforts were in dialogue with the memorial efforts of the allies. In an early section he describes the ABMC's post–Great War thought process, "Also, the American monuments must be of such a nature and so sited as to recall the widespread use of our troops during the closing months of the war when their fighting ability and their moral effect on the tired allied forces was of major importance; understandably, this was no longer being emphasized in Europe."

17. Anne Leland and Mari-Jana Oboroceneau, "American War and Military Operations Casualties: Lists and Statistics," Congressional Research Service, February 10, 2010. Of the 116,516 Americans who died in the Great War, between 77,000 and 80,000 died in Europe.

18. Ralph Hayes, *The Care of the Fallen: A Report to the Secretary of War on American Military Dead Overseas* (Washington, D.C.: Government Printing Office, 1920), 19–30; Michael Stern, "The National Cemetery System: Politics, Place, and Contemporary Cemetery Design," in Wolschke-Bluhman, *Places of Commemoration*, 109, n. 9. According to Stern, only 12.5 percent of those who chose repatriation buried their loved one in a national cemetery. Two ABMC workers told me that while the majority of those who opted for repatriation chose the United States

as the destination, significant numbers of families also chose European countries—
Ireland, Italy, Sweden, Norway, and Greece—as the final resting places for their
sons or daughters.

19. Hayes, *Care of the Fallen*, 35.

20. North, *General North's Manuscript*.

21. Beekman Scrapbook, Archives of the American Cathedral, Paris (hereafter
AACP).

22. Memo from Beekman, "For the Clergy: Ten Reasons for Special and Immediate Church Support of the War Memorial and Endowment Fund of the American Church of the Holy Trinity, Paris," Beekman Scrapbook, AACP.

23. Letter from Beekman, Beekman Scrapbook, AACP. "In Memory of America's Dead of the Great War"; confidential letter from Beekman to fellow clergy,
January 1, 1920, Beekman Scrapbook, AACP.

24. Beekman Scrapbook, AACP

25. North, *General North's Manuscript* (emphasis in original).

26. Hayes, *Care of the Fallen*, 24, 12; Grossman, "Architecture for a Public
Client," 120.

27. Thomas North, "Memorandum for Members of the Commission,"
March 24, 1950, George C. Marshall Papers, box 164, folder 17, George C. Mar-
shall Library, Lexington, Virginia (hereafter Marshall Papers, Marshall Library).
North's memo discusses at length the importance of denying all requests for repa-
triation after permanent burial has been accomplished; Stern, "National Cemetery
System," 111.

28. "Durable Markers in the Form of Crosses for Graves of American Soldiers
in Europe," *Hearing Before the Committee on Military Affairs, House of Representatives*, 68th Cong., March 13 and March 24, 1924 (Washington, D.C.: Government
Printing Office, 1924); Grossman, "Architecture for a Public Client," 136. Paul
Cret designed the Latin cross and the Star of David headstones.

29. See also Linenthal, *Sacred Ground*, 4.

30. "Durable Markers in the Form of Crosses," 19, 31. The testimony recorded in the hearing is generally supportive of the use of Stars of David for fallen
soldiers "of Jewish faith" or "Hebrews." Mr. H. L. Gluckman, representing the
Jewish Welfare Board, supported this iconography but noted that the practice of
attaching a Star of David to a Latin cross "would not be satisfactory." An early sug-
gestion regarding headstone policy, dated December 7, 1918, recommended that
permanent marker not be cruciform because "Hebrews object to the use of a cross
and their desire having been made mandatory by official action, it is necessary for
us to employ a different marker for Jewish graves. This introduces the element of
diversity in grave marking and prevents the desirable harmony that should charac-
terize national cemeteries."

31. Grossman, "Architecture for a Public Client," 135. The original plan called
for a chapel at Meuse-Argonne only.

32. Allen, *Until the Last Man Comes Home*, 118–20; Hayes, *Care of the Fallen*,
35; Sloane, *Last Great Necessity*, 114.

33. Hayes, *Care of the Fallen*, 41–42. In his report Assistant Secretary Hayes argued for the importance of keeping the cemetery at Romagne-sous-Montfaucon based on its proximity to ground over which Americans fought and died. Linenthal uses the phrase "patriotic orthodoxy" in Linenthal, *Sacred Ground*, 4–5.

34. ABMC, "Meuse-Argonne American Cemetery and Memorial," 15; Files of the Superintendent, Meuse-Argonne American Cemetery, "Chaplains" (undated) and "List of Women Buried in Cemetery," November 3, 1988.

35. Psalm 135:4 reads, "For the Lord hath chosen Jacob unto himself and Israel for his peculiar treasure." 2 Corinthians 5:19 reads, "To wit, that God was in Christ reconciling the world unto himself, not imputing their trespasses unto them; and hath committed unto us the word of reconciliation."

36. William M. Hammond, *Normandy* (Washington, D.C.: Department of Defense, U.S. Army, Center of Military History, 1994), 31. This publication is available online at http://www.history.army.mil/brochures/normandy/nor-pam.htm. Some estimates of combat deaths range higher, but all agree that the number killed was far lower than expected.

37. Lemay, "Forgotten Memorials."

38. Edith Morton Eustis to George C. Marshall, July 24, 1952, Marshall Papers, box 161, folder 6, Marshall Library; see North, *General North's Manuscript*, 10–11. North shared his thoughts on architecture critics' reactions to the World War II cemeteries. He wrote, "And the Commission did feel that because a high proportion of the American visitors would be relatives of the dead, still bearing their burden of grief, many of them people of simple background, they should not be confronted with extremes in architectural design. On rare occasions avant-garde 'experts' have criticized the architects' creations as unimaginative, pedestrian, but do they not reveal more inspiration by far than the dreary monotony of human files cases that have come to line our city streets in recent years?" General George C. Marshall, "Our War Memorials Abroad: A Faith Kept," *National Geographic* 61, no. 6 (June 1957): 731–38.

39. ABMC pamphlet, "Normandy American Cemetery."

40. Guest Register, Normandy American Cemetery, April 24, 2010.

41. "U.S. War Victims Honored in France," *New York Times*, May 31, 1937.

42. John 10:27–28. Jesus is recorded speaking these words to a group of "Jews" who asked him to declare whether he was the Messiah. Jesus's full response draws a sharp distinction between believing "sheep" and the non-believing Jews.

43. George C. Marshall to Dean Acheson, August 1, 1952, Marshall Papers, box 161, folder 43, Marshall Library; David Bruce to Marshall, August 13, 1952, Marshall Papers, box 161, folder 43, Marshall Library; "Allied Chiefs Hail American Dead in Cemetery Near Paris," *New York Times*, September 14, 1952.

44. "Report of Robert G. Woodside, Vice-Chairman," to Thomas North and George C. Marshall, August 1, 1949, Marshall Papers, box 161, folder 2, Marshall Library. Woodside notes, "In Suresnes all bodies of World War I dead authorized by the Commission to be moved, have been located in new graves without any appearance at all to indicate a removal has been made. World War II unknowns have

been moved into positions authorized by the Commission. Everything is now ready for the architect to proceed with the new work to make this a World War I and World War II Shrine [*sic*]."

45. Thanks to Kate Lemay who corrected the ABMC brochure for Suresnes, which confuses the names of the statues and their sculptors.

46. See Peter Brown, *Cult of the Saints,* for a discussion of the sanctification of cemeteries in the late antique period and the struggle in the ancient world to control power derived from saints' remains.

47. Sheldrake, *Spaces for the Sacred,* 16; Linenthal and Chidester, *American Sacred Space,* 1–32.

48. Sheldrake, *Spaces for the Sacred,* 18. See also Linenthal, *Sacred Ground;* Robin, *Enclaves of America,* entire.

49. For a brief discussion of these early layout plans see *Stars and Stripes,* April 4, 1919, "A.E.F. Dead To Be Taken to America If Kin So Wishes"; Sloane, *Last Great Necessity,* 83–95. Equality and democracy were also important values to planners and proprietors of rural cemeteries in the nineteenth century, but the gap between ideal and reality was large; Faust, *This Republic of Suffering,* 249.

50. "Cromwell Twins End Their Lives by Leap from Ship," *New York Times,* January 25, 1919; "Cromwell Deaths Now Confirmed," *New York Times,* January 26, 1919.

51. Mosse, *Fallen Soldiers.* Mosse's work provides an excellent example of a much longer study with similar goals for the German and, occasionally, the broader northern European context.

52. See Homans, *Symbolic Loss,* 1–38 for a discussion of the many ways in which twentieth-century monuments have worked to accomplish this very task.

Chapter Four. Saint Francis the Fallen

1. John Bodnar, *The "Good War" in American Memory* (Baltimore: Johns Hopkins University Press) and Andrew Huebner, *The Warrior Image: Soldiers in American Culture from the Second World War to the Vietnam Era* (Chapel Hill: University of North Carolina Press, 2008) provide especially compelling accounts of the ways in which public memory of wars has been shaped by official and popular forces. See also Haberski, *God and War;* and Edward Linenthal, *Changing Images of the Warrior Hero in America* and *Sacred Ground.*

2. A series of articles in the *New York Times* has covered the personal lives of veterans of the wars in Afghanistan and Iraq. A recent installment looked at mental illness and violent crime through the lens of one soldier's rape and murder of a sixty-five-year-old Delaware woman. See Nicholas Kristoff, "When War Comes Home," *New York Times,* November 11, 2012; See Bodnar, *"Good War" in American Memory;* Haberski, *God and War;* Huebner, *Warrior Image;* and Linenthal, *Changing Images of the Warrior Hero in America;* Bodnar's work is helpful in bringing the "private" sphere into conversations about war memory, but he insists on treating actions that happen in and around the home or as part of a private sphere

as authentic reflections of war's effects and those that happen in public as manufactured and propagandistic. This is a tidy but false distinction.

3. Ute Hüsken "Ritual Dynamics and Ritual Failure," in Ute Hüsken, ed. *When Rituals Go Wrong: Mistakes, Failure, and the Dynamics of Ritual* (Leiden: Brill, 2007), 337. Similar sentiments are expressed by Schiefflein in the introduction to the same volume.

4. Francis Gary Powers, with Curt Gentry, *Operation Overflight: The U-2 Spy Pilot Tells His Story for the First Time* (New York: Holt, Rinehart and Winston, 1970). Biographical information on Francis Gary Powers comes from Powers, *Operation Overflight*, an autobiographical account of his involvement in the U-2 program.

5. Ibid., 15.

6. Linenthal, *Changing Images of the Warrior Hero in America.*

7. Bodnar, *"Good War" in American Memory.*

8. Timothy Snyder, *Bloodlands: Europe between Hitler and Stalin* (New York: Basic Books, 2012); Norman Davies, *No Simple Victory: World War II in Europe, 1939–1945* (New York: Penguin Books, 2008); Tony Judt, *Postwar: A History of Europe since 1945* (New York: Penguin Books, 2006).

9. Bodnar, *"Good War" in American Memory;* Huebner, *Warrior Image;* Linenthal, *Changing Images of the Warrior Hero in America.*

10. http://www.imdb.com/title/tt0036868/.

11. Jean Bethke Elshtain, *Women and War* (New York: Basic Books, 1987). Elshtain develops and deploys the concept of the "beautiful soul" to describe the role many women have played in war opposite men who are imagined as and asked to embody the "just warrior."

12. Deborah Dash Moore, *G.I. Jews: How World War II Transformed a Generation* (Cambridge: The Belknap Press of Harvard University Press, 2004). Moore's look at the Jewish American experience of World War II describes Jewish soldiers who embraced the forced ecumenism of army life and those who were deeply troubled by the challenges to their faith lives. She argues, however, that the experience of service was transformative in largely positive ways for a generation of Jewish Americans.

13. Brad D. Lookingbill, ed., *American Military History: A Documentary Reader* (Malden, Mass.: Wiley-Blackwell, 2011), 272.

14. *The U.S. Fighting Man's Code* (Washington, D.C.: Office of Armed Forces Information and Education, 1955), 8, vi.

15. Pash, *In the Shadow of the Greatest Generation,* 141.

16. Ibid., 142, 156.

17. *U.S. Fighting Man's Code;* for revised, gender-neutral wording, see http://www.archives.gov/federal-register/codification/executive-order/10631.html (last accessed September 8, 2014).

18. Ibid., vii.

19. Powers, *Operation Overflight,* 17; Pash, *In the Shadow of the Greatest Generation,* 7–15.

20. Powers, *Operation Overflight*, 17, 18.

21. Powers intended to return to the air force and, he claimed, had an agreement with the air force that when he returned his time flying for the C.I.A. would count toward his overall time in service. It seems entirely appropriate to consider Powers a "soldier" not only because of these formal contractual arrangements, but also because of his military training, his self-understanding, and the famously diverse "fronts" on which the Cold War was waged.

22. Ibid., 20, 26. Powers reports having made $400 per month in the air force. He was paid $1,500 per month while training to fly the U-2 and $2,500 per month once deployed overseas.

23. Ibid., 38, 80.

24. Ibid., 80, 82.

25. Ibid., 34–35, 82–83.

26. Ibid., 88.

27. Ibid., 90–91. In his memoir Dwight Eisenhower wrote of the U-2: "A final important characteristic of the plane was its fragile construction. . . . This led to the assumption (insisted upon by the CIA and the Joint Chiefs) that in the event of a mishap the plane would virtually disintegrate. It would be impossible, if things should go wrong, they said, for the Soviets to come in possession of the equipment intact—or, unfortunately, of a live pilot. This was a cruel assumption, but I was assured that the young pilots undertaking these missions were doing so with their eyes wide open and motivated by a high degree of patriotism, a swashbuckling bravado, and certain material inducements." Cited in ibid., 352.

28. For an account of the various cover stories considered by those who knew about the program and the mishap, see David Wise and Thomas B. Ross, *The U-2 Affair* (New York: Random House, 1962), 28–39; Powers, *Operation Overflight*, 38; Harold J. Berman, "Introduction," in *The Trial of the U2: Exclusive Authorized Account of the Court Proceedings of the Case of Francis Gary Powers Heard before the Military Division of the Supreme Court of the U.S.S.R., Moscow, August 17, 18, 19, 1960* (Chicago: Translation World, 1960), iii. Berman, a professor of law at Harvard Law School, wrote much on Soviet law.

29. See for example, William H. Stringer, "Washington Pits Value of Spy Flights against Worldwide Hail of Criticism," *Christian Science Monitor*, May 9, 1960, 1; Russell Freeburg, "U.S. Reports Plane Spying: Reds Report Pilot Confesses," *Chicago Daily Tribune*, May 8, 1960, 1; Arthur Krock, "The Enigmas in the Pilot Powers Case," *New York Times*, May 9, 1960, 36; James Reston, "The Political Consequences Following the U-2," *New York Times*, May 13, 1960, 30; "Picking up the Pieces" (editorial), *Washington Post*, May 18, 1960, 16; "Our Brinkmanship Threatens Peace" (editorial), *Christian Century*, May 18, 1960, 596–97. For a more pro-Eisenhower presentation of the case, see the editorial "We May Be a Little Ahead," *Los Angeles Times*, May 19, 1960, B-4. "Opinion of the Week: At Home and Abroad," *New York Times*, May 22, 1960, E-13, presents views on the U-2 incident compiled from newspapers across the nation.

30. "Stand Firm America," *Cincinnati Enquirer*, May 12, 1960, from Allen W. Dulles Papers, series 5, Subject Files, box 110, folder 2, U-2 Incident, 1959–1962,

Public Policy Papers, Department of Rare Books and Special Collections, Princeton University Library (hereafter Dulles Papers). Indeed, the *Code of Conduct* was framed primarily as a military code but also as one that should apply to the nation at large in the event that "the problem of survival should ever come to our own main streets" (*U.S. Fighting Man's Code*, v).

31. *Hearing Before the Committee on Armed Services United States Senate on Francis Gary Powers*, 87th Cong., 2d Sess., March 6, 1962 (Washington: U.S. Government Printing Office, 1962), 12.

32. Powers, *Operation Overflight*, 70–71.

33. Universal News Reel reportage of the trial and Eisenhower's response to it is available on YouTube, http://www.youtube.com/watch?v=3pxCqUcYT_c& feature=related (accessed February 20, 2010).

34. Berman, *Trial of the U2*, 118. For a recent history of the Central Intelligence Agency, see Tim Weiner, *Legacy of Ashes: The History of the CIA* (New York: Doubleday, 2007). His brief discussion of the U-2 incident and the fallout for the Eisenhower administration can be found on pages 159–60.

35. Berman, *Trial of the U2*, 141–42.

36. Ibid., 149. See also Powers, *Operation Overflight*, 190; "Preface," in Hüsken, *When Rituals Go Wrong*.

37. Barbara Gay Powers, *Spy Wife* (New York: Pyramid Books, 1965), 113. Barbara's description of their time alone in his prison cell is colorful to say the least.

38. Powers, *Operation Overflight*, 199.

39. *Los Angeles Times*, September 5, 1960, B5.

40. "Powers Blasted for Attempt to Save Self," *Los Angeles Times*, August 26, 1960, 5.

41. Allen Dulles to Mrs. Samuel Sonenfield, August 30, 1960, Dulles Papers, U-2 Incident, 1959–1962.

42. Powers, *Operation Overflight*, 254–55.

43. Berman, *Trial of the U2*, ii. The negative comparison began long before the exchange. Writing in the wake of Powers's trial in 1960, one analyst stated baldly, "[Powers], then, was no Rudolph Ivanovich Abel. . . . Though grilled ceaselessly by the F.B.I. for five days without sleep, and then daily for weeks, Abel gave no information concerning his activities as a Soviet agent . . . Powers, on the other hand, pleaded guilty, took the stand, described his activities in detail, and admitted that he was a spy."

44. Powers, *Operation Overflight*, 295, 299, 299–301.

45. *Hearing Before the Committee on Armed Services United States Senate on Francis Gary Powers*, 87th Cong., 2d Sess., March 6, 1962, 1, 2.

46. Ibid., 6.

47. Powers, *Operation Overflight*, 88–90; *Hearing Before the Committee on Armed Services United States Senate on Francis Gary Powers*, 87th Cong., 2d Sess., March 6, 1962, 8, 12.

48. *Hearing Before the Committee on Armed Services United States Senate on Francis Gary Powers*, 87th Cong., 2d Sess., March 6, 1962, 16, emphasis added;

ibid., 18; Powers, *Operation Overflight,* 330. According to Powers, Senator Barry Goldwater slipped him an envelope with a note that read, "You did a good job for your country. Thanks. Barry Goldwater"; *Hearing,* 17. Stennis prefaced this by saying, "You have understood, I suppose, that at the time this occurred there was some publicity here, not a great deal, but some that was not altogether favorable to you. Did you know that?"

49. *Hearing Before the Committee on Armed Services United States Senate on Francis Gary Powers,* 87th Cong., 2d Sess., March 6, 1962, 19.

50. "The Hot and Cold Wars of Allen Dulles," *CBS Reports,* Eric Sevareid reporting, Thursday, April 26, 1962, transcript in Dulles Papers, U-2 Incident, 1959–1962.

51. Powers, *Operation Overflight,* 301.

52. Ibid., 343–45; Pash, *In the Shadow of the Greatest Generation,* 156–59. This treatment runs parallel to the treatment American POWs suspected of collaboration or treason received upon their return from the Korean War. Pash writes that the army "continued investigations long after the end of the war, denoting some POWs as collaborators in their records and secretly issuing less than honorable discharges to others."

53. Smith, *Imagining Religion,* 59–63; and *Relating Religion,* 145–56.

54. Powers, *Operation Overflight,* 143

55. Hüsken, *When Rituals Go Wrong,* 354.

56. Check-Six.com; "Former U-2 Pilot Powers Killed in Helicopter Crash," *Los Angeles Times,* August 2, 1977, and "The Final Doomed Flight to Los Angeles of a Storied U-2 Pilot" October 20, 2009; http://latimesblogs.latimes.com/afterword/2009/10/milan-miskovsky-and-francis-gary-powers-.html.

57. Wise and Ross, *U-2 Affair,* 8, 22–23; Powers, *Operation Overflight,* 30–33; Albanese, *America: Religions and Religion,* 449. Throughout his book Powers describes the many difficulties that attended taking off, flying, and landing the U-2. The secrecy of the program certainly had much to do with the absence of such information from public discussions of Powers's actions. One might also look to the words of Catherine L. Albanese in her discussion of American civil religion, "Whether looking to past of future, under God or America, deliberate or spontaneous, hypocritical or sincere, the civil religion revolved around what were considered memorable deeds that Americans had performed to initiate an age unknown before in history. Here, actions had to be striking to be seen; events had to make history to be meaningful."

Chapter Five. The Vietnam War as a Christological Crisis

1. Stanley Karnow, *Vietnam: A History* (New York: Penguin Books, 1984); George C. Herring, *America's Longest War: The United States and Vietnam, 1950–1975* (New York: Alfred A. Knopf, 1986 [1975]).

2. Jon Nordheimer, "From Dakto to Detroit: Death of a Troubled Hero," *New York Times,* May 26, 1971.

3. http://www.cmohs.org/recipient-detail/3317/johnson-dwight-h.php (accessed October 28, 2013).

4. Nordheimer, "From Dakto to Detroit."

5. Michael L. Krenn, ed., *The African American Voice in U.S. Foreign Policy since World War II* (New York: Garland, 1998). Three chapters from this volume are particularly relevant to an understanding of the Vietnam War, the civil rights movements, and African-American political involvements more broadly. They are James A. Moss, "The Civil Rights Movement and American Foreign Policy"; Adam Fairclough, "Martin Luther King, Jr., and the War in Vietnam"; and Peter B. Levy, "Blacks and the Vietnam War."

6. Nordheimer, "From Dakto to Detroit."

7. Ibid.

8. Ibid.

9. Ibid.

10. Ibid.

11. Henry Scarupa, "They Carry the War Home in Their Heads," *Baltimore Sun*, September 19, 1971.

12. Nordheimer, "From Dakto to Detroit."

13. Haberski, *God and War*, 57. Ray Haberski titled his chapter on the period "Civil Religion Redeemed," noting in that chapter, "If civil religion is about anything it is about war and the people who sacrifice and die in it." Paul Hendrickson, *The Living and the Dead: Robert McNamara and Five Lives of a Lost War* (New York: Vintage Books, 1996); Stanley Karnow, *Vietnam: A History;* George Herring, *America's Longest War.*

14. Robert Bellah, "Civil Religion in America," in Bellah and Tipton, *Robert Bellah Reader.* In terms of reach and prophetic voice Bellah's fellow public intellectuals Martin Marty and Reinhold Niebuhr certainly did their share of shaping as well.

15. Ibid., 241.

16. Linenthal, *Changing Images of the Warrior Hero in America*, 145. Linenthal writes of the Vietnam moment, "The warrior would take on shapes never popularly associated with classic American warriors."

17. The title of this chapter fuses the titles of two books, each germane in different ways to the conversation about soldiering, civil religion, and the Vietnam War. The first, Richard A. Norris, ed., *The Christological Controversy* (Philadelphia: Fortress, 1980), is a collection of writings from the ancient church representing different views on the nature of Christ. The introduction, written by Norris, describes the various disputes, their tributaries, and their implications down to the establishment of an orthodox Christology, or "an adequate christological language" (Norris, 31) at the Council of Chalcedon in 451. See also F. L. Cross and E. A. Livingstone, eds., *The Oxford Dictionary of the Christian Church* (Oxford: Oxford University Press, 1997). The terms I use in this chapter, "adoptionism" and "voluntarism," are not organic to the ancient period, though the former has been imposed by more modern scholars on ancient groups ranging from the Ebionites to

such proponents of the Antiochene (*logos anthropos*) Christology as Theodore of Mopsuestia and Nestorius ("Adoptianism" [*sic*], in Cross and Livingstone, 19–20). As I use the term "adoptionism" here, it has some of the implications one might identify with ancient Alexandrian *logos sarx* Christology, i.e., that in Christ/the soldier, the *logos*/the nation merely clothes itself in flesh. "Voluntarism," to the extent that it may have figured in the ancient church, would certainly have been marginal and then anathematized. Though as I develop the term here it harmonizes somewhat with ancient "adoptionist" positions, which leaned heavily on the duality of Christ's natures in the interest of avoiding the conclusion that the *logos* had experienced limitation and suffering. The second book, Mark A. Noll's *The Civil War as a Theological Crisis* (Chapel Hill: University of North Carolina Press, 2006), examines the ways in which the American Civil War—the central issues, the fighting, the conclusion—challenged theological assumptions not just in the United States but in the Christian West more broadly. The aims of this chapter are necessarily more modest, but I appreciate the heavy lifting that Noll and Harry S. Stout have done in establishing that America's wars both express and shape America's theologies

18. Linenthal, 151, *Changing Images of the Warrior Hero in America*. Linenthal draws on Caputo to demonstrate the absence of a sacrificial framework for soldierly death in Vietnam.

19. Philip Caputo, *A Rumor of War* (New York: Picador, 1977), xvii, xvi. See also Ebel, *Faith in the Fight*.

20. Caputo, *Rumor of War*, 4, 6.

21. Caputo's feelings map interestingly onto the sense of "evasive banality" described so eloquently by T. J. Jackson Lears in *No Place of Grace: Antimodernism and the Transformation of American Culture, 1880–1920* (Chicago: University of Chicago Press, 1994). Similar sentiments are evident in the words of Francis Gary Powers and Pat Tillman.

22. Bernard Rostker, *I Want You!: The Evolution of the All-Volunteer Force* (Santa Monica, Calif.: Rand Corporation, 2006), 19–33.

23. Caputo, *Rumor of War*, 12, 19–21.

24. Ibid., 234, 232, 96, 127. See also Linenthal, *Changing Images of the Warrior Hero in America*, xiii. Linenthal uses language very similar to Caputo's in his introduction.

25. Caputo arrived in Vietnam as part of a combat unit, was transferred to a staff job, and then sought transfer back to a combat unit.

26. Caputo, *Rumor of War*. At various points in the memoir Caputo references the war movies of the 1950s and 1960s, in particular *The Sands of Iwo Jima*.

27. Ibid., 10, 21.

28. Ibid., 118–19.

29. Ibid., 233, 239.

30. Huebner, *Warrior Image*; Herring, *America's Longest War*.

31. John Kerry and Vietnam Veterans Against the War, *The New Soldier* (New York: Macmillan, 1971).

32. Two discussions of guerrilla theater published during the Vietnam War are R. G. Davis, "Guerilla Theater," *Tulane Drama Review* 10, no. 4 (Summer 1966): 130–36; and Richard Schechner, "Guerilla Theater, 1970," *Drama Review: TDR* 14, no. 3 (1970): 163–68.

33. Kerry, *New Soldier*. In the foreword to *The New Soldier*, the authors express their frustration at the lack of media attention to Operation RAW and the Winter Soldier Investigations. Operation Dewey Canyon III, they say, developed as a way to draw greater attention to VVAW and its message.

34. Huebner, *Warrior Image*, chapter 6; See also Linenthal, *Changing Images of the Warrior Hero in America*. Linenthal's chapter "The Executioner: The Experience of Vietnam" provides an excellent account of the effects of the war on the place of the soldier in American civil religion. More than anything else, I think, the different historical perspectives from which we write account for the differences between Linenthal's and my readings of the crisis.

35. Kerry, *New Soldier*. See also Huebner, *Warrior Image*, chapter 7.

36. Ronald Sullivan, "Veterans for Peace Simulate the War," *New York Times*, September 5, 1970.

37. Linenthal, *Changing Images of the Warrior Hero in America*, 153. Projecting what I would call an adoptionist reading of the massacre, Linenthal writes, "My Lai is an event which, like Hiroshima and Auschwitz, raises questions that go far beyond the massacre itself, questions directed at the core institutions and values of America."

38. Huebner, *Warrior Image*, 229; Kerry, *New Soldier*.

39. Kerry, *New Soldier*. Reconnaissance by fire is a direct repudiation of the just war tradition's *ad bellum* criterion requiring discrimination between combatants and noncombatants.

40. Ibid.

41. Ibid., emphasis added.

42. Ibid., 225–26. See also Grossman, *On Killing*, which gives a more robust accounting of the social forces that enabled American soldiers in Vietnam to kill as they did.

43. Huebner, *Warrior Image*, 229; Pilati, "The Vietnam Veterans' March on Washington," *Boston Globe*, May 30, 1971.

44. "Veterans Turn Minor Prelude into a Major Antiwar Event," *Washington Post*, April 24, 197; George Ashworth, "The Mission Was Impossible, but Veterans Made Their Point" *Christian Science Monitor*, April 26, 1971.

45. Pilati, "Vietnam Veterans' March on Washington."

46. Kerry, *New Soldier*. See also Huebner, *Warrior Image*, 229.

47. Kerry, *New Soldier*.

48. "Veterans Turn Minor Prelude into a Major Antiwar Event," *Washington Post*, April 24, 1971; Pilati, "Vietnam Veterans' March on Washington."

49. http://www.wintersoldier.com/index.php?topic=KerryONeill (accessed November 10, 2013).

50. Ibid.

51. *New York Times*, September 8, 1970.

52. Nick Thimmesch, "Most Vietnam Veterans Will Join Ranks of Middle America," *Los Angeles Times*, April 27, 1971.

53. Ibid.

54. See Hendrickson, *Living and the Dead;* Herring, *America's Longest War;* and Karnow, *Vietnam,* for accounts of popular support for the war in its early stages; Huebner, *Warrior Image,* 171–82; Herring, *America's Longest War.*

55. Linenthal, *Changing Images of the Warrior Hero in America,* 149, 156, 158; see also Huebner, *Warrior Image,* 237. Huebner writes, "The warrior image became murky and troubling between 1969 and 1973."

56. Richard Slotkin, *Gunfighter Nation.* The third volume of Richard Slotkin's history of the frontier myth discusses its influence through the twentieth century and the Vietnam era.

57. Robert L. Turner, "Military Morale Suffered, Survived," *Boston Globe,* January 28, 1973.

58. Huebner, *Warrior Image,* 231–40; Rostker, *I Want You!,* 15–37.

59. Rostker, *I Want You!,* 43–58.

60. Harry A. Marmion (1971) cited in ibid., 33.

61. Morris Janowitz (1967) cited in ibid., 33. On the riots in Houston, East St. Louis, and Washington, D.C., see Arthur Barbeau and Florette Henri, *The Unknown Soldiers: Black American Soldiers in World War I* (Philadelphia: Temple University Press, 1974); Milton Friedman (1967), cited in Rostker, *I Want You!,* 33.

62. Martin Anderson, "An Analysis of the Factors Involved in Moving to and All-Volunteer Armed Force," unpub. paper, July 4, 1967, cited in Rostker, *I Want You!,* 34.

63. Ibid., 34. Though more quietly than many, Anderson is working with warrior images described by Linenthal, the Minuteman in particular.

64. Ibid., 35.

65. Huebner, *Warrior Image,* 231–40.

66. Kerry, *New Soldier;* Pilati, "Vietnam Veterans' March on Washington."

67. Rostker, *I Want You!,* 183.

Chapter Six. Safety, Soldier, Scapegoat, Savior

1. Bacevich, *New American Militarism;* Rostker, *I Want You!;* Dempsey, *Our Army.*

2. I am borrowing the phrase "fantasy echo," again, from Joan Scott; Bacevich, *New American Militarism;* James Turner Johnson, "Contemporary Warfare and American Efforts at Restraint," in John D. Carlson and Jonathan H. Ebel, eds., *From Jeremiad to Jihad: Religion, Violence, and America* (Berkeley: University of California Press, 2012).

3. *Recruiting, Retention, and Future Levels of Military Personnel* (Washington, D.C.: Congressional Budget Office, 2006). Army accessions exceeded initial goals

in active, reserve, and national guard branches in 2002 and in active and reserve branches in 2003.

4. Smith, *Imagining Religion*, xi–xiii.

5. Jon Krakauer, *Where Men Win Glory: The Odyssey of Pat Tillman* (New York: Anchor Books, 2010); Mary Tillman and Narda Zacchino, *Boots on the Ground by Dusk: My Tribute to Pat Tillman* (New York: Modern Times, 2008). See also Mike Freeman, "Tillman's Bold Career Move," *New York Times*, July 14, 2002; and Len Pasquerelli, "Tillman to Serve Three-Year Term in Army," ESPN.com, May 23, 2002.

6. Jon Krakauer, *Where Men Win Glory*.

7. Video of the interview is available as part of a tribute to Tillman at http://www.youtube.com/watch?v=kBM2hiXRZA0. It has also been excerpted in the documentary film *The Tillman Story* (2010). Unsurprisingly, the YouTube tribute, which lists a production date of 2004 and an upload date of 2008, leans heavily on how exceptional Tillman was.

8. Krakauer, *Where Men Win Glory*, 162–64; See also Mary Tillman, *Boots on the Ground by Dusk*.

9. Krakauer, *Where Men Win Glory*, 159.

10. For scholarly treatments of this understanding of masculinity see Gail Bederman, *Manliness and Civilization: A Cultural History of Gender and Race in the United States, 1880–1917* (Chicago: University of Chicago Press, 1996); Clifford Putney, *Muscular Christianity: Manhood and Sports in Protestant America, 1880–1920* (Cambridge: Harvard University Press, 2003); and Richard Slotkin's trilogy cited above. Two influential figures in developing and disseminating this gender and racial ideology at the turn of the twentieth century were Theodore Roosevelt and G. Stanley Hall.

11. Krakauer, *Where Men Win Glory*, 368–69; Barry A. Kosmin and Ariela Keysar, *American Religious Identification Survey [ARIS 2008] Summary Report* (Hartford, Conn.: Trinity College, 2009), 5–7.

12. Lieutenant Colonel Raymond S. Hilliard, "United States Army Recruiting Command: From Zero to Hero-status," unpub. research paper, U.S. Army War College, July 4, 2003.

13. Krakauer, *Where Men Win Glory*, 182–83; 167–69. Krakauer describes the relationship that developed between the Tillman brothers and another older-than-average recruit, Túlio Tourinho, a former high school teacher from Winchester, Kentucky.

14. Ibid., 185.

15. Ibid., 192.

16. Ibid., 199, 251.

17. Catherine M. Webb and Kate J. Hewett, *An Analysis of U.S. Army Fratricide Incidents during the Global War on Terror: 11 September 2001–31 March 2008* (United States Army Aeromedical Research Laboratory, March 2010), http://www.fas.org/man/eprint/fratricide.pdf.

18. Reports of the investigation are archived at ESPN.com. See http://sports .espn.go.com/espn/eticket/story?page=tillmanpart1 (accessed January 5, 2014). These reports also figure prominently in the Krakauer, *Where Men Win Glory*, and in Mary Tillman, *Boots on the Ground by Dusk*.

19. Amir Bar-Lev, *The Pat Tillman Story* (2010); Krakauer, *Where Men Win Glory*, 319–41. Much of the fourth and final part of Krakauer's book discusses cover-up efforts. In a representative paragraph, he writes on page 336, "According to federal statute and several Army regulations, Marie Tillman, as next of kin, was supposed to be notified that an investigation was under way, even if friendly fire was only suspected, and 'be kept informed as additional information about the cause of death becomes known.' Instead, McChrystal, Nixon, and the soldiers under their command went to extraordinary lengths to prevent the Tillman family from learning the truth about how Pat died."

20. See the Congressional Medal of Honor Citation for Marine Corps Corporal Jason L. Dunham for an example of self-sacrifice presented and interpreted during the war in Iraq. Dunham was wounded when he threw himself on a grenade on April 14, 2004. He died on April 22, the same day as Pat Tillman. http://www .cmohs.org/recipient-detail/3458/dunham-jason-l.php.

21. Krakauer, *Where Men Win Glory*, 246, 354. See also Bar-Lev, *Pat Tillman Story*.

22. Scott, "Fantasy Echo."

23. This is the narrative thrust of Jon Krakauer's book and also of Amir Bar-Lev's documentary film. It is also a feature of almost every bit of reporting on the incident since the summer of 2004. See, in particular, "Two Years after Soldier's Death, Family's Battle Is with Army," *New York Times* and nytimes.com, May 21, 2006, and "An Un-American Tragedy," http://sports.espn.go.com/espn/eticket/ story?page=tillmanpart1 (accessed January 5, 2014).

24. Leviticus 16:5–22, quoted in Carolyn Marvin, "Scapegoating and Deterrence: Criminal Justice Rituals in American Civil Religion," in Stewart M. Hoover and Lynn Schofield Clark, eds., *Practicing Religion in the Age of Media: Explorations in Religion, Media, and Culture* (New York: Columbia University Press, 2002), 206–7. See also Marvin and Ingle, *Blood Sacrifice and the Nation*, 9–40.

25. See René Girard, "Sacrifice as Sacral Violence and Substitution," and "The Scapegoat as Historical Referrent," in James G. Williams, ed., *The Girard Reader* (New York: Crossroad, 1996), 69–93, 97–106.

26. "Countdown with Keith Olbermann," July 25, 2007. Video of the interview with General Wesley Clark in which Clark discusses the possibility that Tillman was murdered is available at http://www.youtube.com/watch?v=gpGK6WidRy o&feature=related.

27. In his extensive treatments of religious violence, René Girard points out three characteristics common among ritual sacrifices. He notes, first, that ritual sacrifices are a response to a communal problem and, second, that they involve a designated "victim" who stands in for members of society whose suffering might be more costly. Third and finally, he argues that when successful, ritual sacrifice

functions as an outlet for social tension. Girard writes, "The function of sacrifice is to quell violence within the community and to prevent conflicts from erupting." Williams, *Girard Reader*, 83.

28. "Tillman Killed while Serving as Army Ranger," ESPN.com, April 23, 2004.

29. Ibid.; see also Freeman, "Tillman's Bold Career Move."

30. Freeman, "Tillman's Bold Career Move." See also "Tillman Begins Boot Camp, Not NFL Camp," *USA Today*, July 8, 2002; "Tillman Killed While Serving as Army Ranger," ESPN.com, April 23, 2004.

31. Ibid.

32. www.frontpagemag.com. December 31, 2004, "Highlights and Lowlifes" by Ann Coulter.

33. For an adulatory take on Tillman's decision to enlist before his death, see David Kindred, "After 9/11, Public 'Hero' Move on to Private, True Heroism," *USA Today*, August 19, 2002.

34. *National Review Online*, May 4, 2004, "Courage and Honor."

35. Austin Cline, "Pat Tillman, Christian Supremacism in the Military, and Atheists as Worm Food," About.com, April 26, 2007.

36. Mike Fish, "An Un-American Tragedy," ESPN.com, July 19, 2006, http://espn.go.com/espn/eticket/story?page=tillmanpart1.

37. Faust, *This Republic of Suffering*.

38. Dave Zirin, "Pat Tillman, Our Hero," *Nation*, October 6, 2005.

39. Ibid.

40. Cline, "Pat Tillman, Christian Supremacism." See also Stan Goff, "Playing the Atheism Card against Pat Tillman's Family," www.truthdig.com, July 28, 2006; and Michael Stephens, "Pat Tillman—Non-Christian," www.futureofthebook.org, July 23, 2006.

41. Cline, "Pat Tillman, Christian Supremacism."

42. Slotkin, *Gunfighter Nation*.

43. Krakauer, *Where Men Win Glory*, xxx.

44. Slotkin, *Gunfighter Nation;* Krakauer, *Where Men Win Glory*, 19.

45. Bederman, *Manliness and Civilization;* Putney, *Muscular Christiainity;* Slotkin, *Gunfighter Nation*.

46. Krakauer, *Where Men Win Glory*, 22.

47. Ibid., 47.

48. Ibid., 46.

49. Ibid., 103.

50. I am drawing here on Girard's theories of scapegoating and mimetic violence. See, for example, "The Surrogate Victim," in Williams, *Girard, Reader*, 20–29.

51. "Barrage of Bullets Drowned Out Cries of Comrades," *Washington Post*, December 5, 2004.

52. Mike Freeman, "Tillman's Bold Career Move," *New York Times*, July 14, 2002.

53. Kevin Tillman, "After Pat's Birthday," Truthdig.com, October 19, 2006.

Conclusion

1. A description of the Oshkosh honor flight program is available at https://www.eaa.org/en/airventure/features-and-attractions/special-events/old-glory-honor-flight (accessed September 24, 2014).

2. Charlie Savage and Andrew W. Lehren, "Can Bowe Bergdahl Be Tied to 6 Lost Lives? Facts Are Murky," *New York Times*, June 3, 2014

3. *New York Times*, September 4, 2014, http://www.nytimes.com/2014/09/04/world/europe/obama-calls-russia-ukraine-moves-brazen-assault.html (accessed September 22, 2014).

4. Congressional Medal of Honor Citation, Staff Sergeant Salvatore Giunta. The full citation is available at http://www.cmohs.org/recipient-detail/3471/giunta-salvatore-a.php (accessed December 17, 2013); Leo Shane III, "Obama: Medal of Honor Recipient Giunta 'as Humble as He Is Heroic,' *Stars and Stripes*, November 16, 2010.

5. Associated Press Wire Service, January 2, 2011; http://www.usatoday.com/story/news/nation/2012/11/30/medal-of-honor-winner/1738663/ (accessed June 11, 2013).

6. James Risen, "Several Warnings, Then a Soldier's Lonely Death," *New York Times*, January 1, 2011.

7. The *New York Times* and National Public Radio have been especially attentive to this story. See the reporting of Elisabeth Bumiller and Lizette Alvarez and the online forum "At War" in the *Times* and the reporting of Quil Lawrence for NPR. In June 2013 Lawrence presented a multipart series on soldiers and suicide as part of *All Things Considered*. It is available online at http://www.npr.org/series/200142121/life-after-war (accessed 17 December 2013).

8. Pauline Jelinek, "Army Suicide on Track to Top '08, Hit New High in '09," *USA Today*, November 18, 2009.

9. Bellah, "Civil Religion in America," in Bellah and Tipton, *Robert Bellah Reader*, 229.

10. Elisabeth Bumiller and Thom Shanker, "Pentagon Is Set to Lift Combat Ban for Women," *New York Times*, January 23, 2013; Andrew Rosenthal, "Women in Combat," *New York Times*, January 24, 2013.

11. Because the wars in Afghanistan and Iraq have departed so dramatically from models of warfare that persisted into the mid-twentieth century, it is an open question whether permitting women to be assigned to combat roles will actually increase dramatically the number of women who are involved in combat. In many ways the 2013 policy change simply caught up with the military's lived realities.

12. Melani McAlister, "Saving Private Lynch," *New York Times*, April 6, 2003. See also Krakauer, *Where Men Win Glory*, 201–17. McAlister provides a typically insightful and succinct analysis of the connection between Lynch and the colonial abductee and diarist Mary Rowlandson.

Credits

Sections of chapters 2 and 4 were published previously as "Of the Lost and the Fallen: Ritual and the Religious Power of the American Soldier," *Journal of Religion* 92, no. 2 (April 2012): 224–50.

Sections of chapter 3 were published previously as "Overseas Military Cemeteries as American Sacred Space: Mine Eyes Have Seen *La Gloire*," *Material Religion: A Journal of Art, Objects and Belief* 8, no. 2 (2012): 184–215.

Index

Illustrations are indicated by italicized page numbers.

Abel, Rudolf Ivanovich, 124, 221n43
ABMC. *See* American Battle Monuments Commission
ACLU (American Civil Liberties Union), 30
Adams, Mary Frances, 212n36
AEF (American Expeditionary Force), 85
Afghanistan War, 16, 192, 194, 218n2, 230n11
African-American soldiers, 97, 158–61, 223n5
Albanese, Catherine, 19, 205n27, 208n37, 222n57
Alexander, Holmes, 123, 124, 130
Alexander, Robert, 210n10
All-volunteer military, 143, 155–63, 164
American Battle Monuments Commission (ABMC), 73–75, 77, 81–91, 215n12, 215n16
American Civil Liberties Union (ACLU), 30
American Expeditionary Force (AEF), 85
American Graves Registration Service, 83
American Legion, 28–33, 35, 37, 44–45, 66, 154–55
American Revolution, soldier image associated with, 3
Anderson, Benedict, 64, 205n24
Anderson, Martin, 161–62, 226n63
Annapolis (United States Naval Academy), 5
Antiwar movement, 142, 147–55. *See also* Vietnam Veterans Against the War

Argonne Forest offensive (World War I), 49–50, 55, 85. *See also* Meuse-Argonne American Cemetery
Arlington National Cemetery, 46, 82, 83, 148, 163. *See also* Tomb of the Unknown Soldier
Armistice Day, 25–28, 32, 44–45, 47, 55, 58, 212n36
Army Nursing Corps, 70
Ashworth, George, 151–52
Astoria, Oregon, 26–27, 31
Atheism, 182–83
Atonement, 9, 20, 42, 166, 176, 177, 179
Attitude of soldiers: on capture by enemy in Cold War, 120; expected attitudes, 3; in Vietnam War, 155; in World War I, 56
Averill, Nelson K., 63, 212n25
Ayers, Louis, 87

Bacevich, Andrew, 202n10
Baker, Newton, 76
Balkan conflicts, 165
Baltic states, 193
Bar-Lev, Amir, 188, 228n23
Barton, James F., 67
Basic training in the military, 12, 40, 142, 169, 172–73
Battle Memorial Cloisters (American Cathedral, Paris), 78, *79–80*, 81

Beecher, Lyman, 32

Beekman, Frederick, 78–81

Bellah, Robert, 17, 140–41, 197, 203–4n23, 208n29, 208n32, 223n14

Bergdahl, Bowe, 192

Berkovitch, Sacvan, 17

Bidwill, Michael, 178, 179

Bill Maher Show, 188

Bjornson, John, 151

Bodnar, John, 108, 218nn1–2

Boot camp. *See* Basic training in the military

Brainwashing, 113–14, 124, 151

Brandon, John F., 54

Brent, Charles, 35, 81

Britain: cemeteries of war dead, 215n13; Unknown Warrior, 59; World War II alliance with U.S. and Soviet Union, 107

Browne, Dolores M., 90, *91*, 97

Bruce, David, 92

Brutality, 148, 149, 150

Bullis, H. Edmund, 67

Bullitt, William C., 92

Bureau of Indian Affairs, 47

Bush, George W., 182, 186

Bush, Prescott, 126

Calley, William, 153

Caputo, Philip, 142–47, 157, 208n33, 224n21, 224nn25–26

Casagranda, Ben, 25

Catholicism, 17, 32, 104, 106, 142

Cemeteries. *See* Graves and cemeteries of fallen soldiers

Centralia, Washington, anti-union violence (Armistice Day, 1919), 25–26, 28, 30, 32, 44–45

Changing Images of the Warrior Hero in America (Linenthal), 19, 202n11, 208n38, 223n16, 224n18, 224n24, 225n37, 226n55

Chapels at cemeteries. *See* Graves and cemeteries of fallen soldiers

Cheney, Dick, 4

Chiarelli, Peter, 195–96

Chomsky, Noam, 181

Christ, analogies to, 9, 19, 23, 27–28, 33, 43, 59–60, 90, 98–99, 144, 188, 191

Christianity: chapels constructed at cemeteries and, 84–85, 89–90; dangers in applying to soldiering, 43–44; early martyrs, 69, 71–72; G.I. Messiah in 1917–60 and, 22–23; influences in civil religion, 20, 23;

ritual sacrifice and Crucifixion, 176; role in connecting military and society, 6–7; sacrifice, theology of, 31; Tillman's lack of interest in, 180–81; Unknown Soldier and, 60, 65

The Christological Controversy (Norris, ed.), 223n17

Chrysler Corporation, 16

Church of the Holy Trinity (Paris), 78, 80–81

CIA and U–2 program, 115–19, 127–28, 131, 220n27. *See also* Powers, Francis Gary

Civil religion, 17–22; American Legion and, 35; antiwar movement and, 149, 151, 152, 160; Christian norms reflected in, 20, 23; human cost of war and, 98–99; as lived tradition, 18, 22, 33, 208n37; martial tradition, memory of, 4–5, 140–41, 166; multiple views of, 21–22; persistence in America, 20, 191; post-9/11 terrorist attacks and, 165; in private vs. in public sphere, 101, 218–19n2; relationship between God and the American soldier, 105; sanctifying of militarism's role in, 7; scope of term, 17, 197, 203n17; soldiering as practice of, 18, 36, 142, 193, 225n34; Tillman as embodiment of, 171; Vietnam War and, 141–42, 156–60

"Civil Religion in America" (Bellah), 140–41

Civil War: challenging theological assumptions, 224n17; compared to World War I, 3–4; Lincoln's descriptions of, 34; sermons in, 32; soldier image associated with, 3

Clark, Wesley, 228n26

Cline, Austin, 182–83

Close-order drill, 40, 41, 110, 129, 143, 163

Code of Conduct, 114, 120, 221n30

Coercion in soldiering, 151, 153, 156, 158, 159, 160

Cold War: as challenge to civil religion, 107–8; change to terms of war, 4; *The Manchurian Candidate* (film) and, 20–21. *See also* Powers, Francis Gary

Collectivism, 39–40, 43, 129

Columbia Conserve Company, 30

Columbia Sheathing Her Sword (Young sculpture), 79, *80*

Commercialism, 15, 38, 203n22

Committee on the War and the Religious Outlook (CWRO), 35, 36, 41

Communalism, 6, 15, 19, 38, 39, 41, 198, 202n7, 208n32

Communists: commitment to struggle against, 159; Marshall speaking at Suresne against, 93; in North Korea, 113; Red Scare, 44; sermons in opposition to, 32; vigilante action against, as American will, 25–26, 32, 44. *See also* Cold War

Congressional Medal of Honor, 7–8, 20, 47, 48, 50, *56*, 57, 135–36, 194, 228n20

Conscription: end of (1973), 160–61, 163; negatives of, 161–62

Cook, Russell, 30

Coolidge, Calvin, 46

Corruption, 159

Coulter, Ann, 178–79, 181, 182, 183

Cram, Ralph Adams, 71, *84*

Cret, Paul, 82

Cromwell, Gladys and Dorothy, 97

Crosses, imagery of. *See* Graves and cemeteries of fallen soldiers

Cult of the fallen soldier, 31, 58

Cummings, Ernest, 149

CWRO. *See* Committee on the War and the Religious Outlook

Dak To incident. *See* Johnson, Dwight

D-Day (June 6, 1944), 88–89, 90

Dean, Bradlee, 211n15

Dearing, Vinton, 71

De Lue, Donald, 90

Democracy as American value, 32, 97, 218n49

Denby, Edwin, 46

Denton-Borhaug, Kelly, 19, 31

Dick Cavett Show (May 1971), 153–54

Dilling, Elizabeth, 30

Dilworth, Richardson, 123

Distance of military from American public, 5–6, 16, 37, 73, 165

Draft. *See* Conscription

Dulles, Allen, 121, 123–24, 127–28, 131

Dunham, Jason L., 228n20

Earthquake relief, 198

Ebola, 192–93, 198

Ecumenism, 19, 103, 104, 111, 191, 219n12

Edwards, Clarence, 57

Edwards, Daniel R., 8

Egan, Timothy, 206n4

Eisenhower, Dwight D., 97, 118, 119, 165, 220n27

Eliade, Mircea, 207n18

Elshtain, Jean Bethke, 219n11

Enders, Stan, 138–39

England. *See* Britain

Eustis, Edith Morton, 89

Evangelism, 17, 31, 32, 34, 41, 106, 182, 211n5

Everest, Wesley, 25–26, 44

Excarnation, 196–99

Executive Order 10631 (1955), 114

Extralegal justice, 30

Faust, Drew Gilpin, 97, 181

Federal Council of Churches of Christ (FCCC), 35–36

Felicitas, 69, 71, 74

Ferguson, Bob, 178, 179

Festa in Italian Harlem, 31

Films: *Battleground,* 104, 108, 110–12, 113, 116, 119, 120; *The Best Years of Our Lives,* 104, 108–9; *The Bridges at Toko-Ri,* 13–14; *God Is My Copilot,* 104, 106–7, 119; *Guadalcanal Diary,* 104–5, 111, 119, 120, 126; Lost Battalion depiction (silent film), 57; *The Manchurian Candidate,* 20–21; *The Pat Tillman Story* (documentary), 188, 227n7, 228n23; as sources, 13–14, 103–20

Fine Arts Commission, 81, 82

Fish, Hamilton, 53–54

Flag, sacred status of, 53

Foreign policy of twenty-first century, 192

Fosdick, Harry Emerson, 36, 37

Foucault, Michel, 215n14

Fourth of July 1834, 31–32

France: cemeteries of war dead, 215n13; memorializing Americans who joined French fight force prior to U.S. entry into World War I, 77–78, *78*. *See also* Meuse-Argonne American Cemetery; Normandy American Cemetery; Suresnes American Cemetery

Freeman, Mike, 187

Freud, Sigmund, 41

Friedman, Milton, 161

Friendly fire, death by, 173, 181

Geertz, Clifford, 211n14

Germany: cemeteries of war dead, 215n13, 218n51; cult of the fallen soldier in, 31, 215n16. *See also* World War I; World War II

G.I. Messiah: Caputo as, 146; in civil religion, 19–22, 74; in Cold War, 102, 104, 110; devotion to, 98, 151, 165; Giunta's story and, 194; interpretation of, 10–17; Johnson as, 138; memorial monuments and, 82–85, 96; Powers failing to meet standards of, 124; suicide and, 196; Tillman's story and, 166–68, 174–75, 183, 184, 188; Vietnam experiences and, 156, 159, 160; women soldiers and, 197. *See also* Myths and symbols; Sacrifice; Salvation; Soldier-savior; Veneration of soldiers
Girard, René, 186, 228–29n27, 229n50
Giunta, Salvatore, 194–95, 196
Gluckman, H. L., 216n30
"God and Country," waging war for, 29, 33. *See also* Nation, in analogy to God
Goldwater, Barry, 222n48
Goodhue, Bertram, 78
Goodpaster, Andrew, 118
Graham, Billy, 32
Gratitude toward soldiers, 190–91, 199
Graves and cemeteries of fallen soldiers, 9, 72–99; ABMC, role of, 73–75, 77, 81–91, 215n12, 215n16; chapels erected at, *84*, 84–85, 87, 89–90, 93–94; Christian imprint on, *10–11*, 74, 89–90, 93, 96; civil religious moments at, 75; crosses as headstones, 83, 89, 216n30; democratic impulses to set up memorials, failings of, 77–81; design, importance of, 82, 83, 86, 97, 214n9, 217n38; epitaphs, 74, 209n5, 211n16, 215n12; grouped graves, desirability of, 76–77; as incarnation of nation's will, 13; information recorded on grave markers, 74; inscriptions in chapels of biblical and liturgical statements, 87–88, 89–90; power of memories evoked by, 98, 214n8; repatriation of dead from overseas burial, 76; as sacred spaces, 86, 91, 96–99; as sources, 12
Graves Registration Service (GRS), 54
Great Depression, 103
Great power of America, 33, 73, 99, 112, 164
Great War. *See* World War I
Gréber, Jacques, 71, 86
Gregory, John, 94, *94*
Grimm, Walter, 25, 31
Grinev, Mikhail, 121, 123
Grossman, David, 208n31
Guadalcanal, 104
Gulf War, 165

Haberski, Ray, 205n26, 223n13
Hagiography, 74, 85, 86, 89, 93, 96, 214n11
Hall, G. Stanley, 227n10
Hall, Mary Frances, 66
Harding, Warren G., 46, 60
Hauerwas, Stanley, 19
Hayes, Ralph, 76, 82
Hecht, Felicita, 70–72, 75, 97, 197
Heist, Aaron Allen, 27–28, 30, 31, 33, 35, 37, 45, 196
Heroism: Caputo's desire to embody, 143, 145; dark side of, 194–95; D-Day (June 6, 1944) and, 90–91; death in combat and, 13, 58; discomfort of heroes, 45, 50–51, 55, 105, 194–95; Johnson as symbol of, 135–40, 158–59; mythology of, 64–65, 140, 157, 167–68, 179, 196; Powers tarnishing tradition of, 123–28; sacred narratives of, 99; Tillman legend, creation of, 167–69, 174–75, 178–79, 181–82, 187; Whittlesey as symbol of, 49–50, 55, 56; in World War I, 8, 47; in World War II, 91. *See also* Congressional Medal of Honor; Sacrifice; Unknown Soldier
Histories/historiographies of war vs. of religion, 1, 201n1
Holderman, Nelson, 7–8
"Homely hero," 3
Honor flights, Washington National Airport, 189–90
Howe, Julia Ward, 90
Hubbard, Dale, 25
Huebner, Andrew, 19, 218n1, 226n55
Huntington, Samuel, 38, 202nn6–7, 202n11, 207n29, 208nn32–33, 208n40, 209n6

Identity: prisoners of war and, 115; rites of passage and, 59; Unknown Soldier and imagined history, 65
Imagined Communities (Anderson), 64
Imagined soldier, 2. *See also* G.I. Messiah; Heroism; Soldier-savior; Veneration of soldiers
Incarnation. *See* "Word became flesh" imagery
Individualism, 6, 10, 19, 97, 124, 171, 198, 202n7, 208n29, 208n32
Industrial Workers of the World (IWW), 25–26, 28, 30, 32, 44–45
Influenza pandemic (1918), 70, 85, 193
Insignia. *See* Military insignia
Intelligence Star, 128

Iraq War, 4, 16, 218n2, 228n20, 230n11. *See also* Tillman, Pat
The Irony of American History (Niebuhr), 134
Irwin, Will, 50, 210n11
Iselin, Louis, 94, *95*
Islamic State in Iraq and Syria (ISIS), 193

Jackson, Andrew, 5, 202n7
Janowitz, Morris, 161
Jeep commercial (Super Bowl 2013), 15–16
Jefferson, Thomas, 5, 202n7
Jenks, Chancellor L., 26
Jewish Advocate, 3
Jews, 3, 17, 60, 84–85, 104, 216n30, 219n12
Johnson, Dwight, 135–40, *137*, 157–59, 162–63
Johnson, Lyndon B., 135, *137*, 160
Joint Resolution 426 to create Tomb of the Unknown Soldier, 53
Judas, analogy to, 124

Kauzlarich, Ralph, 181, 182
Kennedy, John F., 143, 160
Kerry, John, 151–55, 157–59, 178, 181
Khrushchev, Nikita, 119
Kilmer, Joyce, 71
King, Martin Luther, Jr., sermons on civic ideals, 32–33
Korean War, 4, 113–14, 120, 222n52
Krakauer, Jon, 172, 183–86, 227n13, 228n19, 228n23

Lafayette Escadrille, 3, 77; Monument (Parc St. Cloud, France), 77–78, *78*, 80, 81
Landeghem, Charles, 139
Laplander, Robert J., 209n7, 210nn10–11
Lasswell, Harold, 208n33
Lazaron, Morris, 60
League of Nations, 4
Levi-Strauss, Claude, 41
Leviticus, scapegoat ritual in, 176
Liberty as American value, 6, 92
Lincoln, Abraham, Second Inaugural and Gettysburg Address, 16–17
Lincoln, Bruce, 203n17, 211n14
Linenthal, Edward, 3, 19, 202n11, 208n38, 217n33, 223n16, 224n18, 224n24, 225n34, 225n37, 226n55
Lofton, Kathryn, 203n22
Lorraine American Cemetery, 88
Lost Battalion. *See* Argonne Forest offensive (World War I); Whittlesey, Charles White
Lynch, Jessica, 197, 230n12

Manila American Cemetery (Philippines), 88
Manship, Paul, *83*
Marine Corps, 143, 144–45
Marlow, Jess, 132
Marshall, George C., 89, 92
Martial symbols, 51–52. *See also* Myths and symbols
The Martyrdom of Saints Perpetua and Felicitas, 72
Martyrs, 34, 69, 71–72. *See also* Hagiography
Masculinity, 140, 159, 182, 184, 227n10
Mayer, William, 114, 178
McAdoo, William, 55–56
McAlister, Melani, 230n12
McCain, John, 168, 179–80, *180*, 183
McMurtry, George, 50
Memorial Day, 53–54, 81, 85, 205n27
Memorializing of war dead. *See* Graves and cemeteries of fallen soldiers; Tomb of the Unknown Soldier
Memorials, control over, 73–85. *See also* American Battle Monuments Commission (ABMC); Graves and cemeteries of fallen soldiers
Memory (Gregory statue), *94*, 94–95
Meuse-Argonne American Cemetery (Romagne-sous-Montfaucon, France), 13, 85–88, *87*, 217n33
Michener, James, 13
Military. *See* Graves and cemeteries of fallen soldiers; Soldiers/soldiering; *specific wars and events*
Military Academy (West Point), 5
Military insignia, 52, 79
Miller, Perry, 17
Milligan, Mike, 152
Mills, Quincy Sharpe, 71
Minuteman, 3
Miskowiec, Jay, 215n14
Monasticism, 37–39, 207n24
Moore, Charles, 82, *83*
Moore, Deborah Dash, 219n12
Morgan, David, 204n23
Mosse, George, 31, 215n16, 218n51
Mucklestone, Mrs. Melville, 30
Music: "Battle Hymn of the Republic" (Howe), 90; at interment of Tomb of the Unknown Soldier, 59–60; Marines in training and, 144; "Onward Christian Soldiers," 36, 46, 55; "Rock of Ages," 104; "The Supreme Sacrifice," 59; "Taps," 98
My Lai massacre, 149, 153, 225n37

Myths and symbols, 3–10, 24; American prisoners of war in Korean War and, 114; American Revolution, 3; civil religion's reliance on, 100; Civil War, 3; complexity of study of, 23, 198–99; instability in meaning of symbols, 52, 68, 211n14; Johnson's story and, 140; military's and war's mythic qualities, 37, 39, 43–44, 143; mixture of truth and falsehood, 198; Powers's story and, 129–30; relationship between nation (collective) and symbol (soldier), 34–39; symbolic lives, 51–58; Tillman's story and, 167–68, 175; tombs of unknown soldiers as emblems of nationalism, 64; World War I (Great War), 3. *See also* Rituals

Nation, in analogy to God, 23, 33, 41, 156–57
National Geographic on World War II cemeteries, 89
Nationalism, 64, 96, 98, 204–5n24
National Pilgrimage Committee (American Legion), 66–67
National unity, 53–54, 99. *See also* Collectivism
NATO, 193
Natural disasters, soldiers' helping role in, 198
Naval Academy (Annapolis), 5
Negative portrayals of American soldiering, 20, 37, 202n7
Neo-Hamiltonianism, 208n40
New York Herald Tribune on trade of Powers for Russian spy Abel, 125
New York Times: on Bullitt speech at Suresnes (1937), 92; on Centralia, Washington killings on Armistice Day (1919), 34, 207n14; on Johnson's heroism and battle breakdown (1971), 139; on military suicide rate (2013), 230n7; on veterans' lives after returning from Iraq and Afghanistan (2012), 218n2
Niebuhr, Reinhold, 134
Nixon, Richard M., 160, 162, 228n19
Noll, Mark A., 224n17
Nordheimer, John, 138
Normandy American Cemetery (France), *11, 13,* 88–91, *91,* 97
Norris, Richard A., 223n17
North, Thomas, 77, 81, 215n12, 217n38

Obama, Barack, 193, 194
Oise-Aisne American Cemetery (France), 71, 72, *84*

Omaha Beach (D-Day), 88–89
O'Neill, John, 153–54, 157, 159
Operation Dewey Canyon III (VVAW event, 1971), 148, 152, 154–55, 225n33
Operation Overflight (U–2 missions), 115–18, 130. *See also* Powers, Francis Gary
Operation RAW (VVAW event, 1970), 148–49, 225n33
Order and following orders, 40–41, 52, 129
Orthodoxy: of American Legion, 30; vs. antiwar movement, 148; making war into a "good," 108; military cemeteries and, 86; in renderings of G.I. Messiah in 1917–60 conflicts, 22–23
Outlook reporting of Whittlesey's speech, 56

Palmer, Frederick, 68
Parades: as acts of evangelism, 31, 32; Armistice Day 1919, Centralia, Washington, 25–26, 32, 44; order as feature of military in, 41; victory, 59
Parson, Maude, 70
Patriotism, 204n24
Pay of soldiers, 162
Perpetua (Roman noblewoman and saint), 69–70
Pershing, John, 46, 81, 82, 83, 85–86, 87, 93, 95
"Plea for the West" (Beecher), 32
Plenty Coos (Chief of the Crow Nation), 47
Poverty and entry into military service, 158, 160–61
Powers, Francis Gary, 101–4, 106, 108, 115–33, *116, 122;* background of, 102–3; compared to Bergdahl, 192; conditions as U–2 pilot, 132; confusion of "ought" expectations with "must be" understandings, 129–30; criticism by press and the public for failure of duty, 123–24; death of, 132; failure to commit suicide, 117–18, 121, 123, 125–26, 127–28, 130; Intelligence Star and, 128; pay in U–2 program, 116, 124, 220n22; Senate Armed Services Committee, appearance before, 125–26; shot down in U–2 over Russia, 117–19; Soviet imprisonment and trial of, 119–24; trade for Russian spy Abel, 124–25, 221n43; in U.S. Air Force and CIA U–2 program, 115–16, 220n21, 222n57
Powers, Oliver, 103

"Present Day Incarnation" (Heist's sermon), 27–28, 33, 35, 196
Prisoners of war, 113–15, 120, 222n52
Private Soldiers and Sailors Legion of the United States of America, 208n42
Professionalization of military, 5–6. See also All-volunteer military
Progressive Era, 6, 35
Protestantism: call for churches to become more like military, 36, 37; Episcopalian funding and support to memorialize American World War I troops in France, 80; World War I soldiers' religious experiences and opinions and, 35–36, 41. See also Civil religion
Protestant Pope's Day observances, 31
Providence Journal's publication of Brandon poem on Unknown Soldier, 54–55
Pruyn, John Bayard, 48, 61
Public celebration in America, mixed civic and religious messages of, 31–32, 33–34, 59
Public opinion of all-volunteer military, 165

Race, 31–32, 41, 158–61, 223n5
Radicals, reaction to, 25–26, 30, 32, 44–45
Rall, Ted, 183
Random fire on civilians, 150
Reconnaissance by fire, 150, 225n39
Redemptive power of the military, 38
The Red Network: A "Who's Who" of Radicalism and Handbook for Patriots (Dilling), 30
Red Scare, 44
Reintegration, 19, 58, 59, 60, 63–64, 108–9, 191
Religion among American Men: As Revealed by a Study of Conditions in the Army (FCCC), 35–36, 38–39, 42, 43
Religious symbols. See Myths and symbols; Sacrifice
Remembrance (Iselin statue), 94–95, 95
Repatriation of war dead from overseas burial, 76, 88, 89, 215–16n18
Return of medals by Vietnam veterans, 148, 153, 154, 178
Richardson, Elliot, 163
Righteousness, 28, 32, 37, 72, 87, 103, 105, 107, 108, 110, 112, 129, 156, 195
Riley, William Bell, 30
Rites of passage, 58–59, 172–73
Rituals, 16, 38, 39–43; boot camp as, 171–72; disconnect from reality of waging war,

129; effects of, 208n30; failures, 101–2, 108, 119–24, 131; in hunting, 128–29; suicides and, 196; of symbols, 58–61. See also Sacrifice
Roosevelt, Theodore, 227n10
Rosas, Darin, 185
Rowlandson, Mary, 230n12
Rudenko, Roman, 121, 123
A Rumor of War, Philip Caputo, 142–147
Runyon, Damon, 50, 210n11
Russell, Richard B., 126
Russian incursion into Ukraine and Baltics, 193

Sachs, Rusty, 152–53
The sacred: flags, sacred status of, 53; sacred spaces of cemeteries, 86, 91, 96–99
Sacrifice, 3, 8, 20, 29, 40, 96, 191, 228–29n27; Christian theology of, 31, 42, 60, 176; "no greater love than to serve their country and die in battle," 42, 144, 174, 180, 190; requirements placed on living by, 97; Tillman's story and, 168, 174, 175–83, 184, 188
St. Mihiel American Cemetery (near Thiaucourt, France), 83
Saltonstall, Leverett, 126
Salvation, 16, 88, 96, 97, 105, 158, 159, 165
Scapegoating rituals, 175–76, 229n50. See also Sacrifice
Scarupa, Henry, 140
Schorr, Samuel, 149–50
Scott, Joan, 3
Scott, Robert Lee, Jr., 106
Second Weather Observational Squadron (Provisional; Detachment 10–10), 116
Secularization, 19
Senate Armed Services Committee, 102, 125–27
Senft, David, 195
September 11, 2001 terrorist attacks, 165, 169
Sermons: civic themes in, 31–33; in Civil War, 32; Heist analogizing World War I soldiers to Christ, 27–28, 33, 35, 196
Service to the nation, 96, 156
Sevareid, Eric, 127, 131
Sheldrake, Philip, 36, 37, 43, 96, 207n24
Sixty-Ninth Regiment Armory in Manhattan, 55
Slotkin, Richard, 209n6, 210n10, 226n56
Smith, Jonathan Z., 16, 17, 41–42, 128–29
Smith, Levi, 67

Soldier-savior: in 1917–60 conflicts, 22–23; Heist's sermon using analogy of, 27–28, 33, 35, 196; nation's need for, 16, 29; recognition of, 7, 33, 93; society's failure to recognize, when soldiers return home, 109–10; in war film, 13–14. *See also* G.I. Messiah

Soldiers/soldiering: basic training, 12, 40, 142, 169, 172–73; dangers of identifying with religion, 43–44; education of officers, 5; future trends in, 198–99; image over time, 5–6; as incarnations of religious tradition, 2–3, 142; monasticism compared to, 37–38; purity, nobility, and honor of, 29, 35, 179; religious power of, 33, 35; stereotyping of, 3. *See also* G.I. Messiah; Graves and cemeteries of fallen soldiers; Sacrifice; Soldier-savior; Unknown Soldier; Veneration of soldiers

Sonenfield, Mrs. Samuel, 123

Sons of the American Revolution, 26

Spaces for the Sacred: Place, Memory, and Identity (Sheldrake), 36

Spanish flu. *See* Influenza pandemic

Speer, Robert, 29

The Spirit of American Youth Rising from the Waves (De Lue statue), 90

Stalin, Josef, 107–8

Standing military force, acceptance of idea of, 6

Stars and Stripes, 3, 32, 50, 76, 86, 92

Stars of David, 12, 71, 74, 83, 90, 216n30

Stennis, John, 126–27, 132, 222n48

Stern, Michael, 215n18

Stevenson, Markley, 89

Stewart, Pamela, 208n30

Stout, Harry S., 31, 224n17

Strathern, Andrew, 208n30

Suicide: Johnson's death as possible, 140; military suicide rate of twenty-first century, 195–96, 230n7; Powers's failure to commit, 117–18, 121, 123, 125–26, 127–28, 130; of Senft, 195; of Whittlesey, 51, 61–64, 212n34

Super Bowl commercial (February 2013), 15–16

Suresnes American Cemetery (France), 9–10, 13, 74, 92–96, 94–95, 217–18n44

Survival and self-preservation, 101, 124

Symbols. *See* Myths and symbols

Taft, William Howard, 47

Tertullian, 34, 69

Thimmesch, Nick, 155

Tillman, Kevin, 187

Tillman, Pat, 165–83, *170*, 193; boot camp experience of, 171–72; civil religion and, 180–81; compared to Bush administration, 186; complexity and unpredictability of, 184, 187–88; cover-up of events leading to death of, 174, 228n19; death of, 167, 173–74; enlisting in military, 166, 169–71; family of, persistence in seeking truth about death of, 188; football career of, 165–66, 169, 178; G.I. Messiah and, 166; Iraq War, reaction to, 181; in Iraq War, 172–73; Krakauer's account of, 183–86, 227n13, 228n19, 228n23; McCain eulogy of, 179–80; murder as possibility, 228n26; national devotion as influence on, 169–70; non-religious nature of, 180–82; ordinary aspects of story of, 167–69; public ownership of his legacy, 177–78, 183–86; in Ranger battalion, 172; sacrificial warrior image given to, 175–83; Silver Star awarded to, 174, 178; violence in life of, 185–86

Tillman, Richard, 180, 188

Time magazine on Bergdahl release (2014), 192

Tomb of the Unknown Soldier: creation and founding ceremony (1921), *48*, 51, 63–65, 212n36; epitaph, 209n5; pilgrimages to, 66–67; purpose of, 93; as window into and mirror of experience of war, 67–68. *See also* Unknown Soldier

Tregaskis, Richard, 104

Truman, Harry, 113

Tsunami relief, 198

Turner, Robert L., 159

U-2 incident. *See* Powers, Francis Gary

United States Air Force, 115, 128

Unknown Soldier: known and unknown dichotomy and, 64–68; lack of identity's effect on rite of passage, 59; Palmer's imagining of, 68; religious identity of, 60; rituals associated with, 58–61; selection and anonymity of, 47, 50, 54, 211n18; unidentified dead in World War I and, 53, 54. *See also* Tomb of the Unknown Soldier

Unknown soldiers: marking graves of, 64, 85, 211n16; World War II dead buried at Suresnes, 93, 217–18n44

U.S.S. *Olympia*, 46

Utopian view of the military, 36–39, 43

VA hospitals, 191–92

Valley Forge, 163

Veneration of soldiers, 18; Christian influences in, 23; complexity of, 195; as longtime tradition, 96; national pervasiveness of, 34–39; post–World War I, 29. *See also* Congressional Medal of Honor; Rituals

Veterans of Foreign Wars, 154–55

Vietnam Veterans Against the War (VVAW), 147–49, 151–55, 157, 160, 163

Vietnam Veterans for a Just Peace, 153

Vietnam War, 22, 134–63; antiwar movement and, 142, 147–55; Caputo's story in, 142–47; civil religious crisis caused by, 141–42, 147–55; described in religious imagery, 144, 146; irony in, 134–35; Johnson's story in, 135–40, *137*; questions of American martial efficacy and, 4, 134–35; returning medals by veterans of, 148, 153, 154; war crimes committed during, 151, 154; warrior image, changes to, 226n55. *See also* Vietnam Veterans Against the War

Vietnam War Memorial, 67

Volunteer military, 143, 160. *See also* All-volunteer military

VVAW. *See* Vietnam Veterans Against the War

Wanamaker, Rodman, 47

War: described in religious imagery, 144, 146; ecumenism of, 103, 104, 111; evangelical powers of, 105, 106; power to transform novice into warrior, 208n38; public memories of, 218n1; as ritual, 42, 124. *See also specific wars and conflicts*

War crimes, 151, 154

War on Terror, 22

Washington, George, 3, 5

Washington Post on veterans protesting against Vietnam War, 151, 153

Weber, Jim, 149–50

Weeks, John, 46, 53

West Point (United States Military Academy), 5, 38

Where Men Win Glory: The Odyssey of Pat Tillman (Krakauer), 172, 183–86, 227n13, 228n19, 228n23

White, Steve, 174

Whittlesey, Charles White, *56*; aiding fellow veterans, 57; in Battle of Argonne (World War I), 47–51; honors for bravery and heroism received by, 50, 56–57, 61; at interment of Unknown Soldier, 51, 63; memory and myth of, 55, 60–61, 193, 210nn9–11, 212n25; price paid by, 58, 209n7, 212n34; suicide of, 51, 61–64, 212n34; tomb as memorial to, 65

"Whole Again" (Super Bowl commercial, February 2013), 15–16

Wickers, John, 125

Wilson, Jerry V., 151

Wilson, Woodrow, 4, 47, 67, 92, 95

Winfrey, Oprah, 15–16, 203n22

Winter Soldier Investigations (VVAW event, 1971), 148, 149, 152, 163

Wobblies. *See* Industrial Workers of the World

Women soldiers, 197–98, 219n11, 230n11

Wood, Lambert, 71

Wood, Leonard, 208n40, 209n6

Woodside, Robert, 93

"Word became flesh" imagery, 28, 33, 43–45, 138, 144, 156–57, 195, 196, 224n17

World War I (Great War): 308th Infantry, 48, 49, 56, 57, 63; ABMC role in memorializing dead of, 73–75, 77, 81–82; Congressional Medal of Honor in, 7–8, 47; imagery associated with soldiers in, 3; training of soldiers for, 6; veneration of soldiers after, 29. *See also* Armistice Day; Hecht, Felicita; Unknown Soldier; Whittlesey, Charles White

World War II: analogizing to September 11, 2001 terrorist attacks, 169; D-Day (June 6, 1944), 88–89, 90; Korean War soldiers responding to images of, 4; nuclear weapon use by U.S. in, 4; remembered as the Good War, 4; soldier image associated with, 3; Soviet role in winning, 107–8; Suresnes Cemetery including dead from, 93; U.S. conduct toward to Japanese citizens in, 4. *See also* Normandy American Cemetery

Wyman, William, 151

Young, Mahonri, 78, 79, *80*

Younger, Edward, 54

Zirin, Dave, 181–82, 183